The Pentateuch in Its Cultural Environment

The Pentateuch in Its Cultural Environment

G. Herbert Livingston

Second Edition

BAKER BOOK HOUSE

Grand Rapids, Michigan 49516

Copyright © 1974, 1987 by
Baker Book House Company

ISBN: 0-8010-5646-2
Library of Congress Card Catalog Number: 73-92978

Second edition issued August 1987
Second printing, November 1988

Printed in the United States of America

To My Wife
Maria

Contents

CONTENTS

PART TWO
Literature, Concepts, and Practices

PART THREE
Assumptions, Critical Methods, and Theories

CONTENTS

List of Photos

Maps

Charts and Graphs

Photo Credits

Preface

To me, the Old Testament has always been a fascinating part of the Bible. Even as a youth, I found its stories enthralling. Through years of academic studies, of pastoral ministry, of teaching Old Testament courses, the appeal of this part of the Scriptures has not dimmed. I have loved the New Testament, too, but it has been the Old Testament that has helped me to understand the New Testament better, and to appreciate its redemptive message.

This volume is the product of twenty years of introducing ministerial students at Asbury Theological Seminary to the Old Testament. Four years ago a change was made in the biblical studies curriculum so that the basic Old Testament course was centered in the Pentateuch. One aspect of the study was focused on the world of the Pentateuch and the problems that have arisen in academic circles in regard to relating the Pentateuch to ancient Near Eastern cultures. The other phase of the study was concerned with a method of analyzing the content of the Pentateuch in its English translations, and relating that content to proclamation. Behind this volume lies the experimental text that was written in 1970 for the study of the Pentateuch's environment.

Apart from the classroom, I have been stimulated by five visits to the Middle East. While assisting Dr. G. Douglas Young, in 1959, in establishing the American Institute of Holy Land Studies in Jerusalem, I traveled widely throughout Palestine and was awakened to the significance of archaeology for Old Testament studies by listening to lectures by Mrs.

Ruth Amiran and assisting Dr. Johanan Aharoni at the excavation of Ramat Rahel.

During the summers of 1966 and 1968, I was further challenged by the contributions of archaeology to our knowledge of the ancient Near East. It was my privilege both summers to serve as a site supervisor under the direction of Dr. Joseph Callaway at Et Tell (Ai). The interest thus sparked has led to careful study of the significant ancient Near Eastern literature now available in English translation.

The overall purpose of this volume is to acquaint ministerial candidates, pastors, and laymen having a basic knowledge of the Bible with the cultural world in which the Patriarchs and the newly-formed Hebrew nation lived. A century and a half ago, little was known of the ancient cultural context of the Israelites, but in the last fifty or so years a knowledge explosion concerning that context has burst upon us. As usual, a lag between the Bible student's grasp of this new knowledge and the transference of it to relatively nonacademic circles has characterized the past several decades. I have sought to describe and to interpret the relationship of this knowledge explosion to the Pentateuch, a portion of the Old Testament of fundamental importance.

Part I of this volume is designed to give a general background to the entire Old Testament. Part II is focused on the thought patterns of the Pentateuch, both in their similarity and their contrast to concepts and practices depicted in ancient nonbiblical literature of religious nature. Part III is structured to speak to problems of basic import related to manuscripts of the Pentateuch now available. Viewpoints of various approaches to these problems are evaluated.

I wish to express gratitude to associates who have provided valued suggestions as this material was gathered and arranged in its present form. Special appreciation is owed to my esteemed colleague Dr. John N. Oswalt, who not only has teamed with me in presenting the content of this volume to successive classes of ministerial students, but has contributed many helpful insights and pointed out changes that needed to be made in the text.

My thanks are due to Miss Juanita Spencer for critically examining grammar and punctuation, to Mrs. Rebecca Sawyer and Mrs. Marilyn James who contributed their typing skills to the project, and to my wife, Maria, for her encouragement and help in proofreading and preparing the indexes.

G. Herbert Livingston
Asbury Theological Seminary
Wilmore, Kentucky

Part One

TIME, PEOPLE, AND COMMUNICATIONS

Black Sea

Caspian Sea

ASIA MINOR

Mt. Ararat

Hittite Kingdom

Lycia

Carchemish
Mitanni
Haran

Hatti

Assyria
Asshur
Nineveh

Media

Cilicia

Kittim
(Cyprus)

Arvad
Amurru
Hamath

Mediterranean
Sea

Phoenicia
Sidon
ARAM
(Syria)

Naharina

Euphrates R.
Akkad
Tigris R.
Elam

Canaan
Tyre
Damascus

Babylon
Babylonia
Susa

Jerusalem
Ammon

Sumer

Moab

Ur
Chaldea

Persian
Gulf

Memphis

Mizraim

ARABIA

Nile R.

Mt. Sinai

EGYPT
Pathros
(Upper Egypt)

Arabian Desert

Thebes

Red Sea

Cush

ANCIENT SEMITIC
WORLD

Copyright by C. S. HAMMOND & Co., N. Y.

Ethiopia

Scale of Miles

0   100   200   300   400

1

A Chronological Frame for the Ancient Near East

There was little interest in a biblical chronology until the Anglican Arch-bishop James Ussher published a system in A.D. 1605. The scheme so impressed the English people that it was early incorporated in the margins of the King James Version and is still so published in many of its editions.

Ussher proceeded in his work on the assumption that the genealogies represented a list of people and dates that strictly followed each other without gaps. Accepted without much question, Ussher's chronology was not seriously challenged until Mesopotamian and Egyptian materials began to pour in during the nineteenth century. Since then, a knowledge explosion has taken place, and the locating of people and events mentioned in the Bible within the greater ancient Near Eastern picture is now easier, though far from complete.

The objectives of this section are to outline the various streams of data that provide a workable framework of chronology; to note the vary-ing degrees of data correlation that are possible at present; to summarize the general historical picture in the ancient Near East in Mesopotamia, Egypt, and the Levant (the eastern Mediterranean coastal region) in each archaeological age; and to relate this to the biblical data where relevant.

Egyptian Dynasties as Reference Points

Because of two factors, the Egyptian dating sequence has come to be used as a major reference in the attempt to form a chronology of the ancient Near East. These two factors are the care with which the ancient Egyptians preserved their king lists and annals, and the coincidence of

1

the Sothic cycle, which makes it possible to assign an absolute date to the major dynasties and to many individual kings in Egyptian history.

An Egyptian priest of the third century B.C., Manetho, has left us the most complete king list. Manetho lists thirty-one different dynasties, or ruling families, giving the total number of years for each dynasty as well as the number of years of the reign of each monarch within the dynasty. In addition, a number of other Egyptian king lists have been recovered. These have served to double-check and, in some instances, correct Manetho. The result is a sequence which, although not without problems, is considered to be highly accurate.

The king lists, then, permit a largely complete *relative* chronology. That is, within Egyptian history we know whether a certain king and the events of his reign preceded or followed some other king. What we do not know from this information is when these things occurred with respect to the absolute reference point that the West has accepted, the birth of Christ. Thus, there is little basis for comparison with other events in the ancient Near East. At this point the Sothic cycle provides help.

The Egyptian calendar was 365 days in length. We now know that the solar cycle takes 365¼ days. We handle this by adding an extra day every four years. The Egyptian calendar, lacking this "year of the leap," fell one day behind the sun (and thus the seasons) every four years. As a result, after 730 years the winter season would occur in summer months on the calendar. After another 730 years, the calendar and the sun would be in phase again for a four-year period.

The event which marked the beginning of the solar year, the rising of the Dog Star, Sothis, would thus coincide with the calendrical New Year's Day only once every 1,460 years. On good evidence, this is reported to have occurred in A.D. 139. The previous occurrence would then have been in 1317 B.C. and the one prior to that, in 2773. With this information in hand, scholars have been able to take the three instances of when the Dog Star is reported to have risen on a certain calendrical day in a certain royal year and, ascertaining where the calendar was in its cycle, assign an absolute date to the royal year. The earliest of these is 1872 B.C.[1]

With these fixed checkpoints and the king lists, it is now possible to date almost all of the pharaohs to within ten or twenty years. Armed with this information, it is possible—whenever other cultures intersect that of Egypt—to establish a fixed checkpoint for *that* culture by which its chronological information can be assessed and arranged. This is especially true for Palestine.

---

1. Alan Gardiner, *Egypt of the Pharaohs* (Oxford: Clarendon Press, 1961), pp. 64-66.

Et Tell from the air. This scene demonstrates the use of elevated sites for defense purposes.

A closer look at Et Tell from the air, which affords a good view of the citadel (right center of photo).

Et Tell, showing the grid layout of site G.

Stratification and Pottery as Dating Indicators

Palestinian archaeologists have discovered that the most reliable means to establish relative dating sequences is to carefully observe and record the layers of soil through which they dig. In these layers of soil, they have also noted that particular types of pottery are repeatedly found in particular layers of soil that have the same sequence. Careful study has revealed that both soil layer and its matching type of pottery were tied with a specific people and their culture.

A German archaeologist, H. Schliemann, was the first man to see the significance of stratification, when he dug into the ruins of Troy (west coast of Turkey) in 1870. Sir Flinders Petrie, an English archaeologist who spent many years in Egypt, was the first scholar to observe the same phenomenon in Palestine while he was digging at Tell el-Hesi in 1890. He also noted the relationship of soil layers to pottery types and was able to identify certain pottery types with Egyptian pottery. He knew that these particular kinds of pottery were made in specific dynastic periods and in no others, so he had a key to dates for both soil layers and pottery types in Palestine. Because most other archaeologists in Palestine were publicity minded and thus more interested in "big finds" for museums, Petrie's insights were mostly ignored until after World War I.

A young archaeologist, W. F. Albright, saw the value of Petrie's clues to dating ancient cultures and, in the 1920s and '30s, made great progress in scientifically gaining information from soil layers and pottery types. Since World War II, the Institute of Archaeology at the University of London has made important contributions toward helping scholars to "read" the soil and the pots of ancient ruins.

Two archaeologists who have risen in fame above all others in this Institute of Archaeology are Sir Mortimer Wheeler and Miss Kathleen Kenyon. Building upon the work of many others and profiting from their mistakes, they devised a system of field excavation and classification of finds that is called the Wheeler–Kenyon method.

Basically, the excavation procedure consists of a layout of an area of ground, where ruins are buried, in a series of squares much like a checker board. Between each square there is a balk, or wall, of earth left, ranging from two to three feet in width, which is not dug unless clearly necessary. This balk serves as a walkway, but, more importantly, it preserves a record of the layers of soil through which the archaeologists dig. Each square is numbered, and each layer of soil is numbered. Each object found

This excavation at Tell Qasila reveals two strata, each from a different period in ancient civilization. Tell Qasila is near Tel Aviv.

is labeled with a tag carrying these numbers so it can always be properly identified and traced to its source. By means of surveying, drawings, and a wealth of pictures taken by photographers, careful records are kept of each phase of the excavation. This procedure is very important, for the work of archaeologists is very destructive, and later evaluations of the results of the dig rest heavily on every item and observation that are thus recorded.[2]

Stratification. More than in most areas of the world, cities in the ancient Near East tended to build upon older ruins, creating mounds (called *tells*) of some size and depth. Since sources of water were scarce and crossroads of commercial routes were important, communities built their shops and

The typical tools of a "digger," for use in archaeological excavations.

2. Sir Mortimer Wheeler, *Archaeology From the Earth* (Oxford: Clarendon Press, 1954) and Kathleen Kenyon, *Beginning in Archaeology* (New York: Frederick A. Praeger, 1961).

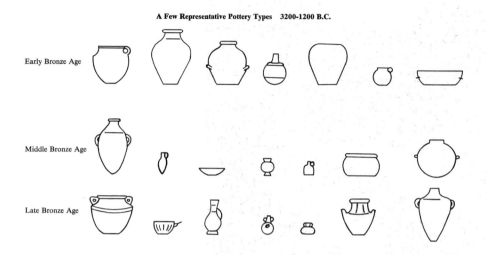

A Few Representative Pottery Types   3200-1200 B.C.

Early Bronze Age

Middle Bronze Age

Late Bronze Age

homes close by them. As the older ruins were located at the most logical spot, the newer city arose on top of the old. The site therefore took on a layer-cake effect.

This layering of the ruins has been a boon to archaeologists, for, obviously, the layers were successively older from top to bottom. At least this has provided a sequence of age; it has not, in itself, told the archaeologist how long a particular people lived on that spot, their identity, or the dates, according to our calendar, that should be assigned to that layer of soil. Nevertheless, the isolation of each layer of soil, the removal of artifacts from it, and the full and proper recording of all facts about each layer of soil are exceedingly important aspects of field archaeology.

Typology of Pottery. The excavation of a number of mounds (tells) of ruins of ancient cities has presented the archaeologist with a mass of pottery, both broken and whole. Careful analysis has revealed that certain kinds of pottery occur in certain layers of soil in the same sequence of strata (soil layers). Hence, like the strata in which they are found, types of pottery represent successively older periods of time, as an archaeologist digs down through a tell. Like stratification, pottery types outline a sequence of age but not the length of time involved, the identity of the potters, nor the precise dating according to our calendar.

7

Opening to underground silos in which calcinated grains of wheat, barley, lentils, and grapes were found. The silos date back to 4000 B.C. and are located near Beersheba.

Pottery chronology has been refined to the extent that archaeologists can, for the most part, come within fifty years, plus or minus, of dating the beginning and end of any occupation of a site. This system is now much more accurate than Carbon-14 dating (see below), and this system can be done best in Palestine. The pottery dates for other areas of the Near East are not so refined for ancient times.

Artifacts That Reveal the Past

A number of human products found by archaeologists aid in identifying people and dating events. These artifacts are mainly buildings, home utensils, implements used for hunting, farming and manufacturing, weapons of war, art objects, tombs, bones, weights, coins, and, above all, inscriptions.

This wide variety of man-made objects and inscriptions found in many ancient ruins has been correlated with soil layers and pottery types. The result has been a determination of the amount of time to be assigned to each strata; the identity of various people who have lived in the ancient Near East; the allotment of certain or nearly certain dates to nations, rulers, and events back to at least the eighth century B.C.; and relative dates back to about 3000 B.C.

Ideally, as many of these artifacts as possible should combine to give a fund of knowledge about the people who lived in the ancient Near East at any period of history. Since the Bible is set in the context of the ancient Near East, this knowledge has greatly enriched our understanding of the ways of thinking and practice that are sometimes described or sometimes only alluded to in the Bible. The resultant chronology has also provided a much more stable framework to which a student can relate biblical materials.

Carbon-14 and Other Promising Techniques

The discovery of the isotope C-14 in 1941 and its use in 1948 as a means to date ancient wood, fibrous material, and seeds has been exciting for archaeologists. The new method was quickly applied to confirm dates

An ancient Egyptian model of a plowman and oxen.

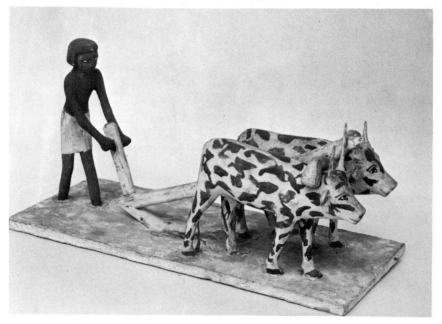

arrived at by other means. It also was found that the C-14 method could upset pet theories about dates that were based more on logic than on data.

The carbon-14 dating method involves radioactivity with a complicated chemistry. The procedure requires extreme care and sophisticated equipment. The method is not foolproof, it has weaknesses, though it is valuable. Its basic assumption is that the amount of isotopes of C-14 in the atmosphere has been constant over a long period of time. Some evidence, however, seems to indicate that there have been fluctuations of amounts of C-14 in the atmosphere. The fluctuations can cause inaccuracy in dating materials older than about 1000 B.C. For example, comparison of tree-ring dates with C-14 dates for 5000 B.C. show a deviation of about 750 years.

Another element of uncertainty in C-14 dating has to do with the half-life of the isotope. The journal, *Radiocarbon,* has published its data on the assumption that the half-life of C-14 is 5568 plus or minus 30 years, but

This cult object, which depicts snakes and birds, was recovered from the southern temple at Beth-Shan, level 5.

These lamps are typical of those commonly used in the ancient Near East. They burned oil, and illumination was by means of a lighted wick.

the Fifth Radiocarbon Dating Conference in 1962 established 5730 plus or minus 40 years as a standard.[3]

Kathleen Kenyon notes that the results of several laboratories in Europe and America gave her variants ranging as much as 500 to 800 years for objects taken from Mesolithic and Neolithic strata at Jericho.[4] Hence, the method can spotlight a span of time but not an exact date.

So far, the oldest date (C-14 can't reach back farther than about 40,000 years) for the ancient Near East is about 30,000 B.C. on some materials from the Shanidar Cave in Iraq. For Palestine, old dates come from the lowest levels of Jericho. The average of the results obtained by this method is about 9000 B.C., which is a thousand years older than anticipated. Materials from strata Miss Kenyon has assumed to be Neolithic have been dated by C-14 to be a full thousand years earlier than Neolithic is supposed to have begun. After pottery was invented, about 5000 B.C., the correlation has been much nearer to that accepted by pottery dating. After 3000 B.C., pottery dating and C-14 dating have been remarkably close together, with the former the more efficient method.

The C-14 method of dating is becoming more and more refined and reliable, hence a valuable tool. Other methods have recently been devised which are highly promising because they date artifacts that C-14 cannot.

---

3. Elizabeth K. Ralph, "Carbon-14 Dating," in *Dating Techniques for the Archaeologists* (Cambridge, Mass.: The MIT Press, 1971), p. 3.
4. Kathleen Kenyon, *Archaeology in the Holy Land* (New York: Praeger Publishers, 1970), pp. 330-334.

11

A few of the more significant are obsidian hydration rates, archaeomagnetism, thermoluminescence, tree-ring dating, and pollen flotation. More attention is centered on environmental and demographic factors. Field excavations have become training grounds for students and professors from many countries, with academic credits granted. Computerization of record keeping, data sorting, and statistical analysis will hopefully reduce the time lag between excavation and publication. The more methods used the better, for they will serve to check each other, thus producing dates by which a more reliable chronology can be constructed.

The Interrelation of Tradition, Inscription, and Archaeology

In spite of these advances toward setting up a clearly defined chronological scheme, we are still plagued with a paucity of data. To highlight how meager our knowledge still is, E. M. Yamauchi, of Miami University, Ohio, has summarized what has yet to be done to gain maximum information.[5]

Yamauchi points out that only a fraction (possibly as much as 10 percent) of what man has made or written survives. Only a fraction of the sites where these things can be found have yet been surveyed and noted on maps, and only a fraction (as little as 2 percent) of those identified have been touched by the excavator's spade. Furthermore, only a small percent of the total area of those sites dug into have been excavated. Finally, only a small percentage of the materials and information obtained by excavation has been published. Often, as much as forty to fifty years lapse between excavation and publication. What has been made available is extremely valuable, but much more is needed.

To show how evidences for ancient history may stand alone or overlap, Yamauchi presents a diagram with traditions, inscriptions, and materials, each in a circle that overlaps the other two.

Traditions represent late manuscripts bearing upon the ancient Near East. In this sense, biblical manuscripts, especially those of the books of the Pentateuch, can be called traditions because many centuries have elapsed between Moses' time and the oldest extant manuscript. In these manuscripts (i.e., Hebrew and Greek), there are many references to ancient peoples and events about which no non-Hebrew materials reveal a shred of information as yet.

---

5. Edwin M. Yamauchi, "Stones, Scripts, and Scholars," *Christianity Today* 8 (1969): 432-437; idem, *The Stones and the Scriptures* (New York: L. C. Lippincott Company, 1972), pp. 146-166.

Of the thousands of inscriptions of all sorts found in the Mesopotamian valley, the Nile valley, and the Levant, which come from the time-span represented by the Pentateuch, by far the greater majority of them provide data on people and events not mentioned at all in the Pentateuch. The same could be said of the materials other than inscriptions that archaeology has brought to light. Both inscriptions and other materials have supplied us with a picture of the world in which the Hebrew lived and moved that is invaluable.

In regard to the Pentateuch, non-Hebrew inscriptions to date have touched upon its content to a limited extent. There are some similarities in vocabulary and phrasing between the biblical and nonbiblical stories about creation, man, confusion of languages, and the flood in the Mesopotamian valley. There are some technical terms and basic concepts that are to be found both in the Patriarchal practices of marriage, adoption, and covenant making and in legal documents preserved on clay tablets. This includes a few names as well. Titles, names, and some customs are found in Egyptian inscriptions and in the Pentateuch, especially in regard to Joseph and Moses. Also, some laws are much alike.

The relation between inscription and archaeology is more obvious because most, but not all, inscriptions have been found by archaeologists. The translation and analysis of inscriptions have normally been the task of specialists who may or may not be archaeologsits.

The correlation between the Pentateuch and man-made products excavated by archaeological methods is still scanty. As far as we know, no items in museums can be identified directly with any of the men and women mentioned in the Patriarchal stories or any of the Hebrews involved in the Exodus. No site yet excavated has revealed a layer of soil, with artifacts, which can be said to be the remains of Hebrew occupation prior to the Conquest. It is known, however, that many of the places mentioned in the Pentateuch existed in ancient times. Perhaps under the mosque at Hebron there are bones and artifacts of the Patriarchs in the Cave of Machpelah, but archaeologists are not allowed to touch this spot that is so sacred to Islam.

The correlation of Pentateuchal material, non-Hebrew inscription, and archaeological artifact in regard to any one item is, up until now, rare. It may be that the buildings at Tell er-Ratabeh, which from bottom to top have bricks with adequate straw, bricks with little straw, and bricks with no straw, were built by the Hebrews; but this identification is still far from certain.

In summary, it may be said that we do not have as close a tie between the Pentateuchal witness and archaeology as we do for the Hebrew Kingdom period (1000-587 B.C.) or the New Testament period, but the cor-

13

relation is constantly becoming more closely knit together. A scholar can no longer prudently dismiss items in the Pentateuch as nonhistorical just because at the present time its witness stands alone. Archaeologists and specialists in the history and culture of the ancient Near East are busy people, and a knowledge explosion is now happening.

Recovering History from Archaeology

Since archaeological activities provide much of the raw data for historians of ancient eras, the constant challenge for researchers is to organize this data in such a way that the facts tell a credible story of past events. Several procedures have been commonly used in this type of research.

Circumstantial evidence obviously plays an important role because no one has survived and no voice recordings have been preserved. Inscriptions and artistic representations of people and their activities have been recovered, but in most cases they are meager in number.

To accurately describe the events of any ancient era, a historian must first bring together every scrap of evidence from geography, from the relationships between strata in a mound of ruins (what is below is earlier, what is above is later), from artifacts, and from inscriptions. From this evidence the historian describes the who, how, when, and where of human affairs in a certain period.

The historian often must move from what is definitely known to what is partially known or not known at all. For example, a structure with unusual features may be found. Ancient works of art, inscriptions, and reports of other archaeologists are then searched for clues to the identity of the structure. Perhaps an inscription with a strange script form and/or an unknown language is discovered. Then experts in decipherment are asked to apply their skills in unlocking the secrets of the strange inscription. Making analogies (comparing something point by point with something else) is often helpful in studies of society, government, trade, religion, and military artifacts.

On a broader scale, a historian may select a developmental model which results in an understanding of the movement of events over a long period of time. A model that regards human affairs as happening according to rigid laws of cause and effect may serve as a framework about which the raw data are molded. A theory of how social and cultural changes take place may be the model with which the researcher may compare rather limited data and then perhaps fill in the blanks with interpretations influenced by the model. For example, efforts have been made to understand the tribal system of the Israelites during the period of the judges by studying the amphictyonies of ancient Greek and Italian tribes, in which the states shared a common religious center. Modern theories of changes in trade practices may be applied to ancient times in an effort to make sense out of limited factual evidence. A Hegelian concept of thesis, antithesis, and synthesis may be utilized to explain how various religious beliefs, practices, and literature changed and matured over the years.

In the pages which follow, illustrations and explanations of many analogies and models will be found. The reader may wish to analyze how these tools of the historian are used as he studies the contents of this book and those listed in the bibliographies.

ARCHAEOLOGICAL AGES IN THE ANCIENT NEAR EAST

The following discussion will endeavor to sketch briefly the highlights of each period of time that archaeologists have constructed to which they can peg the information they discover. This framework is chosen as basic because it extends further back than the beginnings of the Egyptian dynasties and further forward than the significant dynasties. It can incorporate all of the ancient Near East, not just one area of it.

Archaeologists have customarily labeled the periods of time according to the dominant implements associated with those preceding the Greek period. At the turn of the century, some archaeologists (and most Israeli archaeologists now) designated the periods following 3000 B.C. in terms of the people who dominated Palestine. This variation will be noted where appropriate. The discussion will range from the Mesolithic Age through the Iron Age. through the Iron Age.

An effort will be made to correlate dates according to our present calendar, Egyptian dynasties, and Mesopotamian, Levant, and Asia Minor culture periods with these archaeological ages. The Old Testament as a whole will also be tied in with this chronological scheme.

The Mesolithic (Middle Stone) Age

The beginning point of the Mesolithic Age is obscure and varies between 12000 and 9000 B.C. and ends at approximately 6500 B.C. Some would suggest a proto-Neolithic or pre-pottery Neolithic beginning about 9000 B.C. This would make Mesolithic earlier, perhaps 14000 to 9000 B.C.

Most information comes from the caves of Mount Carmel and the bottom layers of soil at Jericho, where carbon-14 dating goes back to the beginning of the period. This age has also been called Natufian by Miss Dorothy Garrod because she first found evidence of it in Wadi en-Natuf. Somewhat similar stone implements have been discovered at Helwan, Egypt. The continuous stratification in the mound of debris at Jericho offers no evidence of a flood (Gen. 7–8), so some would rule the Flood to be earlier, perhaps at the beginning of the period.

The Neolithic (New Stone) Age

In round numbers the dates of this period are 6500-4000 B.C. Jericho is the main source of artifacts, with a limited number provided by a few other sites in Palestine. The earlier strata are sometimes called the Tahunian phases.

The big event of this age was the invention of pottery about 5000 B.C.; some would push this date back to 6000 B.C. This pottery is referred to as Yarmukian, for it was first found by the Yarmuk River near the village of Sha'ar Hagolan. The excavation of Jericho supplied archaeologists with quantities of this pottery, taken from an unbroken sequence of soil layers. Miss Kenyon has been able to obtain a goodly number of carbon-14 datings for this span of time. Jarmo, Hassuna, Tepe Gawra, and Nineveh in Mesopotamia; Ras Shamrah (Ugarit), Tell ej-Judeideh, and Byblos in the upper Levant; and El-Fayum, Deir Tasa, Merimdeh, and Beni Salameh in Egypt have contemporary levels.

The Chalcolithic (Copper-Stone) Age

Approximately a thousand years are assigned to this age, namely 4000-3000 B.C. Archaeologists are not in full agreement about the dates, however. Copper smelting and copper working was the big advance of this period.

Knowledge about this age is not extensive but is steadily increasing. Jericho and Ghassul in the lower Jordan valley have been the biggest producers of artifacts, but a dozen or more other sites in Palestine have provided their share. Tell Halaf, Tepe Gawra, and Tell el-Ubeid are the most important sites in the Mesopotamian valley. Three places in Egypt, El-Badari, El-Amrah, and Nagada, had contemporary cultures.

The Early Bronze (Canaanite) Age

This age spans almost the entire third millennium B.C. and is characterized by the building of cities all over the ancient Near East. The earliest written records of human activity come from the beginning of this period, both from the Mesopotamian and the Nile valleys.

In Egypt, the organization of the entire Nile valley to somewhat beyond the first cataract into a political unit was accomplished early in this period. City states developed in the Mesopotamian valley and did not combine into a short-lived empire until late in the Early Bronze Age. This is the thousand-year period immediately before the time of the Patriarchs.

Most of the Palestinian cities, such as Beth-Shan, Megiddo, and Lachish, began somewhat before or around 3000 B.C. and grew rapidly. Almost all settlements of any size were completely destroyed toward the end of the Early Bronze Age.

This age is customarily divided into four periods labeled by the symbols I, II, III, IV. Early Bronze I is dated from 3200 to 3050 B.C. on one side to 2900 B.C. as its close. It is parallel to the predynastic period in Egypt and the settlement of Jemdet Nasr in Mesopotamia.

EB II spans 2900 to 2650 B.C. and is paired with the first and second dynasties of Egypt. The Sumerian early dynastic period was just beginning in the Mesopotamian valley.

EB III covers the time span of 2650 B.C. to about 2400 B.C. The third through fifth dynasties were in power in Egypt. This is sometimes called the Old Kingdom (or the Pyramid) Age. In Mesopotamia the Sumerian culture was at its high point, with Ur, Akkad, Erech, and Lagash as its great cities.

EB IV reaches from about 2400 to 2200 B.C. It was a time of chaos in Egypt with rapid decay of central power beginning in the Seventh Dynasty and continuing until the Eleventh Dynasty. In contrast, the Semites who conquered the Sumerians set up the first Akkadian empire under Sargon I. Some important fortresses in Palestine, such as Beth-Yerah, Beth-Shan, Tell el-Farah, and Ai were destroyed early in this period.

The Early Bronze Age is also the era of the newly discovered Eblaite Empire.[6]

CORRELATION OF EGYPTIAN DYNASTIES AND ARCHAEOLOGICAL PERIODS 3200 to 1200 B.C.		
Dates (B.C.)	**Egypt**	**Archaeological Periods**
3200-2900	Predynastic	Early Bronze I
2900-2650	Dynasties I, II	Early Bronze II
2650-2400	Dynasties III-V	Early Bronze III
2400-2200	Dynasties VI-X	Early Bronze IV
2200-1900	Dynasty XI	Middle Bronze I
1900-1750	Dynasty XII	Middle Bronze IIa
1750-1650	Dynasties XIII-XIV	Middle Bronze IIb
1650-1550	Dynasties XV-XVII	Middle Bronze IIc
1550-1350	Dynasty XVIII	Late Bronze I
1350-1200	Dynasty XIX	Late Bronze II

NOTE: It should be understood that the dates in the left column are approximate. Considerable disagreement still exists in regard to these dates.

6. Giovanni Pettinato, "The Royal Archives of Tell Mardikh-Ebla," *Biblical Archeologist* 39:2 (May 1976). Basic information about this recent discovery is given in this article.

The Middle Bronze (Canaanite) Age

The dates 2200-1550 B.C. mark the beginning and the end of this age, which is divided into MB I (2200-1900 B.C.), MB IIa (1900-1750 B.C.) and MB IIb (1750-1550 B.C.) by most archaeologists. A variation is MB IIb (1750-1630 B.C.) and MB IIc (1630-1550 B.C.).

In regard to Egypt, MB I spans the end of the Old Kingdom and the beginning of the Middle Kingdom, also called the First Intermediate Period.

MB IIa marks the growing power of the Twelfth Dynasty of Egypt, often referred to as the Middle Kingdom, which soon controlled most of the Levant, i.e., the eastern coastal area of the Mediterranean Sea.

MB IIb designates the span of time during which the Semitic invaders, the Hyksos, dominated Egypt. They represent the Fifteenth and Sixteenth dynasties. Some would include the Seventeenth Dynasty. Another designation of this period is Second Intermediate.

The Late Bronze (Canaanite) Age

The Late Bronze Age begins with the expulsion of the Hyksos, roughly 1550 B.C. to the coming of the Philistines, which is roughly 1200 B.C.

The Eighteenth and the Nineteenth dynasties constituted the powerful New Kingdom of Egypt, which ruled all of the eastern coastline of the Mediterranean Sea to the Orontes River. During this time, the Late Bronze Age is divided into LB I (1550-1350 B.C.), which is the Eighteenth Dynasty, and LB II (1350-1200 B.C.), which is the Nineteenth Dynasty. A variation is LB I (1550-1400 B.C.), LB IIa (1400-1300 B.C.), LB IIb (1300-1200 B.C.).

The Iron (Israelite and Persian) Age

Starting with the Philistine invasion, about 1200 B.C., the Iron Age goes to the Greek invasion in 333 B.C. It is split into Iron Age I (1200-900 B.C.), and Iron Age III (600-300 B.C.). Some have argued that Iron I should close with the division of the kingdom in 932 or 922 B.C., that Iron II should extend to the Fall of Jerusalem in 587/6 B.C., and Iron III with the Greek invasion 333 B.C. This would give more preciseness to the dating sequence. A variation is Iron I (1200-1000 B.C.), Iron II (1000-840 B.C.), Iron III (840-587 B.C.), Persian (587-330 B.C.)

Suggested Books for Further Study

Aharoni, Yohanan. *The Archaeology of the Land of Israel.* Philadelphia: Westminster Press, 1978.

Albright, W. F. *The Archaeology of Palestine.* Baltimore: Penguin Books, 1961.

Daniels, G. *The Origins and Growth of Archaeology.* New York: Thomas Y. Crowell, 1971.

Dever, William G. *Archaeology and Biblical Studies: Retrospects and Prospects.* Evanston: The Winslow Lectures at Seabury-Western Seminary, 1973.

Gardiner, Alan. *Egypt of the Pharaohs.* Oxford: Clarendon Press, 1961.

Kenyon, Kathleen. *Archaeology in the Holy Land.* New York: Praeger Publishers, 1970.

_____. *Beginnings in Archaeology.* New York: Frederick A. Praeger, 1961.

Lapp, Paul. *The Tale of a Tell.* Pittsburgh: The Pickwick Press, 1975.

Mellaart, James. *Earliest Civilizations of the Near East.* London: Thames and Hudson, 1965.

Michael, H. N. and Ralph, E. K. *Dating Techniques for the Archaeologist.* Cambridge, Mass.: The MIT Press, 1971.

Schoville, Keith N., *Biblical Archaeology in Focus.* Grand Rapids: Baker Book House, 1978.

Wheeler, Mortimer. *Archaeology from the Earth.* Oxford: Clarendon Press, 1954.

Wilson, John. *The Culture of Ancient Egypt.* Chicago: The University of Chicago Press, 1958.

Wright, G. E. *Biblical Archaeology.* Philadelphia: The Westminster Press, 1960.

Yamauchi, Edwin M. *The Stones and the Scriptures.* New York: J. B. Lippincott Co., 1972.

The figure of Gudea, an enlightened Sumerian ruler who occupied the throne of Lagash.

2

The People
of the Ancient Near East

The center of interest in the Pentateuch is the ancestors of the Hebrews and the beginnings of their nation. Other people are mentioned only in passing, as they fit into genealogies or into stories. Up until the nineteenth century more was known about the Egyptians than about others, but, even then, information was meager. Many people mentioned in the Pentateuch were totally unknown from any other source. That situation has radically changed. True, the record on some is incomplete, but details are coming in steadily. Extrabiblical account on a few are still practically nonexistent.

The purpose of this section is to summarize basic data that has accumulated about people mentioned in the Pentateuch and a few that are not mentioned, and to list a bibliography to which the student can turn for details. The hope is that this background will illuminate otherwise obscure passages in the Scripture.

THE MESOPOTAMIAN VALLEY

The Sumerians

The Sumerians are not mentioned in the Bible and were totally unknown until the nineteenth century. The first evidence of their culture was found at Tell ul-Ubaid in the lower Mesopotamian valley, and they are first mentioned by name in an inscription dated about 2400 B.C.

The Sumerians probably came into the valley from the north toward the end of the fourth millennium B.C. but this is not certain. Their important cities were Eridu, Ur, Larsa, Isin, Adab, Kullah, Lagash, Nippur, and Kish.

A remarkable people, the Sumerians were skilled in the arts and crafts,

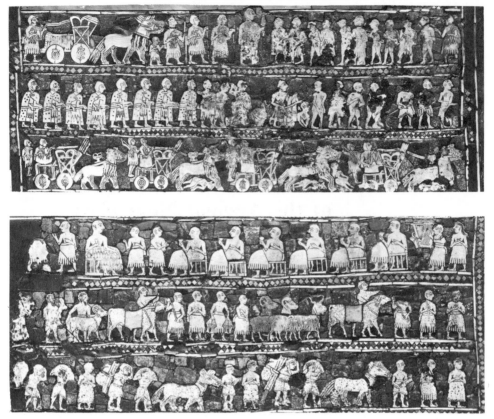

The standard of Ur: the top panel shows scenes of war and the bottom panel depicts scenes of peace.

built massive structures, developed an irrigation system, devised a system of writing, and set up formal education centers. They produced a varied literature, including religious mythology and ethical thought, mathematics, epics, hymns, and law.

The invading Akkadians (Semites) conquered the Sumerians about 2400 B.C. and borrowed heavily from their culture. The Sumerians were able to regain their independence for a short time (2100-2000 B.C.). The Sumerians created the impressive urban centers of Isin, Erech, Lagash, and especially Ur, from whence Abraham is said to have emigrated (Gen. 11:31). The influx of more and more Semites, which culminated in Hammurabi's rise to power, removed the Sumerians from history.

The Hurrians

In the Pentateuch, the name *Horites* (possibly Jebusites and, in some instances, Hivites) seems to refer to the Hurrians. This people lived all over the upper Mesopotamian valley but were concentrated in the upper Tigris valley. The excavations at the city of Nuzi in that area have provided the bulk of our information about the Hurrians.

The Hurrians learned much from the Sumerians and taught the Hittites their new-found culture. Some moved into Palestine and influenced the Canaanites. They were politically strong from about 2500-1000 B.C., but were at their peak during the Mitanni Kingdom (1470-1350 B.C.).

For additional information on Nuzi, see pages 299–301 in the appendix.

The Elamites

The name occurs in Genesis 10:22 and 14:1, 9. They are more commonly known to us as Persians. Living in the mountains to the east, they were the plague of the nations in the Mesopotamian valley. The Elamites destroyed the Third Dynasty of Ur about 2000 B.C. and ruled other cities in the valley until they were evicted by Hammurabi. They came back in to destroy the Kassites about 1155 B.C. at Babylon.

The Assyrians

The land of Assyria is mentioned four times in Genesis, but the nation does not come into the Bible narrative until the Hebrew divided kingdom

An Assyrian, fishing with a line, stands in a pond and supports a basket of caught fish on his back. The relief was found at Nineveh.

period. They were an active people as far back as 3000 B.C. in the upper Tigris valley. The Assyrian king list found at Khorsabad includes seventeen nomadic kings up till they were subjugated by Sargon I. Later, the Third Dynasty of Ur ruled their land.

Regaining some independence about 1950 B.C., the Assyrians pushed their trade routes into Anatolia, providing military protection for their merchants. One of the strong rulers of Assyria at this time was Shamshi-Adad I, who seems to have been more powerful than Hammurabi. Only after Shamshi-Adad's death was Hammurabi really able to dominate Meso-

Assyrian relief of horses' heads, which was recovered from Sargon's palace in Khorsabad.

potamia. The Hittites blocked Assyrian expansion in the eighteenth century and the Assyrians were harassed by a series of foreign nations for several hundred years. They recovered freedom in the fourteenth century, and slowly rebuilt their power to the point of being the dominant force in the ancient Near East from the tenth to the end of the seventh centuries B.C., becoming actual ruler of the ancient Near East for roughly a century between 725 and 625 B.C.

The Akkadians

Only the main city of this people, Akkad (Accad, or Agade), is mentioned in Genesis 10:10. These Semites came into the lower Mesopotamian valley from the north about 2400 B.C. Their first strong ruler was Sargon I, who carved out an empire from Elam (Persia) to the Euphrates River.

The Akkadians absorbed the Sumerian culture with little change. Their specialty was commerce and their trading routes covered the ancient Near East. Their empire was destroyed by the Gutians, who swarmed down from the Caucasus about 2250 B.C. and ruled for about a century.

The Amorites

The Amorites are mentioned fairly often in the Pentateuch but are not always clearly distinguished from the Canaanites. Research in the past century has shown that they were Semites who migrated west from the lower Mesopotamian valley to the upper Euphrates valley and on into Palestine. Their name literally means "Westerner," and the Gutian invasion seems to have been the reason for their move.

The Amorites succeeded in capturing Mari, on the south bank of the Euphrates, and made it their wealthy capital. They were powerful from about 2000 B.C. to the rise of Hammurabi, who destroyed Mari completely.

Archaeologists have discovered about twenty thousand clay tablets at Mari. Some of these inscriptions are of a legal nature but most are about everyday domestic and business affairs. Their content throws much light on Patriarchal customs. For more information on Mari and the tablets discovered there, see pages 296–98 in the appendix.

The Babylonians

In Genesis, the main city of the Babylonians, Babel, is mentioned in 10:10 and 11:9, whereas their land is referred to as Shinar in 11:2 and 1:1, 9, or as Chaldees in 11:28, 31 and 15:7. The first Babylonian empire was created by Hammurabi about 1728 B.C. and continued until its destruction about 1530 B.C. by the Kassites.

The empire stretched from the Zagros Mountains to the northeast corner of the Mediterranean Sea. It was the second attempt to unite that area under one ruler. Some have attempted to identify Hammurabi with the Amraphel of Genesis 14:1, 9, but no general agreement has been reached on this problem.

During the time of this empire, a great deal of ancient literature was copied on new clay tablets. This was religious material of a practical type. The corpus of law called the Code of Hammurabi comes from this time. It has several laws which are strikingly like some Mosaic laws.

The Kassites

The KJV, in Genesis 2:13, translates the Hebrew word, *Cush,* as Ethiopia, but leaves it untranslated in 10:6, 8. The context would seem to indicate that in 2:13 and in 10:8 it refers to an area and a people in the northern Tigris valley, whereas in 10:6 the Cush mentioned may indeed be Ethiopia.

It is now known that a people called the Kassites did indeed live far to the north and moved into the lower Mesopotamian valley about 1530 B.C. to destroy the Babylonian Empire. They controlled the area for almost four hundred years, after which they were defeated by the Assyrians in the thirteenth century. Their death blow came when the Elamites came into the valley in the middle of the next century.

THE NILE VALLEY

The Egyptians

As far as we know, the first settlements of Egyptians began about 5000 B.C. and developed along the Nile valley as an agricultural society. These people soon learned how to irrigate their lands, and by the end of the fourth millennium B.C. had established trade with the Mesopotamian valley.

The Egyptians first organized as forty-two districts (*nomes,* comparable to the Sumerian city state), then as two nations: Upper (southern) Egypt and Lower (delta) Egypt. A clever people, they early devised a calendar and a system of geometry.

The first ruler over all Egypt was Menes of Thinis in Upper Egypt. He soon saw that he could rule more effectively by building a capital at Menfe (Memphis) at the southern end of the Nile delta. The cemeteries of these first two dynasties were at Abydos in the south and Sakkara in the north.

The powerful Old Kingdom ruled for at least five hundred years and constructed the amazing pyramids. During this period was fixed that approach to life that would characterize Egyptian thought for the next two

The famous sphinx of Egypt, with two of the great pyramids in the background.

Bust of the Egyptian Queen Nefertiti.

thousand years. The Old Kingdom was followed by a century or more of chaos, after which arose the feudal Middle Kingdom with the main capital at Thebes. Abraham's visit to Egypt (Gen. 12:10-20) may have occurred early in this period. It was the golden age of Egypt's classical literature.

Early in the eighteenth century, the Middle Kingdom fell apart. By 1750 B.C., the invading Hyksos took over control of the land. They ruled for two centuries before being expelled by princes from Thebes, about 1550 B.C.

The New Kingdom of the Eighteenth and Nineteenth dynasties provided the Egyptians with their high point of international power. The first pharaoh of this period was probably the one "who did not know Joseph" (Exod. 1:8).

The Eighteenth Dynasty is characterized by the remarkable Queen Hatshepsut, the imperialist Thutmosis III, and the heretic Amenhotep IV, also known as Akhnaton (Ikhnaton).

The Nineteenth Dynasty produced the outstanding Rameses II, who, for almost seventy years, ruled Egypt and the Levant. During this dynasty, the capital was moved to Avaris (Tanis).

The Hyksos

Coming from the northeast, the Hyksos were basically Semitic, but their leaders seemed to be Aryans and possibly some Hurrians. Manetho describes them as savage destroyers. He called them "Shepherd Kings," but in Egyptian the name means "rulers of foreign lands."

The Hyksos conquered Egypt about 1720 B.C. They soon put Semites in official positions and seemed to have some kind of relationship with the Habiru, or Apiru/Aperu in the Egyptian language. Two of the Hyksos leaders had the names *Jacob-el* and *Jacob-baal*. Joseph and the migration of Jacob's family to Egypt may have taken place early during the Hyksos rule of Egypt.

The Hyksos set up a feudal state in Palestine and built forts of packed earthwork at Sharuhen, Jericho, Shechem, Tell Beit-Mirsim, and at Hazor. At the end of their rule, all the land of Egypt except temple property belonged to the pharaoh. They were expelled from Egypt by the princes of Thebes, who had finally developed the horse chariot and mastered the composite bow, in 1570 B.C.

ASIA MINOR AND THE LEVANT

The Eblaites

Until 1975, scholars had no hint of an extensive empire of West Semitic people that had been centered at Ebla, now known as Tell-Mardikh in northern Syria. Interestingly, one of Ebla's strong leaders was Ebrum, who is associated by some with Eber in Genesis 10:21. Note also that Obal (Gen. 10:28) may be a variant of Ebla. Eblaite power spanned the period from 2400 to 2250 B.C.

The Hittites

The Hittites are referred to as Heth in Genesis 10:15 and as Hittites in Genesis 23:3-20 and in 27:46. In some instances the people called Hivites may have been Hittites. Though some of these people were in Palestine, their center of power was in Anatolia (Turkey).

The Hittites seem to have come from southern Russia and were the first Indo-Europeans to move into Anatolia. There they mingled with people called Khatti. They slowly built up a nation, which became the so-called Old Kingdom that ruled from 1750-1450 B.C. Their capital was Khattusas (Boghazkoy), where their culture was first excavated in A.D. 1906.

The Hittites were weak for about fifty years; then they established the powerful empire (1400-1200 B.C.) of thirteen kings, who stopped the Egyptians and conquered the Babylonians and Hurrians, only to be destroyed by the Greeks who were fleeing the Doric invasion of their land.

The Hittites had a levirate marriage arrangement much like the Hebrews, and built casement walls, which were also used by the Hebrew kings. Their covenant forms were much like those described in the Old Testament.

Hittite soldier on a sculptured slab, from Carchemish.

29

The Beni Hasan tomb painting shows Semites entering Egypt during the nineteenth century B.C.

The Habiru

The ancient relationship between the Hebrews and the people whom the Akkadians called the Habiru/Hapiru and the Egyptians named Apiru/Aperu has been a difficult puzzle for scholars to solve. Phonetically, the name is equivalent to the word *Hebrew*. In the Pentateuch is a Hebrew ancestor named Eber (Gen. 10:21-25; 11:14) and Heber (Gen. 46:17; Num. 26:45). Abraham is called a Hebrew in Genesis 14:13, and his descendents receive the same label in Genesis 39:14; 40:15; 43:32; Exodus 2:6; and Deuteronomy 15:12.

In the nonbiblical literature, the Habiru appear all over the ancient Near East, going back before 2000 B.C. Albright calls them "donkey caravaneers." At least they were nomadic and filled such roles as bandits, servants, craftsmen, and even musicians. In the Tell el-Amarna letters, they are depicted as attacking Palestine from the east much as the Hebrews under Joshua did. Much more needs to be known about them.

The Philistines

A small group in southwest Palestine is called Philistines in Genesis 26:1-33 (cf. 20:1-18), and in Genesis 10:13-14 they are related to Egypt. They do not appear on the scene in force until the migration of a number of them to the same part of Palestine about 1200 B.C.

The Philistines came from the Aegean Sea area. Some destroyed the Hittite empire and moved on into the Levant from Anatolia. Others seemed to have come by boat. The Egyptians called them "People of the Sea," who tried to invade their land but were repulsed. They settled in five cities: Gaza, Gath, Ashkelon, Ashdod, and Ekron. The Philistines had learned new methods of tempering iron from the Hittites and held a monopoly on the metal for several hundred years. This privilege gave them a strong economic and military advantage over the Israelites. Lacking a strong central leadership, they were unable to profit long from this power. King David was able to reduce them to servitude in his kingdom.

The Greeks applied their name to all the land of Canaan, so it has come down to us as Palestine to this day. Only two Philistine names have survived —Goliath and Achish—and only one word, *seren*, meaning military lord.

The Canaanites

The Canaanites were the people with whom the Hebrews had the most continuous interrelationship, for they were the long-term inhabitants of Palestine. The people and their land are referred to more often in the Pentateuch than any other people or land.

On a wall of the temple at Medinet Habu, this relief depicts two Philistine prisoners being brought to Rameses III, the victor.

The various references in Genesis relate them closely to Egypt (cf. Gen. 10:6) and at times include several subgroups under their name. They are repeatedly depicted as undesirable neighbors.

Whether the inhabitants of the Levant during the third millennium B.C. were Canaanites is a debated question. Some would say that they came into the land about 2000 B.C. and perhaps were the same as the Amorites (cf. Gen. 15:16). The Akkadians used the term to designate the "Land of the Purple" because of a purple dye made of the murex mollusks on the eastern coast of the Mediterranean Sea. The Greeks used their own term for purple dye, and called the inhabitants Phoenicians.

Since the Egyptians dominated the land of Canaan most of the time during the third and second millenniums B.C., the inhabitants were powerfully influenced by them. The Egyptians referred to Byblos as the main Canaanite seaport and carried on extensive trade with that city. The earliest reference to the Canaanites by name in Egyptian records is found in an inscription by Amenhotep II in the fifteenth century. The Egyptians allowed them to build fortresses and establish city-states within a feudal system. These Semites had a marked influence on Egypt through their religion. Much of Baalism was accepted by the Egyptian people.

The bearded Canaanite foes of the Egyptian Pharaoh Seti I are featured on this relief on the exterior of the north wall of the temple at Karnak.

The Arameans

The Pentateuch mentions a people whose ancestor was Aram (Gen. 10:22, 23; 22:21), and notes that Balaam came from the land of that people (Num. 23:7). Their land is also called Paddan-aram (Gen. 25:20; 28:5; see also 24:10 where the same word is translated as Mesopotamian in KJV). Abraham's relatives are called Syrians, which is often the English form of the label Arameans (in 25:20, KJV), and Abraham himself is called such in Deuteronomy 26:5. They lived in the region between the Tigris and Euphrates rivers and later made their capital at Damascus.

The Arameans were basically Semitic and probably come under the more general term *Amorite*. They did develop a culture of their own, which was to have a wide impact on the later Assyrian and Babylonian empires. They had a separate nation called Syria (Aram) during the kingdom period of the Israelites. It was destroyed by the Assyrians about 732 B.C.

A Summary of Ancient Near Eastern Affairs

Since there is little known about what went on in the ancient Near East prior to the Early Bronze Age, this summary will begin with approximately 3200 B.C. to span two millennia until 1200 B.C. According to the contents of the Pentateuch, the events that it records took place mostly during the Late Bronze Age. This survey will only bring out the highlights in terms of leaders and events and will not endeavor to wrestle with controversies over details, of which there are many.

One of the remarkable features of the beginnings of the Early Bronze Age is the almost sudden appearance of major civilizations in the Mesopotamian and Nile valleys. At the same time, new migrations were taking place in Palestine. The earlier Chalcholithic culture disappeared from Palestine, leaving a blank of several centuries in archaeological data. These new migrations seem to have come from the north, and the people comprising these waves of settlement were responsible for building the new fortified cities that sprang into being. The civilizations of Mesopotamia and the Nile bracketed this new influx into Palestine and soon made trade contacts with it.

Two interrelated factors contributed to the growth of cities and of trade at the beginning of the third millennium B.C. In both major valleys, seemingly with no knowledge of each other's activities, communities began to control the supply of water by constructing irrigation systems. This new technology meant that larger groups of people could live together, that a surplus of food was available for trade, and that leaders were required both to manage the irrigation systems and the people who worked them.

Related to the new technology of irrigation were other technologies.

In both Egypt and Mesopotamia, systems of recording numbers and concepts were devised and developed—systems which continued to function for at least three thousand years. Trade organizations were developed to barter surplus food for precious metals and stones. Craftsmen developed skills to turn these raw materials into implements, weapons, and gems, which in turn were traded to neighboring people. There seems to be some evidence of trade contacts between the civilization of the two valleys, but no records have as yet been found of political or military encounters during the third millennium B.C.

The Sumerians organized themselves into a multitude of independent city-states, which often fought with each other. The Akkadians, who swept in from the Arabian desert, conquered them and forged the first empire of the Mesopotamian valley under the leadership of Sargon of Akkad (Agade) about 2350 B.C. The empire comprised all of the Tigris and Euphrates river basin areas, pushed into Asia Minor, and established outposts at harbors along the northeastern coast of the Mediterranean Sea. The empire dissolved about 2150 B.C., and the Sumerians at Ur became the dominant power in the valley.

Quite apart from the events taking place in the Mesopotamian valley, the Egyptians were united as a people of the Nile valley into a nation under the leadership of Menes about 3100 B.C. Basically, Egypt was considered as two parts: Lower Egypt, which is the delta of the Nile; and Upper Egypt, which is the long, narrow valley of the Nile, squeezed by forbidding deserts to the east and the west. As noted earlier, the Old Kingdom was in power for about five hundred years and produced the remarkable pyramids. There are indications that the Egyptians had trade relationships with parts of Palestine and may have controlled Palestine from the mighty fortress, twenty-seven acres in size with forty-five-foot-wide stone walls, at Et-Tell, north of Jerusalem.

A devastating force of unknown origin swept over Palestine about 2400 B.C. and left a number of fortress cities in utter ruins. So complete was the destruction that almost another five hundred years passed before cities were built again. About the same time, the Old Kingdom of Egypt fell apart, and disorder left the land torn by strife. The Egyptians remained isolated and shattered until the end of the Early Bronze Age.

Mostly materials found in tombs make up the testimony we have for the later part of the Early Bronze Age in Palestine. These materials seem to indicate that nomads were wandering to and fro over the land and that others were moving in from the northeast. The settling of these nomads in villages was a slow process, and by 2000 B.C. cities were beginning to reappear.

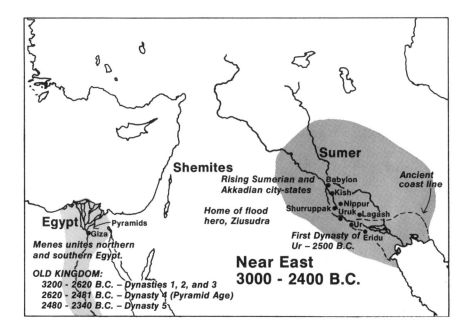

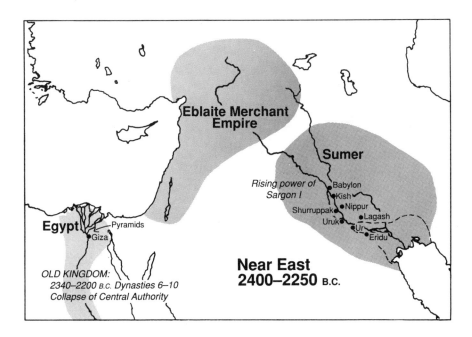

It has been popular to refer to the increasing migration of people from the northeast as the Amorite invasion made up of Semites pushed to the west after the fall of the Sargon empire and the revival of Sumerian power. Trade by means of donkey caravans was moving across the entire area, carrying food, raw materials, and finished products. The Patriarchs seemed to be part of this trade network, although they were more deeply motivated by divine guidance.

The eighteenth century was an important period in the ancient Near East. In the Mesopotamian valley, the Sumerians had been engulfed by invaders by 1900 B.C., and during this century the second great empire was forged by Hammurabi with Babylon as his capital. Before he could realize his empire dream, Hammurabi had to contend with Rimsin, leader of the invading Elamites, and Shamshi-Adad, who controlled the upper Euphrates and Tigris valleys. Shamshi-Adad ruled from Ashur on the Tigris, but through his relations with the Amorite kings at Mari, on the Euphrates, he blocked Hammurabi's moves toward the west. In the thirty-first and thirty-second years of his reign, Hammurabi was able to conquer his enemies and begin to forge his empire into shape. Clay tablet records found at Mari indicate that this took place about 1728 B.C. The empire stretched from the tip of the Gulf of Persia to the northeast corner of the Mediterranean Sea.

After the chaos of the so-called First Intermediate Period, Egypt began to pull itself together into a unified government called the Middle Kingdom, with its capital at Thebes. From this period come the famous Execration Texts and the "story of Sinuhe," which indicate considerable trade with the region of the Levant. The capital was shifted to Memphis and the Fayum was colonized.

The land became prosperous, and huge reservoirs were built to irrigate new land. Mines were developed in the Sinai peninsula, in which, incidentally, the earliest of all alphabetic inscriptions have been found. They were written by Semitic workers in the mines.

This period is, archaeologically speaking, the Middle Bronze IIa and the age of the Patriarchs of Genesis.

After the middle of the eighteenth century B.C., shifts of power took place in the ancient Near East. In the Mesopotamian valley, Hammurabi's empire burst forth into full glory. About the same time a horde of other Semitic people, led by non-Semites, pushed into Egypt. These migrants into the Nile valley were possessors of war materials unfamiliar to the Egyptians, and they were able to defeat the Egyptians fairly easily. The migrants had two-wheeled chariots pulled by horses. They had body armor and the new, powerful composite bow. They constructed large camps surrounded

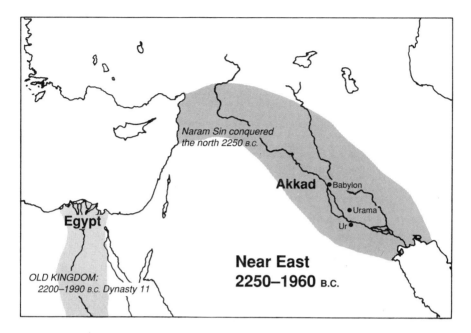

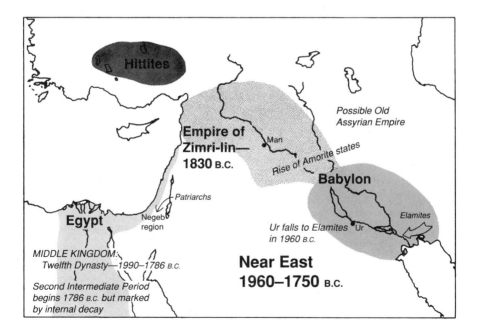

by earthen ramparts. Their capital was established on the northeastern side of the Nile delta at Avaris (Tanis).

There are very few inscriptions from this point of Egypt's history, but later inscriptions tell us that Egypt referred to these Semitic invaders as "rulers of foreign lands." The name commonly given to them is *Hyksos.* Their domination of Egypt was the first time non-Egyptians had been rulers over the isolated Egyptians, who were never to forget the humiliation of the experience.

The Hyksos ruled Egypt about one hundred and fifty years, a span of time fairly comparable to the domination of the Hammurabi, or the Old Babylonian Empire, in the Mesopotamian valley. Many scholars believe that Joseph came to Egypt early in the Hyksos rule of Egypt, but this has not been documented to the satisfaction of all. Many features of Canaanite religion were introduced to the Egyptians during this time and profoundly influenced their understanding of the divine and natural realms.

In the first half of the sixteenth century B.C., while the Hyksos were being expelled from Egypt, the Old Babylonian Empire of Mesopotamia was falling apart. Hurrians from the mountains to the north and Kassites from the mountains to the east were pushing relentlessly into the valley. Farther away to the northwest, the Hittite nation was becoming aggressive. They managed, under Mursilis I, to conquer Babylon in 1531 B.C. and rob the city of its wealth, but it was the Kassite nation that remained to dominate the Mesopotamian valley.

The Middle Bronze Age ended with the Egyptians again in control of their own land and hungry to grab new territory. The Babylonians bowed to the dominion of foreigners, and the Hittites were coming into their own as an international power. Also, another set of migrants were moving into the upper Tigris valley; they were the Hurrians who were determined to hew out their own domain and make a mark in the world.

During the next span of time, the Late Bronze Age, the Kassites made little impact outside of Babylon. The struggle for power shifted to the north between the Hurrians, who built the so-called Mitanni Empire, and the Hittites, who occupied the land now called Turkey. Actually, a three-cornered power hassle developed, for Egypt was on the move up the Mediterranean coast and clashed head-on with the Hittites, who were moving down the coast.

A new day had dawned in Egypt. The pharaohs of the Eighteenth Dynasty were an aggressive lot and, especially under Thutmosis III, made their new-found power felt all the way to the Orontes and Euphrates rivers. But prior to Thutmosis III, Egypt had a most interesting ruler for two decades. Thutmosis I had had only a daughter of pure royal blood, and a

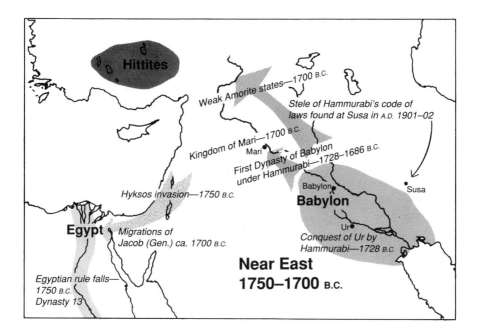

Hittites

Weak Amorite states—1700 B.C.

Stele of Hammurabi's code of laws found at Susa in A.D. 1901–02

Kingdom of Mari—1700 B.C.

Mari

First Dynasty of Babylon under Hammurabi—1728–1686 B.C.

Hyksos invasion—1750 B.C.

Babylon

Susa

Babylon

Egypt

Migrations of Jacob (Gen.) ca. 1700 B.C.

Ur

Conquest of Ur by Hammurabi—1728 B.C.

Near East 1750–1700 B.C.

Egyptian rule falls—1750 B.C. Dynasty 13

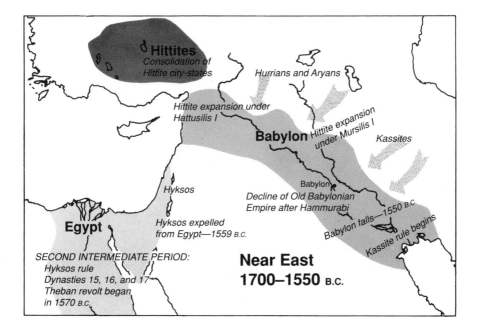

Hittites

Consolidation of Hittite city-states

Hurrians and Aryans

Hittite expansion under Hattusilis I

Babylon Hittite expansion under Mursilis I

Kassites

Hyksos

Babylon

Decline of Old Babylonian Empire after Hammurabi

Babylon falls—1550 B.C.

Egypt

Hyksos expelled from Egypt—1559 B.C.

Kassite rule begins

SECOND INTERMEDIATE PERIOD: Hyksos rule Dynasties 15, 16, and 17 Theban revolt began in 1570 B.C.

Near East 1700–1550 B.C.

crisis arose because Egypt had never before lacked a royal scion to the throne. It was axiomatic that the throne could only be occupied by a male. A son by a concubine was married to the royal daughter, but Thutmosis II did not live long. Another son of a lower-ranked woman was married to the royal daughter, but she refused to yield power to him. Queen Hatshepsut dominated Egypt with an iron fist. Statues and bas-reliefs consistently show her as a male. Her most lasting monument has been her mortuary temple built on the west side of the Nile opposite Thebes (Luxor) at Der el-Bahari. There is a strong suspicion that she met a tragic end. At any rate, her second half-brother husband, Thutmosis III, took over power and carved a niche in history with his many expeditions, inscriptions, and long reign. His sons followed valiantly in his steps, and a grandson, Thutmosis IV, married a princess of the Hurrian nation of Mitanni.

An unusual pharaoh of the Eighteenth Dynasty was Amenhotep IV, who began to rule about 1380 B.C. This pharaoh rebelled against the rising power of the priests at Thebes and forsook the capital to construct a new one of his own, several hundred miles downstream at a place that has come to be called Tell el-Amarna. The new pharaoh replaced the high god Amun of Thebes with Aten (Aton), the sun disk, and replaced his throne name with Akhnaton (Ikhnaton). The new capital was called Akhetaten. From the ruins of this city come the famous Tell el-Amarna letters, which were written on clay tablets, many of which came to Tell el-Amarna from Palestine.

During the nineteen-year reign of the heretic king, the strength of the frontiers at the Orontes and Euphrates rivers weakened and the garrisons in Palestine became ineffective. Not only was Akhnaton more interested in religion than his empire, but also the Hittites were moving out of Asia Minor (Turkey), reducing the Mitanni Empire to vassal status and also pushing down the eastern seaboard of the Mediterranean. Closer at home, the Habiru were crossing the Jordan River from the east, threatening cities in the highlands of Palestine. Appeals for help directed to the pharaoh seemed to fall on deaf ears.

With the death of Akhnaton, agitation grew to change the new direction set by him, to move the government back to Thebes, and to restore traditional religion. Two sons-in-law, Sakare (Semenkhare) and Tutenkhaten, consecutively followed Akhnaton as rulers. The second one changed his name to Tutenkhamun and moved back to Thebes. His father-in-law left a city that soon fell into ruins and was buried under drifting sand.

Tutenkhamun died as a youthful pharaoh, was buried in a deep tomb west of Thebes, and came into fame when that tomb was discovered intact

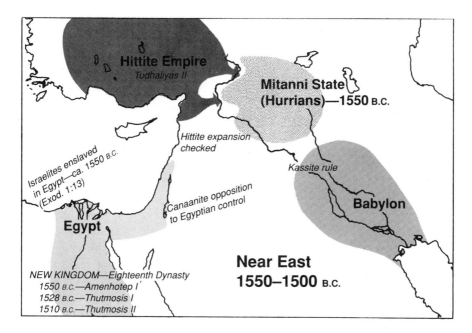

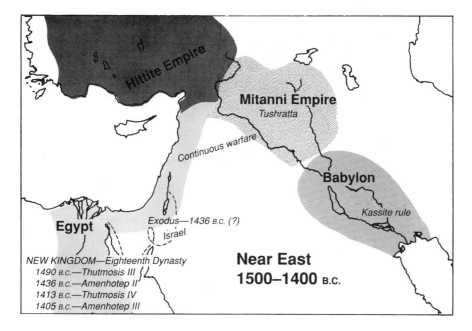

in A.D. 1922 (the first royal tomb ever to be found untouched by robbers).

The last pharaoh of the Eighteenth Dynasty was not an heir-apparent to the throne; and, being an old man, ruled only five years.

The Eighteenth Dynasty was marked by turbulent contacts with restless empires to the far north, but a great deal of trade flourished, involving the islands of Cyprus and Crete. Pottery and artifacts in Palestine reflect this widespread commerce.

Some argue that the Exodus and wilderness wanderings took place during the Eighteenth Dynasty. Factors in this debate will be discussed later; but, at the least, the Hebrews were in dynamic relationship with the Egyptians during this time span.

A new era opened for Egypt under the aggressive leadership of the pharaohs of the Nineteenth Dynasty. These men were generals of the army and had visions of making Egypt a power in the world again. The administrative center shifted from Thebes to the east side of the Nile delta. Two pharaohs, Seti I and Rameses II, were especially empire-minded and tried to establish anew the frontiers of Egypt on the Orontes and Euphrates rivers. The Hittite rulers did not like this move and contested it mightily. The Egyptian goal was not reached.

After a pitched battle at Kadesh in Syria (c. 1296 B.C.), the Hittites

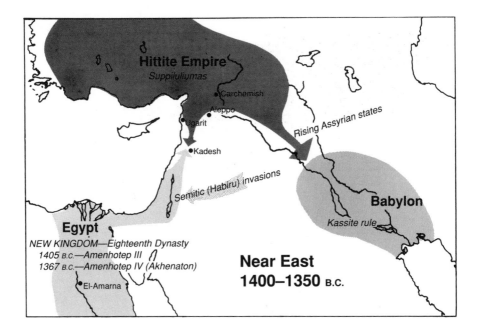

Hittite Empire
Suppiluliumas

•Carchemish

Aleppo

•Ugarit

Rising Assyrian states

•Kadesh

Semitic (Habiru) invasions

Babylon

Egypt
Kassite rule

Egypt

NEW KINGDOM—*Eighteenth Dynasty*
1405 B.C.—Amenhotep III
1367 B.C.—Amenhotep IV (Akhenaton)

•El-Amarna

**Near East
1400–1350** B.C.

and the Egyptians concluded a nonaggression pact in 1280 B.C. It established an uneasy coexistence policy for the two military giants of the day. The original silver plate on which this treaty was engraved has not been found, but Egyptian versions of it were carved on the walls of temples, and cuneiform tablets bearing the Hittite version have been found in Boghazkoy. The treaty was sealed with the marriage of a Hittite princess to Rameses II.

During most of the twelfth century B.C., the close of the Late Bronze Age, commerce continued to flow increasingly along the trade lanes of the ancient Near East. Sea traffic was an integral part of the network; and Palestine, as a land bridge, garnered its share of the wealth. The Canaanites built strong cities, but they also remained divided and contentious, making them easy prey to invaders. And invaders were busy, coming from the east out of the desert and from the west via boats. The Tell el-Amarna letters of about 1380 B.C. tell of attacks across the Jordan, and the Scriptures tell of the Hebrews who pressed into the land. Egyptian inscriptions tell of the "Sea People," who were landing on the coastline of the delta and near Gaza. Some of these new invaders were coming from the north after destroying the Hittite empire and major port cities such as Ugarit (Ras Shamrah). These people were the Philistines who were to bring the opulent Nineteenth Dynasty to its knees, push the Canaanites out of the Plain of Sharon back into Lebanon, and seriously threaten the existence of the Hebrew communities in the highlands of Palestine.

The Date of the Exodus

One of the most vexing problems of early Israelite history continues to be the dates of the Exodus, the wilderness wanderings, and the conquest of Palestine. As far as Israel is concerned, the quantity of data on persons, places, and time is the least for this period, in contrast with most other periods of her history. The data for the Exile, the other vague period, is filling in more rapidly than for the Exodus.

Ussher's date for the Exodus was 1491 B.C., but in more recent years the controversy has centered either in the reign of Amenhotep II of the Eighteenth Dynasty or Rameses II of the Nineteenth Dynasty.

Several date formulae in the Old Testament bear upon the Exodus and the Conquest. Exodus 12:40 states, "The time that the people of Israel dwelt in Egypt was four hundred and thirty years." The Septuagint and the Samaritan Pentateuch reads, "in Egypt and Canaan." Galatians 3:17 also mentions the same period of time, but Genesis 15:13 and Acts 7:6 speak of only four hundred years. The anchor point of either of these dates would be Joseph's relationship with the Hyksos. If he entered Egypt during their domination of Egypt, which began about 1730 B.C., then 430

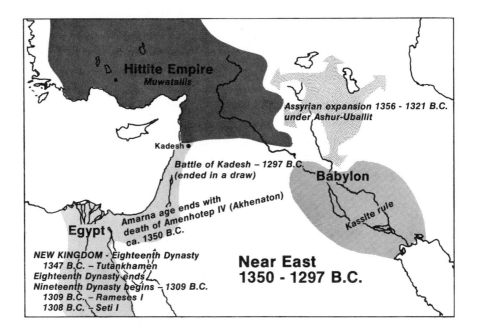

Hittite Empire
Muwatallis

Assyrian expansion 1356 - 1321 B.C.
under Ashur-Uballit

Kadesh ●

Battle of Kadesh – 1297 B.C.
(ended in a draw)

Babylon

Amarna age ends with
death of Amenhotep IV (Akhenaton)
ca. 1350 B.C.

Kassite rule

Egypt

NEW KINGDOM - Eighteenth Dynasty
1347 B.C. – Tutankhamen
Eighteenth Dynasty ends
Nineteenth Dynasty begins – 1309 B.C.
1309 B.C. – Rameses I
1308 B.C. – Seti I

**Near East
1350 - 1297 B.C.**

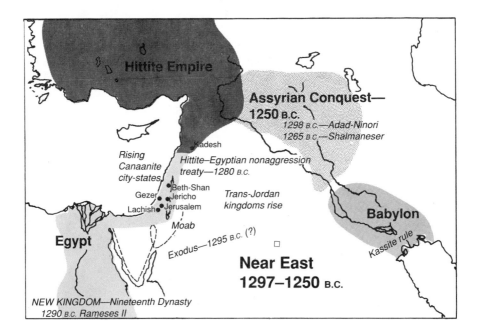

Hittite Empire

**Assyrian Conquest—
1250 B.C.**
1298 B.C.—Adad-Ninori
1265 B.C.—Shalmaneser

Kadesh

Rising
Canaanite
city-states

Hittite–Egyptian nonaggression
treaty—1280 B.C.

Gezer ● ● Beth-Shan
● Jericho
Lachish ● ● Jerusalem

Trans-Jordan
kingdoms rise

Babylon

● Moab

Exodus—1295 B.C. (?)

Kassite rule

Egypt

**Near East
1297–1250 B.C.**

NEW KINGDOM—Nineteenth Dynasty
1290 B.C. Rameses II

years would place the Exodus in the reign of Rameses II. If Joseph was earlier, then the Exodus was earlier.

There is a reference in Judges 11:26 that covers the time of the Conquest on to Jephthah's lifetime. It designates this span of time as three hundred years. Jephthah is dated by many scholars at about 1100 B.C. Hence the conquest of the area east of Jordan took place about 1400 B.C.

Another reference is I Kings 6:1, which declares that four hundred and eighty years had elapsed between the Exodus and the fourth year of Solomon, when he began to build the temple. Since this year of Solomon's reign is dated between 966-62 B.C., the Exodus would come at approximately 1440 B.C.

The biblical data would be much more helpful in our effort to establish a chronological date for the Exodus if the throne name of the pharaoh in Joseph's time, or of the pharaoh who oppressed the children of Israel, or of the pharaoh whose daughter befriended the baby Moses, or of the pharaoh from whom Moses fled, or of the pharaoh whom Moses challenged in the ten plagues, were stated in the biblical text. Consequently, many arguments that support one theory or another must depend heavily on inferences drawn from incidental statements in Scripture, upon possible correlations with pharaohs in either the Eighteenth or the Nineteenth dynasties of Egypt, or upon archaeological evidence found in the ruins of cities connected with Israel's conquest of Canaan.

A theory that places the Exodus at approximately 1440 B.C. and the Conquest at about 1400 B.C. was made popular by the report of John Garstang's excavation (1930-36) of Jericho. He claimed that a fallen wall not far below the surface of the tell was of Late Bronze Age date and that houses nearby had some Late Bronze pottery, as well as a few scarabs of the Eighteenth Dynasty of Egypt. Tombs in a cemetery also had some pottery of the same period. The conclusion was that he had found the city destroyed by Joshua's army.[1]

Because of dissatisfaction with Garstang's digging techniques and dating of Late Bronze pottery, Miss Kathleen Kenyon led an excavation at Jericho during the period of 1952-56. She found that Garstang's fallen wall was Early Bronze in date rather than Late Bronze and was inclined to date the Late Bronze pottery in the fourteenth century rather than the fifteenth century B.C. She noted, as did Garstang, that most of the Late Bronze city had been washed off the top of the mound.[2]

---

1. John Garstang, *The Story of Jericho* (London: Marshall, Morgan & Scott, 1948), pp. 125-130.

2. Kathleen Kenyon, *Digging Up Jericho* (New York: Frederick A. Praeger, 1957), pp. 167-185; 256-265.

Brickmaking in Eighteenth-Dynasty Egypt as depicted on the tomb of Rehkmire, Vizier of Upper Egypt.

Brickmaking along the Nile as it is done today. Wet clay is poured into a wooden frame, which is then lifted to repeat the process. The sun-dried bricks provide long-lasting building material in this land without rain.

Thus the archaeological witness of Jericho for the conquest, and, by inference, for Exodus, is scanty and inconclusive. Two problems in particular are troublesome. Jericho lacked any bi-chrome ware, which was abundant in the valley of Esdraelon and the lower plains of Sharon during the sixteenth and early fifteenth centuries B.C. This pottery has not been found in the Jordan valley. The other problem is the dating of ash layers and the attribution of them to specific invaders. Garstang and Kenyon disagree at this point; so do other archaeologists.

The Tell el-Amarna clay tablets, sent to Ikhnaton (Amenhotep IV) about 1380-70 B.C., were written by Canaanite kings in Palestine who complained about an invasion from the east by the Habiru. They asked for troops to protect them. Some scholars have identified these Habiru with the Hebrews under Joshua, but others are doubtful. Hence, the contribution of these tablets to the dating of the Conquest, and therefore the Exodus, is minimal.

The pharaohs of the Eighteenth Dynasty of Egypt enter into the arguments of those who favor the fifteenth century date for the Exodus. Because Moses was in exile for forty years before the reigning pharaoh died, it is necessary that the pharaoh who oppressed the Hebrews and created fear in Moses' heart reigned for a long time. Thutmose III (1502-1448 B.C.) would seem to qualify for this role; and this, in turn, would make Amenhotep II the pharaoh of the Exodus, and Amenhotep III the pharaoh during the conquest of Canaan by Joshua. But there is no name given to the pharaoh of the Exodus in the Bible; and there are no inscriptions of the Eighteenth Dynasty that mention the Hebrews. Therefore, this type of chronological correlation is guesswork.

The fact remains that the clearest support for the fifteenth-century date of the Exodus are the references in Judges 11:26 and I Kings 6:1. Many conservative scholars have favored this view.

Another scholar in the traditional viewpoint, a Frenchman by the name of Edouard Naville, concluded from his excavations in Egypt that the date of the Exodus must be placed in the late thirteenth century B.C.[3] He based his theory on conclusions which related to the statement in Exodus 1:11b: "And they built for Pharaoh store cities, Pithom and Raamses." Naville believed that he could tie Pithom with a ruins at Tell el-Maskhuta near present-day Ishmailiah. He had found here lower courses of brick with straw, some courses with little amounts of straw and bricks with no straw. He also found some inscriptions with Rameses II mentioned in them. He

---

3. E. H. Naville, *Archaeology and the Old Testament* (New York: Samuel R. Leland, 1937). pp. 93-102.

Rameses II is portrayed as the great victor in this scene from the Great Temple at Abu Simbel.

therefore concluded that this place was Pithom, that Rameses II was the oppressor of the Hebrews, and that Merneptah was the pharaoh of the Exodus. Rameses II (1301-1234 B.C.) would have reigned long enough to cover Moses' exile, and Merneptah's reign was troubled enough to allow the Hebrews to get out of Egypt.

Many scholars, including those in the traditional stream of thought, have followed Naville, but with modifications.

Because of an inscription of Merneptah that mentions Israel as being in Palestine (ANET, p. 378), Rameses II has replaced him as the pharaoh of the Exodus, thus dating that event early in the thirteenth century B.C. and the Conquest after the middle of that century.

Few scholars have accepted Naville's identifications of Pithom with Tell el-Maskhuta. Ancient On, or Heliopolis (Greek name), has been more widely favored as Pithom. Pithom is a shortened form of Per (temple) Atum, and Atum was very important in On.

The city of Rameses has been much more difficult to identify. Five places have vied for the honor. They are Tell er-Ratabeh (which is near Tell el-Maskhuta), Pelusium, Tanis, Qantir, and Tchel. E. P. Uphill, an Egyptologist rejects all sites except Qantir (about fifteen miles south of Tanis)

---

4. E. P. Uphill, "Pithom and Rameses: Their Location and Significance," *Journal of Near Eastern Studies*, 27 (1968): 291-316; and 28 (1969): 15-39.

as Rameses, but admits archaeological evidence for the identification is still inconclusive. Most evidence is based on above-ground inscriptions, and no real excavation has taken place. The inscriptions cover the Early Bronze and the Middle Bronze ages and the Nineteenth Dynasty, but not the Eighteenth Dynasty of the Late Bronze Age.

The results of excavations at Tell Beit Mirsim, Lachish, Hazor, Bethel, and Ai have had importance in the arguments for a thirteenth-century conquest of Canaan and, by inference, the Exodus early in the same century. The interpretation of layers of ash and destruction is significant at each site, and in a few places proper identification is in doubt. The book of Joshua admits only to the destruction by fire of Jericho (6:24), Ai (8:28), and Hazor (11:13).

Lachish has been successfully identified with Tell ed-Duweir and has a

The stele of Merneptah, on which is found the first mention of Israel in Egyptian records.

An ancient cistern at the site of Lachish.

layer of ashes that can be clearly dated to the time of Pharaoh Merneptah (about 1234-1220 B.C.). Some have attributed this destruction to the Israelites, but either Merneptah or the Philistines could have done it.

W. F. Albright had identified Tell Beit Mirsim with Debir, and a layer of ashes, dated about 1230 B.C., has been related to the Israelites. But another layer of ashes that can be dated to the middle of the fourteenth century is not related to them.[5] Recently, a long dissatisfaction with Albright's claim that Tell Beit Mirsim was Debir has found a new lease on life. In 1968, Israeli archaeologists claimed that they had found a much better site for Debir at the Arab town of Raboud, south of Hebron. The site has been partially excavated with the help of students from the American Institute of Holy Land Studies. Two springs near Raboud fit the biblical site much better, for Tell Beit Mirsim had no springs.

Excavations at Hazor have yielded two ash layers for the Late Bronze Age. Hazor has been identified clearly with Tell el-Qeday, nine miles north of the Sea of Galilee. The upper layer of ash has been dated to late thirteenth century B.C., but the ash layer beneath it has been dated to the fifteenth, possibly to the beginning of the fourteenth, century B.C.

---

5. W. F. Albright, "Debir," in *Archaeology and Old Testament Study,* ed. D. W. Thomas (Oxford: The Clarendon Press, 1967), p. 215.

The excavator, Y. Yadin, prefers to relate the upper layer of ash to Joshua, although the lower layer is not an impossible candidate for that honor.[6]

Two problems are involved in the witness of Bethel to the Conquest. It has been identified with ruins on which the modern Arab village Beitin is situated, but this identification is being challenged.[7] The excavation reports show two levels of ash for the Late Bronze Age. The upper one has been dated to about 1230 B.C. and attributed to the Israelites by Albright, but the lower one can be dated to about 1400 B.C.[8] The identification of Ai with a particular site has long been a problem. It has been popular to tie it with et-Tell, but this ruin has only a huge twenty-seven-acre fortress from the

The mound of Hazor, before excavation. Hazor was the chief city of the north at the time of Joshua's conquest.

6. Y. Yadin, "Further Light on Biblical Hazor," *Biblical Archaeologist* 20 (1957): 33-47.

7. See the interesting controversy in the following articles: David Livingston, "Location of Bethel and Ai Reconsidered," *Westminster Theological Journal* 32 (1970): 20-44. Anson F. Rainey, "Bethel Is Still Beitin," *WTJ* 33, (1971): 175-188. David Livingston, "Traditional Site of Bethel Questioned," *WTJ* 34, (1971): 39-50.

8. J. L. Kelso, *The Excavation of Bethel* (Cambridge: American Schools of Oriental Research, 1968), pp. 28-31.

first half of the Early Bronze Age and a three-acre village from Iron Age I. There are no Late Bronze materials at el-Tell; hence the search is still on for Ai.

Nelson Glueck's population studies in Trans-Jordan seemed to indicate that no kingdoms were in existence prior to 1200 B.C. in Moab or Ammon, but this position is being strongly questioned.

The preceding discussion should make it clear that we still lack any solid evidence in Egypt or Palestine that definitely aids in establishing a date according to our present calendar. It does seem clear that the Exodus took place sometime during the Late Bronze Age. Beyond that we presently cannot go.

The foregoing simplified survey of the historical events of the three Bronze ages hopefully has revealed something of the interrelationships of peoples and nations in the ancient Near East. The Pentateuch claims to span this same period of time with its portrayal of the Hebrew people in their origin and transit from one area of the ancient Near East to another, until they arrived at their Promised Land, Palestine, or Canaan, as it is known in the Pentateuch.

It is not possible yet to pinpoint exact dates for biblical events in the Pentateuch, or name with certainty the pharaohs whom the leaders of the Hebrews met. Continued archaeological activity and research in many specialized disciplines may provide clarification of these matters in the future. As never before, however, the overall picture of social, economic, political, and religious concepts and activities is visible. One of the important, pressing tasks of students of the Scriptures is to compare the overall picture with the content of the Bible and to dovetail them as much as is possible. This project is an attempt in that direction.

Suggested Books for Further Study (in addition to previous list)

Clay, A. T. *The Empire of the Amorites*. New Haven: Yale University Press, 1959.

Frankfort, H. *The Intellectual Adventure of Ancient Man*. Chicago: University of Chicago Press, 1946.

Greenburg, M. *The Hab/Piru*. New Haven: American Oriental Society, 1955.

Gurney. O. *The Hittites*. London, Baltimore: Penguin Books, 1952.

Harden, D. *The Phoenicians*. New York: Praeger, 1962.

Harrison, R. K. *Old Testament Times*. Grand Rapids: Wm. B. Eerdmans Publishing Co., 1970.

Hindson, E. E. *The Philistines and the Old Testament*. Grand Rapids: Baker Book House, 1971.

Kitchen, K. A. *The Ancient Orient and the Old Testament*. Chicago: Inter-Varsity Press, 1966.

Kramer, S. N. *History Begins at Sumer*. London: Thomas & Hudson, 1958.
———. *The Sumerians: Their History, Culture, and Character*. Chicago: University of Chicago Press, 1963.

Langdon, S., ed. *Cambridge Ancient History,* vol. 1. Cambridge: The University Press, 1961.

Marek, K. W. and Ceram, C. W. *The Secret of the Hittites*. New York: Knopf, 1956.

Montet, P. *Eternal Egypt*. New York: New American Library, 1964.

Moscati, S. *The Face of the Orient*. London: Routledge & Paul, 1960.

O'Callaghan, R. T. *Aram Nararaim*. Roma: Pontificium Institutum Biblicum, 1948.

Oppenheim, L. *Ancient Mesopotamia*. Chicago: University of Chicago Press, 1964.

Parks, H. M. *Gods and Men: The Origin of Western Culture*. New York: Knopf, 1959.

Schwantes, S. J. *A Short History of the Ancient Near East*. Grand Rapids: Baker Book House, 1965.

Speiser, E. A. *Oriental and Biblical Studies*. Philadelphia: University of Pennsylvania Press, 1967.

Steindorff, G. *When Egypt Ruled the East*. Chicago: University of Chicago Press, 1942.

Turner, R. *The Ancient Cities*. New York: McGraw-Hill Book Co., 1944.

Van Seters, J. *The Hyksos*. New Haven: Yale University Press, 1966.

On this high mountain near Bihistun (Bisitun), the Persian ruler Darius the Great had his military feats carved in rock. This trilingual inscription unlocked the Assyrio–Babylonian system of cuneiform writing.

3

The Languages
of the Ancient Near East

Though scholars a few centuries ago thought the Hebrew language was directly given by God without human antecedents, the Bible never makes such a claim nor does the information now available support it. It is now known that, like the English language, Hebrew is the child of several language parents.

The purpose of this section is to summarize the knowledge now available concerning the major languages of the ancient Near East and to identify the ancestral languages of Hebrew.

The rich literature in non-Hebrew languages now available has clarified the meaning of many words in the Bible that for centuries were beyond the understanding of translators. The same holds true for phrases, idioms, technical terms, and syntax forms. All the mysteries of difficult words in the Pentateuch have not yet been unveiled, but progress is being made.

All of the languages in the ancient Near East may be conveniently grouped under two headings: Semitic and non-Semitic. That is to say, there are nearly a dozen languages in the eastern Mediterannean area that exhibit the same "family" characteristics. This family has taken its name from the Biblical Shem, the forebear of the Hebrew nation. It has been pointed out that the easiest way to account for all of the similarities and differences in the family is to presuppose a common "mother" language, often called "Proto-Semitic."

The second group has no common denominator except that it is non-Semitic. Hittite stems from the Indo-European family (Greek, Indic, etc.), whereas Hurrian seems to be "Caucasoid." Relations between these families are not clear. Egyptian has a number of similarities to Semitic; but if it is finally to be related to that family, a number of very significant alterations must have taken place. Sumerian, most tantalizingly, cannot be related to any known language family.

For a family tree of the languages, see the end of this chapter.

THE MESOPOTAMIAN VALLEY

The Sumerian Language

During the nineteenth century, a people gradually came to light whose language was totally unknown from any source. The language of this people, the Sumerians, quite unlike that of any other, was neither Semitic nor Indo-European, nor Egyptian in character. Their language has been classed as agglutinative (meaning the combining or running together of old words into compounds, but still retaining the original meaning of each part), and it is thus similar to Turkish, Hungarian, and Finnish. Otherwise, it is not like any of these three just named.

The Sumerian language was a living, spoken form of speech from before 3500 B.C. to about 2050 B.C.; then it became a dead, classical language. Fortunately, the language, though dead, was studied by the scribes of the Babylonians, the Assyrians, the Elamites, the Hurrians, the Hittites and the Canaanites. Basically, it was from the Babylonian and the Assyrian literature that the Sumerian language came to light.

The story of how the Sumerian language was recovered is an exciting one. In 1850, an Irishman, Edward Hincks, suspected that behind the newly deciphered Akkadian was an earlier language. He knew that the main trait of Semitic languages (of which Akkadian was a member) was the stability of consonants and the instability of vowels. The cuneiform syllabic system (to be described in the next section) had both stable consonants and stable vowels, but none of the syllabic sign values could be tied to Semitic words. In 1855, H. C. Rawlinson said he had found non-Semitic inscriptions on bricks and tablets from Nippur. The next year Hincks observed that the new language was agglutinative, but thought it was Scythic or a variety of Akkadian.

It was not until thirteen years later that Oppert, a Frenchman, tied the new language to the Sumer mentioned in Akkadian inscriptions, and suggested the name Sumerian for them; but for many years most other scholars continued to call the language "Akkadian."

Until 1877, most of the information available about Sumerian came from bilingual lists that had Sumerian words and phrases with their supposed equivalent in Akkadian. Also, there were Sumerian texts matched by Akkadian translations. But the translations were poor, sometimes farfetched; so when genuine Sumerian material was found, scholars could not read them. It was not until three decades ago that an adequate grammar was devised, though thousands of Sumerian tablets and fragments had been known from excavations in Iraq since the turn of the century.

To date, about one quarter of a million tablets and fragments have been discovered. Because the clay tablets were unbaked for the most part, they break easily. About 95 percent of the tablets are economic texts, the business documents of everyday life. Most of this group of tablets have been easy to translate, but only a few are now published. Some of the tablets date to at least 3000 B.C. and perhaps earlier. About 1 percent of the total are literary texts of poetry dealing with religious and ethical themes. Only about half of these tablets have been published. The literary texts date to about 1750 B.C. and were mostly found at Nippur. The concepts in this material molded the thinking of a large part of the paganism against which the Old Testament protests.

The Akkadian Language

The Akkadians spoke a Semitic language that belongs to the eastern branch of this family of speech. Sargon I, who put together the first empire in Mesopotamia during the third millennium B.C., spread this language far and wide. Later it divided into two dialects: Babylonian and Assyrian.

Akkadian is the earliest recorded Semitic language and became known from the decipherment of cuneiform inscriptions written in three languages on monuments at Persepolis and on the rock of Bihistun in the Zagros Mountains east of Babylon. The Englishman, H. C. Rawlinson, published the first translated Akkadian in 1851; and from that time a new realm of knowledge about the ancient Near East was revealed to the world.

The branch of Akkadian called *Babylonian* became prominent during the empire established by Hammurabi about 1728 B.C. An extensive literature was produced, of which the Code of Hammurabi is most famous. It was found in 1901 at Susa. Some of the older Sumerian myths were rewritten in a much expanded form, but most of the clay tablets found from this period are magical in nature.

Written examples of what is known as Middle Babylonian are quite rare. The Tell el-Amarna letters found in Egypt do show that in the fourteenth century B.C., at least, Akkadian had become the international language of diplomacy in the ancient Near East. There are a few tablets from the Kassite regime that reveal something about Akkadian during the fourteenth and thirteenth centuries.

When Nebuchadnezzar set up the Neo-Babylonian empire at the end of the seventh century, he had most royal inscriptions written in the ancient Babylonian language style; but some of the contemporary vernacu-

Stele of the code of Hammurabi.

lar manages to shine through. The royal inscriptions of the Persian period were in the late Babylonian language style.

Assyrian was the other branch of the Akkadian, but some early samples of the dialect have come from Anatolia. The language of the government during the empire was heavily influenced by Babylonia, though there are tablets in the current Assyrian dialects. The Assyrian language faded out with the empire's destruction in 612 B.C.

Akkadian is one of the major parents of the Hebrew tongue, and many obscure words and phrases in Genesis have been clarified by comparing Hebrew and Akkadian. Some features of Hebrew grammar and vocabulary have been made more intelligible by tracing them back to Akkadian. The contributions of this language to a better understanding of the Old Testament, however, have not been exhausted.

The Hurrian Language

The Hurrian language was first discovered on some of the Tell el-Amarna letters and in inscriptions found in Boghazkoy. The Nuzi tablets of the fifteenth and fourteenth centuries have provided most of the information about Hurrian that is available. The many Hurrian personal names known from the ancient Near East have also contributed information for the grammatical analysis of the language.

The Hurrian language was unrelated to Sumerian, Akkadian, or any Indo-European tongues. It seems to have some affinity with ancient Armenian.

The greatest contribution that Hurrian made to the Hebrew tongue was its tendency to soften the sound of the consonants b, g, d, k, p, and t after vowels. This trait is peculiar to Hebrew among Semitic languages.

THE NILE VALLEY

The Egyptian Language

The origin of the Egyptian language is unknown. It is usually classed as Hamitic (African) in type, but it also has several affinities to the Semitic language. At least by 3000 B.C., it was a language in its own right, and came to its classical form, called Middle Egyptian, during the Old Kingdom of the third millennium B.C. Some words of the primitive tongue did survive in religious and medicinal texts. Middle Egyptian became standard in the literature of Egypt into the Roman period, though it was obsolete before the Eighteenth Dynasty and was a dead language by the fourteenth century.

Middle Egyptian had many words for all aspects of everyday life, but very few abstract words for emotions or ideas as such. Later, abstract words did come into the language. The older literature indicates that speech was in short, independent sentences; but the exact pronunciation of Egyptian words is difficult to ascertain because the script did not have signs for separate vowels. Consequently, the spelling (transliterations) of Egyptian names varies among scholars.

The Egyptian language moved through several stages of development. This development, as in almost all known languages, was in the direction of simplification, such as dropping the final "t" or loss of specialized endings. Because written language tends to be conservative, many of these lost elements continued to be written long after they had ceased being spoken (cf. French *rendezvous, hors d'oeuvres*). Such a situation prevailed in Egypt until the time of Ikhnaton, when it was decreed that the language should be written as it was spoken. This stage is called late

59

Egyptian. It is often written in simplified, cursive hieroglyphics. A later stage of the language, demotic, shows even more simplification, with a still more simplified script.

The final stage of Egyptian is called Coptic. Under the influence of the Hellenistic rulers, the Ptolemies, the Egyptians adapted their language to a Greek-style alphabet. Coptic, then, is Egyptian in Greek letters. Later, when Egypt became largely Christian, many copies of the Scriptures were done in Coptic. These manuscripts are of great value for textual criticism of the Bible, especially the New Testament.

THE LEVANT

The Aramaic and Canaanite languages are often classed as a northwestern branch of the Semitic family. They are fairly closely related, but they developed somewhat differently. Their influence extended in opposite directions: Aramaic to the east and Canaanite to the west.

The Eblaites spoke a Semitic dialect different from the Akkadian language but similar to a group of dialects classified as West Semitic, of which Hebrew is one. It is a language much older than any previously

The Rosetta stone is inscribed in Egyptian hieroglyphic and demotic characters and in Greek with a decree in honor of Ptolemy V, Epiphanes. This trilingual inscription became the key to the decipherment of ancient Egyptian writing.

known Semitic language. Some of the Ebla tablets are vocabulary lists of Sumerian words with Eblaite translations.

The Aramaic Language

In the Pentateuch there occurs one short phrase in Aramaic. Uttered by Laban (Gen. 31:47), it is the name he gave to the heap of stones that was the memorial to the covenant made between him and Jacob. There are traces of Aramaic in some Egyptian inscriptions of the New Kingdom. Otherwise, little is known about the language before its first inscriptions appeared about 1000 B.C.

On the basis of inscriptions covering about a thousand years, scholars have set up these periods of its history: Old Aramaic, on North Syrian inscriptions (tenth to the eighth century); Official Aramaic on Assyrian tablets (eighth to the end of the seventh century); Neo-Babylonian on Babylonian tablets (605-539 B.C.); Persian Aramaic (539-333 B.C.); Levantine Aramaic after 721 B.C. in Syria and Palestine; and Palestinian Jewish Aramaic in later intertestamental and New Testament times.

During the Assyrian Empire, Aramaic replaced Akkadian as the *lingua franca* of international displomacy and continued to enjoy this status during the Neo-Babylonian and Persian periods. It became more and more the language of the common people of the Mesopotamian valley, so that when the Hebrews were taken to that area in exile they gradually adopted the language as their own. In Palestine, Aramaic became increasingly the common tongue and continued such status through New Testament times. A few Eastern Othodox churches still retain the Aramaic and its cousin, Syriac, as their liturgical languages. Aramaic also continued in Jewish circles for a number of centuries.

Sections of two books in the Old Testament are written in Aramaic. They are Ezra 4:8–6:18; 7:12-26; and Daniel 2:4b–7:28. A short sentence is found in Jeremiah 10:11. There has been sharp controversy whether Aramaisms are present in other passages of the Old Testament.

The Canaanite Language

A member of the northwest branch of Semitic tongues, the Canaanite language (called "Phoenician" by the Greeks) appears only sporadically in Egyptian inscriptions. The latter had commercial contacts with Byblos, the port city of the Canaanites. Any early native literature has disappeared because papyrus and leather were more popular as writing materials than stone or clay.

The Tell el-Amarna letters of the fourteenth century have Canaanite names and phrases mixed in the normal Akkadian of the tablets. A few very short inscriptions on stone, metal, and broken pottery give some

61

These Amarna letters, sent by governors of city-states in Palestine, appeal to Egypt for help against rebels and the seminomadic Hapiru.

hints about the language; but since only consonants were used in the script, pronunciation is mainly guesswork.

The big breakthrough came with the discovery of ancient Ugarit (Ras Shamrah) at the northeastern tip of the Mediterranean Sea in 1929. A large number of inscriptions in several different scripts are in Canaanite, dating from before 1200 B.C. Since vowels are employed in many of these inscriptions, and some of the materials are lengthy, rapid advances have been made in understanding the language better. Roman sources indicate that a great library of Canaanite (Phoenician, Punic) literature was in existence at Carthage in A.D. 146, but it was destroyed by the Romans.

Though the limited Canaanite literature curtails research into the language, the Ugaritic materials have revealed that many words and phrases in the poetry of the Old Testament, especially the Psalms and the Wisdom Literature, are basically Canaanite. Parallel phrases and similarities of poetic structure have helped to establish the antiquity of the Song of Miriam (Exod. 15), the Balaam Oracles (Exod. 22–24), the Blessing of Jacob (Gen. 49), and the Song of Moses (Deut. 33).

The Hebrew Language

Except for the few portions of Aramaic mentioned above, the Old Testament has come to us written in the Hebrew language, hence it is the tongue in which a student of that portion of the Bible is interested. The language of the Israelites, however, is never called Hebrew in the Old Testament. It is called "the Jew's language" in II Kings 18:26, 28 and in Nehemiah 13:24, and "the language of Canaan" in Isaiah 19:18.

The Hebrew language is a highly mixed tongue, the child of several parents. It is the result of a fusion of Akkadian, Canaanite, and Aramaic. Some think ancient Arabic was also involved. It is possible that Abraham first spoke a dialect of Akkadian, then Canaanite. Jacob probably learned Aramaic while with Laban. The Hebrew language may have taken its distinctive form while the Israelites were in the land of Goshen. The Bible does not tell the story of its development, but the earliest inscription in Hebrew, the Gezer Calendar from Solomon's time, was written in good Hebrew.

Hebrew was the living language of the Israelites until the Exile. Then they gradually limited it to their religious activities and employed Aramaic for everyday speech. The nonbiblical literature of the Qumran sect and the Bar Kochbah letters show that Hebrew had not altogether become a dead language in New Testament times, but it did become obsolete after the Second Revolt ended in A.D. 135. Through the centuries it has been the language of piety for the Jewish people, until it was revived and became a living language again in modern Israel.

Hebrew is a typical Semitic language. Words are formed from a basic set of three consonants called a "root," which carry the fundamental meaning of those words. Highly variable vowels tend to modify the root meaning as need requires. It is even possible that the same set of three consonants can represent different meanings. One set carries eight meanings, but this is rare.

The Hebrew manner of thinking was not like ours in the western world, and this is reflected in its structure. We, taught by the Greeks, tend to think with logical syllogisms; but the Hebrews thought optically, that is, with many similes and metaphors. The ancient language had a few particles, adjectives, and adverbs. Like English, it lost most of its case endings. Many sentences are short and blunt.

The Hebrew verb system differs from that found in Indo-European systems. Hebrew verbs are not based on tense and mood. The time element must be gained mostly from context. Instead, the Hebrew verb stresses completed action, incomplete action, continuous action, intensive action, or caused action. Its conjugation differs from that in English, for example. There is a strong emotional element in the average Hebrew verb and in many nouns. This emotional tone is often completely lost in translation into English.

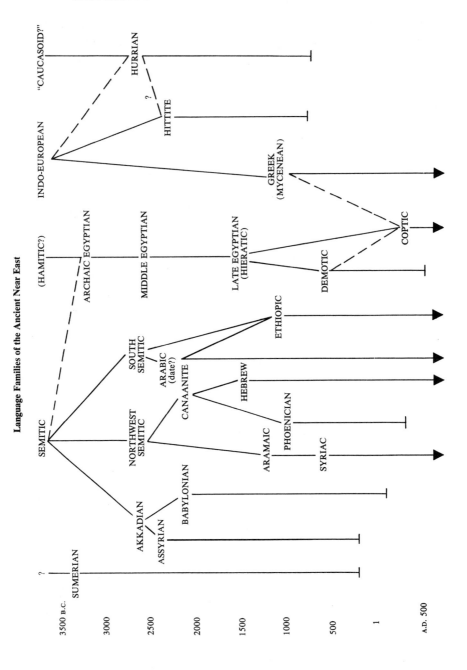

Language Families of the Ancient Near East

Hebrew words do not always coincide in meaning with words in other languages; sometimes the Hebrew meaning is broader, sometimes more limited, in scope. This makes a proper choice of words for translation purposes a difficult task. Hebrew has some important words that have no exact English equivalent. It lacks some words that we take for granted: for example, "religion," "person," "brain." Idioms are the most difficult to translate, and Hebrew has its share of them. Probably it has some we do not yet even recognize as idioms. Weights and measures are not the same as in English, and hence are not usually translated. They are transliterated and then explained in a footnote (e.g., *shekel, omer, ephah*). Names that are loaded with meaning in Hebrew lose their significance when transliterated into English. Usually they are so hard to pronounce that they are skipped over by English readers.

Hebrew is a vital, dynamic language. It can be learned fairly quickly; it just requires hard work. Actually, three Hebrew words are so well known among Christians that they are universal. They are "sabbath," "amen," and "hallelujah."

Suggested Books for Further Reading
Read pertinent sections of books already listed.
Consult articles on languages of ancient Near East in standard encyclopedias and Bible dictionaries.

Writing equipment of an Egyptian scribe. A palette, with two circular sections hollowed out, is attached to a writing reed and a water jug. This arrangement of writing equipment served as the hieroglyph for the word "scribe."

4

The Scripts
of the Ancient Near East

More than one ancient community probably possessed a rich fund of oral literature that was passed from generation to generation through recitation from memory. Because the community had no effective way to record their thoughts, their literature has been lost forever.

The major breakthrough in learning to write happened about 3000 B.C. Whether this occurred first in the Mesopotamian valley or the Nile valley has not yet been fixed. Three great systems of writing, however, did develop in the ancient Near East. They are the cuneiform style in the Mesopotamian valley, the hieroglyphic form in the Nile valley, and the alphabetic form in the Levant.

The inhabitants of the Mesopotamian valley learned early that clay was cheap and, when baked, provided durable material for writing purposes. Stone was scarce in the valley, but it was increasingly imported for inscribed monuments. The Nile valley had stone near at hand, in the desert bordering the river, and they employed it plentifully as a surface upon which to write. They soon found that papyrus and leather were also cheap and effective, but these proved to be extremely perishable. Fortunately, the dry sands of Egypt have preserved some inscribed papyrus from the third millennium B.C. In the Levant, papyrus and leather seemingly were popular as writing materials, but its damper soils have destroyed all specimens of such inscriptions from before the time of the Dead Sea Scrolls. There have been a few inscribed stones (stelae) found in Palestine and also some inscribed pottery fragments (ostraca), but not nearly so many as in other areas of the ancient Near East.

The science of studying ancient inscriptions is called *epigraphy*. The science of analyzing the forms of scripts is called *paleography*.

Scripts have been classified according to several types. *Pictographs* are symbols that can be "read" in almost any language because they represented ideas and actions in a simple story sequence. *Ideographs* are signs that convey abstractions, subtle modifications of an idea, or a complex of ideas. A variety of ideographs, more advanced in function, may represent words in a given language. Such ideographs have a phonetic element in them. This kind is sometimes called "analytic transitional script." *Phonemes* are graphic symbols for speech sounds, and thus cease to be self-interpreting pictures. Phonemes are intimately tied to the mechanics of speech in a particular language.

The aim of this chapter is to describe the nature of the several scripts utilized in the ancient Near East, to trace their development and influence, to list some of the most significant literature written in each script in the several areas of the ancient Near East, and to relate what is known about ancient scripts to the writing of the Old Testament, especially the Pentateuch.

THE MESOPOTAMIAN VALLEY

The Sumerian Pictograph and Cuneiform

The oldest samples of Sumerian come from Erech, dating about 3000

Selected Specimens of Sumerian Writing

EARLY PICTOGRAPHS	EARLY CUNEIFORM	MEANING
		Boat
		Ax
		Plow
		War Club
		Sled

This tablet, of the Babylonian chronicle, confirms the conquest of north Arabia by Nebuchadnezzar.

B.C. and numbering about one thousand tablets. These tablets were poorly baked and come out of the ground in fragmentary condition. The signs were pictographs drawn on the clay tablets with a stylus, probably a reed. The making and inscribing of tablets were done at temples to record its resources and activities.

As the years passed, the pictograph forms were replaced by similar signs impressed on the clay surface by the tip of a stylus, which left wedge-shaped marks. More and more, this new procedure stylized the signs so that they looked little like the originals. Another change also crept into the system: instead of pictures representing ideas and acts, the signs became increasingly phonetic. The signs did not represent *either* a consonant *or* a vowel, but rather consonant *and* vowel: i.e., ba, bi, bu, ub, ib, ab. Since a different sign was needed for each possible combination, hundreds of syllables were depicted by hundreds of signs, resulting in a complicated form of writing. About nine hundred different symbols were found at Erech (Uruk) alone.

By the time the Semitic Empire under Sargon I was formed, toward the end of the third millennium, the Sumerians had forged a system of writing that was an effective means of communication and preservation of records and literature. Scholars have given the name *cuneiform* (a Latin compound meaning "wedge-shaped") to the symbols produced by this style of writing.

Originally the writing was arranged like Chinese or Japanese—in columns. Eventually, for reasons not entirely clear, the columns were turned on their sides, to run from left to right across the writing surface. Interestingly enough, this meant turning the original signs on their sides, as well.

The Eblaite Cuneiform

In 1975 and 1976 nearly twenty thousand clay tablets were excavated from a royal archive at Ebla. Eighty percent of these tablets are in a Sumerian cuneiform script. The remarkable aspect of the discovery is that 20 percent of the tablets are in a proto-Canaanite dialect in cuneiform. For more information on the Ebla tablets, see pages 293–96 in the appendix.

The Akkadian Cuneiform

The Semitic Akkadians, led by Sargon I, borrowed heavily from the Sumerians and adapted the cuneiform to their own language. This could be done quite easily since already the signs represented syllables and had phonetic values.

The Old Babylonian Empire of Hammurabi made extensive use of cuneiform in the late eighteenth and early seventeenth centuries B.C. By the fourteenth century, it was utilized widely as an international means of communication. The Hurrians, the Hittites, the Assyrians, and the Canaanites found that the system could be adapted to their own languages. This is most graphically illustrated by the collection of diplomatic correspondence from the fourteenth century B.C. found at Tell el-Amarna. Coming from every corner of the ancient Near East, all are written in cuneiform. During the Assyrian, Neo-Babylonian, and Persian empires, the script was standard. It steadily declined in popularity during the Greek Empire and disappeared about A.D. 75 during the Roman Empire. The Persians had devised a mixture of alphabetic and syllabic signs; but centuries before, almost a millennium in fact, the scribes at Ugarit had invented a pure alphabet script utilizing cuneiform signs. More about this will be presented later.

THE NILE VALLEY

The Egyptian Hieroglyphs

At least by 3000 B.C., the Egyptians were recording and communicating their thoughts by means of pictographs. Scholars have labeled this form of writing *hieroglyphic* (a compound of two Greek words meaning "sacred writings") and applied the term to all Egyptian forms that were pictorial. The pictures represented everything found in ancient Egyptian life, but they also stood for the actions and uses of each object pictured. The Egyptians soon learned to regard their hieroglyphic as more than ideograms; they gave signs phonetic values and made some into determinatives or modifiers of other ideas. The sign could be written from top to bottom, from right to left, or from left to right. From right to left was the normal direction of writing. There were 604 basic symbols in the system.

In hieroglyphic writing, there were no separate signs for vowels, as was true of cuneiform, but there were a few signs for groups of three consonants, about seventy-five for two consonants, and twenty-four signs (later as many as thirty) for single consonants. The latter actually could have provided the Egyptians with an alphabetic script, yet they mixed all these signs together as needed. They never did take the step of creating an alphabet, though some of their signs found their way into the one that was devised by other people.

Hieroglyphic writing was an artistic medium. It was used for virtually all the monumental inscriptions, beautifully carved on stone monuments or on stone or plastered walls of temples and graves. The carvings were then painted in brilliant colors that have survived the ages. Hieroglyphics became more and more confined to religious matters, continuing in use among the priests until a small group of priests of Isis on the island of Philae composed the last-known inscription in A.D. 394. Probably because of its complexity, hieroglyphics never became an international means of communication.

Developments of Hieroglyphic Script

Hieratic writing is an abbreviated kind of hieroglyphic script that scribes used for religious literature and somewhat for business documents. In this

Horemhab with a papyrus scroll on his lap. The future Egyptian king is reading a psalm to Thoth. The cuneiform on the base includes prayers to Thoth and other gods.

71

script, the signs were simplified to outlines or even to mere strokes. In time, many of the signs became linked with ligatures. This script was mainly on papyrus, wooden boards, and pottery from the middle of the third millennium B.C. It received a great impetus through the reforms of Ikhnaton.

Demotic writing was a popular style that developed sometime before 700 B.C. and was widely employed in Egypt during the Greek and Roman domination of that land. It is an even more abbreviated form of hieroglyphic writing than is hieratic. Its use was limited almost totally to secular communication on papyrus, wood, and pottery. The latest-known inscription in this script dates to A.D. 476. It was written from right to left, as was hieratic.

THE LEVANT

The Proto-Sinaitic Alphabetic Script

Near some ancient turquoise mines in the Sinaitic peninsula, an Egyptian archaeologist, Sir Flinders Petrie, actually an Englishman, found twelve inscriptions of a peculiar script. Thirty-eight other inscriptions were located during expeditions in 1927, 1929, 1930, 1935, and later years, but they are in poor condition. Many are fragments. Two Semitic words have been identified: *Ba'alat,* a feminine form of Baal, designating Hathor, the Egyptian mother goddess; and a word meaning "gift offering." There are at least twenty-five signs on the inscriptions of which nineteen have been identified. Scholars regard the system as alphabetic. Some of the signs are like some Egyptian hieroglyphic signs, but they follow the acrophonic principle (i.e., the sign represents the first sound in the name of the sign, as c for "cat").

There has been dispute about the date of the Sinaitic inscriptions. A. H. Gardiner gave them an approximate 1800 B.C. date, whereas W. F. Albright has proposed a date of about 1500 B.C. So far there has been no agreement.

Some scholars have held that Semitic workers in the mines operated in Sinai by the Egyptians borrowed directly from hieroglyphic symbols and invented an alphabet that was the ancestor of all other alphabets. Others hold that the invention was a product of Semites in Canaan, and that the Sinaitic script is a variety of the earlier form.

Canaanite and North Semitic Alphabetic Script

There is general agreement that the alphabetic script was invented by Semites in the Levant sometime between 2000-1700 B.C. Diringer regards the Hyksos as the likely candidates for this honor, but the claim cannot be proved. The actual origin of the alphabet is still shrouded in mystery. One thing is clear: the earliest inscriptions available utilize a fully developed system of writing. The two basic hallmarks of an alphabet, the one-sign, one-sound principle and the acrophonic principle, are present in these inscriptions.

The Canaanite Script

Our knowledge of a script is dependent on inscriptions that provide specimens of it. The specimens of early Canaanite script are limited but are extremely significant. They have all been found in the Levant since 1929 and are comprised of three chronological groups.

In the oldest group are three samples, dated in the eighteenth to seventeenth centuries B.C. They are (a) the Gezer Potsherd found in 1929, (b) the Shechem Stone Plaque found in 1934, and (c) the Lachish Dagger discovered in 1934. Joseph Naveh holds that these three inscriptions are older than those found in the Sinaitic peninsula, thus proving that the Canaanites invented the alphabet.[1]

The next group belongs to the late fifteenth to early fourteenth centuries B.C. They are (a) the Oblong Seal of Lachish, uncovered in 1935; (b) a similar seal found at Lachish; (c) Lachish Censer Lid found in 1936; (d) the Lachish Bowl No. 1; (e) the Tell el-Hesi Potsherd discovered in 1891; (f) the Tell el-'Ajjul Pot discovered in 1932; and (g) the Beth-Shemesh Ostracon brought to light in 1930.

The latest group is from the thirteenth century and includes (a) the Lachish Ewer found in 1934; (b) the Lachish Bowl No. 2 from the same year; (c) Lachish Sherd No. 6, also 1934; (d) a few bowl fragments; (e) Megiddo Golden Bracelet; (f) Jerusalem Temple Foundation Stone Inscription; and (g) the Raddana Jar Handle found near Ramallah in 1969.

Diringer notes the curious parallel of the first group with the Patriarchal period, the second group with the Conquest, and the last group with the period of the Judges. Although he refrains from claiming that these inscriptions were written by Hebrews, they certainly show that a full-fledged alphabet was being used as a means of recording items of interest during the time contemporary to the events recorded in the Pentateuch. G. E. Mendenhall has observed, "It is not widely enough known that in the time of Moses the Canaanites were familiar with at least eight languages recorded in five completely different systems of writing."[2]

---

1. Joseph Naveh, "Incriptions of the Biblical Period," in *Recent Archaeology in the Land of Israel,* ed. Hershel Shanks (Washington, D.C.: Biblical Archaeology Society), p. 60.
2. G. E. Mendenhall, "Biblical History in Transition," in *The Bible and the Ancient Near East,* ed. G. E. Wright (Garden City, N.Y.: Doubleday and Company, Inc.), p. 50, footnote 23.

The Moabite Stone, a black basalt stele, commemorates the revolt of Mesha, king of Moab, against Israel. The inscription also mentions Omri's conquest of Moab. The stele dates from the last days of King Ahab.

The North Semitic Script

Before 1923, there were a limited number of specimens of the North Semitic script available for study. Included in this small group were the Mesha Stele, or Moabite Stone, found in 1868 at Dhiban and dated about 850 B.C. An inscription written on bowl sherds was found on the island of Cyprus but dedicated to the Baal of Lebanon. Some specimens from Zinjirli in Syria also are dated to the ninth and eighth centuries B.C.

The breakthrough came with the unearthing at Byblos of the so-called Ahiram epitaph dated to about the twelfth century B.C.

More recently, these inscriptions have come to light: (a) the Abdo pottery fragment, fourteenth century B.C.; (b) the Shafatba'al inscription of the fourteenth to thirteenth centuries B.C.; (c) the Asdrubal spatula, about the twelfth century B.C.; (d) the Yehimilk of the eleventh century B.C.; (e) the Roueisseh spearhead of the same time; (f) the Abiba'al inscription; and (g) the Eliba'al inscription, both of the tenth century B.C.

The North Semitic alphabet was the writing medium of the people who lived in Syria and was essentially the same as that used in Palestine.

There were twenty-two letters, all consonants, in the alphabet, and the script was written from right to left. It was this alphabet that the Greeks adopted about 1100-1000 B.C.

The Ugaritic Alphabetic Script

After ancient Ugarit (Ras Shamrah) was rediscovered and excavation begun in 1929, a series of spectacular "finds" of clay tablets bearing cuneiform inscriptions opened a new frontier of study. But these were different from the Akkadian cuneiform tablets. It was soon recognized that instead of a syllabic system, these tablets had thirty-two signs of an alphabetic style of writing. There were twenty-seven consonantal signs, three vowel signs, and two others of minor value. The only similarity with cuneiform was that the signs were impressed on clay with the end of a stylus, making wedge-shaped marks. The direction of writing was the same, from left to right. The language of the inscriptions was Canaanite.

A remarkable discovery in 1949 was a tablet with the oldest A B C list on it. It has thirty letters, twenty-two of which are equivalent to the twenty-two in the North Semitic alphabet and in the same order. Two other fragmentary A B C lists have been found in Ugarit since, and they confirm this order of the alphabet.

Adze with an Ugaritic alphabet inscription

No specific evidence points to the precise origin of the cuneiform alphabet. Scholars are generally agreed that the North Semitic alphabet lay behind it and that some genius invented the system. A sizeable amount of literature was written in this script at Ugarit from about 1500 B.C. to about 1200 B.C., when Ugarit was totally destroyed. Two specimens have been found in Palestine: a clay tablet from Beth Shemesh dates from 1400-1300 B.C.; a copper knife found on Mount Tabor dates from 1300-1200 B.C. The writing on these samples are from right to left.

Whereas the Ugaritic cuneiform alphabet ceased with the destruction of the city of Ugarit, the Canaanite and North Semitic alphabets continued in popularity among the Hebrew and Phoenician peoples.

The Palaeo-Hebrew Script

Actually the type of script on the inscriptions definitely known to have been authored by Hebrews was only slightly different from that employed by the older Canaanites. The older signs were more conventional, angular, and pronglike in palaeo-Hebrew; but the consonants were the same, the direction of writing was the same (right to left), and there were no vowels.

All the inscriptions so far discovered that date from the kingdom period were written on stone or on potsherds. In the Scripture, there is

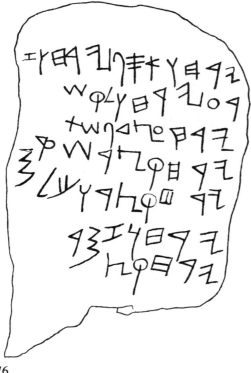

Gezer agricultural calendar as redrawn from an original fragment. The text describes the main periods of planting and harvest.

The Lachish letters are communications between Lachish and its military outpost during the time of the Babylonian invasion of Judah. The message in this letter reported that Azekah had ceased sending signals. Evidently Azekah had capitulated. Soon afterward, both Lachish and Jerusalem were occupied by Nebuchadnezzar's troops.

only one description of the writing process (Jer. 36), and it relates that the scribe Baruch wrote on a scroll, probably made of papyrus. It is known that papyrus and leather were cheap and popular during the kingdom period, so few of the everyday documents would likely survive the dampness of the wet seasons. Of all the things written on these materials, only the Old Testament has come through to us, by means of carefully, repeated copying of its content.

The number of Hebrew inscriptions from the kingdom period is limited. A recently published fragment found at Lachish in 1938 is now considered to be the oldest sample and is dated to the twelfth or eleventh century B.C. Other than this fragment there are the following inscriptions:

(a) The Gezer Calendar dates from 1000-950 B.C. and was found in 1908 at the ruins of ancient Gezer. It gives the agricultural operations in Palestine for eight months of the year, beginning with October. Some think the hand-sized limestone slab, on which the calendar was written, was a school boy's exercise slate.

(b) The Samaritan Ostraca are a group of about eight pieces of broken pottery on which records were written with brush and ink. They are dated at about 750 B.C.

(c) The Siloam inscription was found on a wall of a water tunnel beneath ancient Jerusalem in 1880. It tells of the completion of the tunnel in the time of King Hezekiah and the prophet Isaiah. It dates from about 700 B.C.

(d) Near the Siloam tunnel the first-known Hebrew tomb inscription was uncovered. It is dated from about 700 B.C.

(e) The Metsad Hashavyahu inscription was found near Tel Aviv and dates about 650 B.C.

(f) The Lachish Ostraca unearthed in 1935 and 1938 are twenty-one in number and are dated between 600-589 B.C.

In addition to the foregoing, hundreds of inscribed jar handles have been found, along with one hundred and fifty stone seals and many inscribed stone weights and measures. Dozens of lumps of clay inscribed with seal impressions have been found. A number of Israelite names appear on these seals, but only a few are biblical, with their counterparts in the Book of Jeremiah. Only one piece of papyrus, found in a cave at Wadi Murabaat, bears an Israelite inscription. This specimen dates from the seventh century B.C. A few burial inscriptions chiseled on stone, some of a dedicatory type, and a few graffiti cut or painted on rock have been found in Judea, all dated before the Exile.

The palaeo-Hebrew script was largely discarded during the Exile, but the fact that some of the older Dead Sea Scrolls are written in this script and that Jewish coins of the Maccabean period were inscribed in this script suggests that some Jewish scribes retained a knowledge of it and revived the use of it, to a limited degree, just before the New Testament period.

There is inscriptional evidence that the neighboring Moabites, Ammonites, and Edomites employed the same script as the Hebrews. Other than the famous Mesha Stele of the mid-ninth century B.C., there are only two Moabite seals.

There are but a few Ammonite specimens. The oldest is the Balu'al Stele found in 1930, which is dated from the thirteenth century B.C. Another inscription was found in Kerak in 1958, and it is dated to the ninth century B.C. A so-called Amman Citadel inscription was published in 1969 and dated to the ninth century also. In 1972 a bronze juglet was found at Amman bearing the names of three generations of kings. Part of a clay vessel with a short ink inscription was found the next year at Heshbon, near Amman. A very short inscription, on a statuette found at Amman, dates to the fifth century B.C. Dozens of seals have also been identified as Ammonite. Careful study has revealed that Ammonite and Aramaic scripts were very nearly alike.

Only a few samples of Edomite script have been found, and they differ little from the Hebrew script. A jug found at Ezion-geber in 1938 bears six letters of an inscription, and there are twelve other jar handles with seal impressions. These specimens have been dated to the seventh century B.C.

Pottery pieces with inscriptions (ostraca) recovered from the ruins at Arad Beersheba contain Edomite and Arabic names. They are dated in the Persian period (539–332 B.C.).

The Samaritan community, which formed in the hills of Ephraim after the fall of North Israel in 721 B.C. and which still continues with a few hundred members, developed a variation of the palaeo-Hebrew script. This style of writing has been preserved in the Samaritan Pentateuch, scrolls of which can still be viewed at their sanctuary at modern Nablus.

The Phoenician Script

The type of alphabetic writing common among the Phoenicians of Tyre and Sidon and their colonies scattered throughout the Mediterranean Sea islands and along its shores remained remarkably similar to the palaeo-Hebrew for many centuries.

Two very short inscriptions have been discovered, one at Tel Dan and one near Tel Avia. They appear to date from the time between the fall of Samaria, 721 B.C., and the fall of Jerusalem, 586 B.C. A few samples of Phoenician script appear on jars and ostraca found at several places in Palestine. Less than a dozen samples of this script have been found in Phoenicia; most are from the Persian period and are brief. The longest, found in 1869 at Byblos, is about Yehawmilk (Yehimilk) of Byblos and is dated in the fifth to fourth centuries B.C. Elsewhere, three were found in Zinjirli, Syria. Two of these were produced by Kilamuwa and are dated in the ninth century B.C. They were found in A.D. 1902, but were not published until 1943. The other was made by Barrakab and dated in 730 B.C.; it was found in 1891 A.D.

Three versions of a Phoenician inscription were found at Karatepe, Anatolia (Turkey), in 1946-47 and are dated in the ninth to eighth centuries B.C. Three inscriptions have been found on the island of Sardinia. One, the Nora Stone, is significant, for it is dated to the early ninth century B.C. It was found in 1838 A.D. The earliest inscription on Cyprus has been dated to the ninth or eighth century B.C. A five-line inscription from Spain dates to the eighth century B.C.

The Phoenician developed into a variety called the Punic script. Samples of this type were found at Marseilles, France, in 1845, dating to the third or second century B.C. Of the same time, there is an inscription found at Carthage. Others have been found in Malta, Sicily, and Greece.

The Phoenician script was the father of all the Western scripts, mainly through the Greeks, who started to borrow the alphabet as early as 1000 B.C. They retained nineteen of the Phoenician characters, made vowels out of several of them, and added new characters up to twenty-four. In the early period, their direction of writing varied. Some inscriptions proceed from left to right. In others, one line goes one way and the next goes to the opposite direction. In still others, the lines go from right to left. It was not until the fourth century B.C. that the Athenians established the left to right direction, using the uncial form. It was this style that the Jewish translators of the Pentateuch employed in the third century B.C. to render the Hebrew text into the Greek Septuagint.

The Aramaic Alphabetic Script

While the Phoenician script was moving west, fathering the scripts of that part of the world, the Aramaic script was moving east, engendering the scripts of the Orient. It even persuaded the Hebrews to forsake the Phoenician style and rewrite, or better, transliterate, their Scripture into a derivative of the Aramaic form of writing.

Actually, the early Aramaic writing looked very much like palaeo-Hebrew or Phoenician, but it developed differently. The earliest inscription was found at Tell Halaf. It is dated to about 1000 B.C. and was published in A.D. 1940. The first royal inscription bears the name of Ben Hadad and is dated to the late ninth century B.C.; it was found in 1941. An ivory tablet uncovered in 1928 at Arslan Tash in Cappadocia is dated to the late ninth century B.C. The Zakir stele was discovered in 1904 near Aleppo and is dated about 775 B.C. Several hundred short inscriptions are scattered across the next centuries from as far away as northwest India. Many Aramaic papyrus scraps and inscribed pieces of broken pottery have been found in Egypt. The famous Elephantine papyri from the fifth century B.C. were written by Jews.

In Israel a short Aramaic inscription was found at Ein Gev, and one at Tel Dan, both belonging to the ninth century B.C. Another has come to light at Hazor; it dates back to the eighth century B.C. A large number of ostraca with Aramaic inscriptions from the Persian period have been recovered. Only one coin in the same script can be dated to this period, but a number of seal impressions and stamped jar handles have come to light. A group of sixty-five bullae stamped with twelve different seals, and two actual seals, join the collection.

Up to the seventh century B.C., the Aramaic script was mostly limited to the Aramaeans themselves. But increasingly in the eighth and predominantly in the seventh centuries, the script was adopted by the Assyrian government, along with the Aramaic language, as the international means of communication. Assyrian sculptures show two scribes sitting side by side, one using the cuneiform method of writing, and the other, brush and ink on a scroll. The latter is presumably writing with the Aramaic script. Tablets in Ashurbanipal's seventh-century library show that they were catalogued by means of the symbols of the Aramaic script. The Aramaic script remained important during the Neo-Babylonian and the Persian empires and was adopted widely by the common people. This is a remarkable achievement for the Aramaic nation. Syria was destroyed in 732 B.C.

The Square Hebrew Script

Sometime during the Exile of the Jews (sixth-fifth centuries B.C.), the Hebrew people decided to transliterate their Scripture into the Aramaic script, which by that time had developed to the extent that it looked somewhat different from the palaeo-Hebrew. Parts of Daniel (2:4b–7:28) and Ezra (4:8–6:18; and 7:12-26) were originally written in Aramaic.

The Aramaic script was taken by the returning Jews to Palestine, where a few coins and seals in the Hebrew script can be dated to the Persian period and a few to the Greek period (332–63 B.C.) There are inscriptions on Jewish ossuaries (burial boxes containing bones) from the second and first centuries B.C. Until the discovery of the Dead Sea Scrolls, the Nash Papyrus (dated about 100 B.C.) was the oldest biblical inscription known. The Dead Sea Scrolls will be discussed in more detail later.

The Jews developed the Aramaic script into a more nearly square form. The alphabet still remained at twenty-two letters, all consonants; but two ceased to have a sound value, and four increasingly were used as signs for long vowels as spoken Hebrew died out, except in the synagogue and the school.

During the Middle Ages, vowel-systems did develop in Jewish circles. They are known as the Babylonian, the Palestinian, and the Tiberian systems. In the Babylonian system, small consonantal letters were written above the line of the text to represent basic long and short vowels. The Palestinian system utilized dots, also placed above the line of the text, to represent various vowels. Both of these schemes are represented in but a few manuscripts.

The Tiberian manner of symbolizing vowels was to arrange dots and dashs in varying combinations and to place them both above the line of text and below it. Some dots were placed within or beside the consonants. It is a highly efficient and logical method and has been the kind which has been preserved in most texts of the Hebrew Old Testament. The Tiberian mode also had a group of markings to indicate the accent patterns of each word. Synagogue scrolls never have any of these symbols.

During the years, cursive styles have developed among the various Jewish communities scattered throughout the world. Only one of these has become popular in modern Israel. It comes from the Polish-German communities and is used mostly in handwriting.

To the present time, Hebrew has managed to remain fairly close to the ideal of an alphabet, namely, one sign equals one sound. It has failed in two instances where two signs have lost their sounds, and in two cases where two signs stand for one sound. Only Turkish, Norwegian, Finnish, Spanish, and Korean scripts have successfully retained a one-sign, one-sound relationship. This is much better than English, which has twenty-six

THE SCRIPTS OF THE ANCIENT NEAR EAST

Selected Specimens of Alphabetic Script

SINAITIC Ca. 1700 B.C.	PHOENICIAN Ca. 1200 B.C.	O.T. HEBREW Ca. 700 B.C.	PRINTED Modern	GREEK Ca. 500 B.C.	LATIN Printed	ENGLISH Printed
			א	A	A	A
			ב	B	B	B
			ג	Γ	C G	G
			ד	Δ	D	D
			ה	E	E	E
			ו	Y	F,UVY	F,U,V,W
			ז	I	Z	Z
			ח	H	H	H
			ט	Θ		
			י	J	I	I
			כ	K	K	K
			ל	Λ	L	L
			מ	M	M	M
			נ	N	N	N
			ס	Ξ	X	X
			ע	O	O	O
			פ	Π	P	P
			ץ	M		
			ק	Q	Q	Q
			ר	P	R	R
			ש	Σ	S	S

letters, forty-four sounds, and two hundred fifty-one spellings. Try this sentence: "The rough-headed, dough-faced ploughman went coughing and hiccoughing through the village after houghing the thoroughbred horse which he had bought for his brougham" (Diringer). Or, read this sentence: "Oh, no, you sought the toy cow thoroughly below the bureau, on the oboe, the boat, behind the door to sew the poor toe for Otto too." To top it off, our letter "c" has no sound of its own but is pronounced as either "s" or "k." By comparison, Hebrew is relatively easy.

Other Varieties of Script

A group of ten inscriptions were found at Byblos in 1929, only three of which are of any length. The total of signs on the inscriptions is 1038, but there are only 114 different symbols, which are heavily influenced by Egyptian hieroglyphics. The Frenchman, Edouard Dhorme, claimed in 1946 that he had deciphered the script and found it to be made up of syllables. He said the language was Phoenician and that the script should be dated about 1500 B.C. Other scholars, however, disputed his conclusions.

The Hittites had a sort of hieroglyphic script, which was employed by them from about 1500-600 B.C. The earliest inscription was found in A.D. 1812, but the script was not deciphered until the 1930s. Since this script had no impact on the productions of the Scripture, the student is directed to the bibliography for further details.

Suggested Books for Further Study

Diringer, D. *The Story of Aleph Beth.* New York: Philosophical Library, 1958.
―――. *Writing.* New York: Praeger, 1962.
―――. *The Alphabet.* New York: Funk & Wagnalls, 1968.
Driver, G. R. *Semitic Writing.* London: Oxford University Press, 1954.
Gelb, I. J. *A Study of Writing.* Chicago: University of Chicago Press, 1969.

Part Two

LITERATURE, CONCEPTS, AND PRACTICES

Cuneiform tablet containing part of the Babylonian creation story.

5

The Literature
of the Ancient Near East

The previous chapters have sketched some aspects of the life and practice of people in the ancient Near East that have come to light in recent decades. Hopefully, you have been made aware of the possibilities for understanding better the Pentateuch because this knowledge is now available. Up to this point nothing has been said of the religious concepts and practice of these ancient peoples.

The religious literature of the ancient Near East is not widely known apart from the inner circle of scholars who have particular interest in it. During the past decade, efforts have been made to publicize this literature more widely in English translation, but as a whole, students of the Bible are still poorly informed about the relationship of this material to the Old Testament.

This chapter will deal with the most important mythological literature produced by the peoples of the ancient Near East, with notations as to where they may be found in standard reference books. There will be a brief description of the basic content of this material and a summary of the nature of ritual in the various religions of the ancient Near East. The mythological literature will be related to the ritual of the cult. The salient features of religious organization and practice will be correlated with the myths. A résumé will be made of the historical material that is available in this ancient literature, and an evaluation of its significance will be presented.

The Religious Literature of the Ancient Near East

Most of the mythological materials from the ancient Near East that bear upon the content of the Pentateuch come from the Mesopotamian valley.

However, the literature from Egypt and the Levant have provided information about the religious thinking and practices of the times of the Patriarchs and of Moses. This pagan material throws a great deal of light upon the Pentateuch and fills in huge gaps in the knowledge of Biblical scholars of a century, or even fifty years, ago. The writers of the Old Testament assumed this pagan environment was known by their readers and challenged it. Western people have been ignorant of this environment and so often have misunderstood some of the material in the Old Testament. Few evangelical scholars have been familiar with the content of the mythological and institutional data discussed in the following pages.

The Sumerian Myths

Only about 1 percent (about five thousand tablets and fragments) of the total Sumerian literature available touches upon mythological concepts or contains mythological material. Most of these tablets and fragments were found at Nippur by the University of Pennsylvania about sixty years ago. Much of it has been published by S. N. Kramer only recently.[1] The literature that refers to the activities of the gods or describes them to some extent ranges from short hymns to stories that have as many as a thousand lines. They are dated mostly to 1750 B.C., but a catalogue of literary compositions dating to 2000 B.C. indicates that they go back into the third millennium B.C. This literature constitutes the oldest corpus of written expressions of human thought to be found in the world to date.

The compositions that come nearest to presenting information about the Sumerian's concept of creation are only two in number. Kramer entitles them "Enlil and Ninlil: The Begetting of Nanna" and "The Journey of Nanna to Nippur." Seven other stories provide further details. They are "Emesh and Enten: A Disputation Between Summer and Winter," "The Creation of the Pickax," "Cattle and Grain," "Enki and Ninhursay: The Affairs of the Water God," "Enki and Sumer: The Organization of Earth and Its Cultural Processes," "Enki and Eridu: The Journey of the Water God to Nippur," and "Inanna and Enki: The Transfer of the Arts of Civilization from Eridu to Erech." In addition, the introduction of the story "Gilgamesh, Enkidu, and the Nether World" adds a few details. These can be found in English translation in the books listed at the end of the chapter.

Since none of the compositions listed above are primarily concerned with creation, one can only gather the scraps of information together and rather arbitrarily group them into a composite picture.

---

1. S. N. Kramer, *Sumerian Mythology* (New York: Harper & Row Publishers, 1961).

Basically, this is how the Sumerians understood the origin of all things. First of all, there was a primeval sea. Whether the Sumerians regarded the sea as eternal and uncreated is not known. The primeval sea gave birth to a united heaven and earth, which was thought of as a mountain. An expanding gaseous air separated the heaven and earth, then the air gave birth to the moon and the sun. The creation of plants, animals, and man then took place, sometimes as the result of command, but more often by procreation between the air, earth, and water. The same is true of other gods and goddesses, who were regarded as various aspects of nature.

Concerning the creation of man, there is a two-line statement in the essay "Cattle and Grain" which tells us that, "For the sake of the good things in their pure sheepfolds/Man was given breath." This indicates that man's role in life was to feed the gods and goddesses in order to provide them leisure. Another damaged tablet has a portion that says that the gods needed someone to produce bread for them so they got the primeval sea, a female goddess, and the water god to fashion man out of clay. The lines are damaged but there is indication that the primeval sea produced man of clay. This included six abnormal types of man, fashioned while the god and goddess were drunk with wine. The god tried his hand and came forth with a sickly creature who the goddess tried to help, but she ended cursing the god for his ineptness.

Only one broken tablet (published in 1914) describing a flood on the earth has been found at Nippur. It consists of six columns, none of them complete. The first two columns tell of a previous destruction of men, their restoration and the establishment of five cities for them. After a break of about thirty-seven lines, we learn that, for some reason, the gods had decided to destroy man by means of a flood. Some goddesses were unhappy and pled for mercy. As a result, the high gods had some regrets. The water god, Enki, revealed the threat of a flood to a king-priest, Ziusudra, through a dream.

After a break of forty lines, the story describes the fury of the flood, which lasted seven days and nights. The king-priest was riding in a huge boat. When the sun came shining through the clouds, Ziusudra opened a window, worshiped the sun, and sacrificed an ox and a sheep. Obviously, these animals were with him in the boat.

The priest-king worshiped the god of heaven and the god of air, who conferred on him immortality so that he became a god himself.

Early reports concerning the Eblaite archives refer to tablets bearing myths on creation and a flood, but details of their contents have not been released as yet.

The Akkadian Myths

The basic stories about the gods and goddesses familiar to the Assyrians came to light during the excavation of Nineveh from 1848-1876. Many clay tablets were found in the library of Ashurbanipal, emperor of Assyria, and were recognized as possessing materials that are somewhat similar to Genesis. The so-called Epic of Creation, or *Enuma Elish,* the first two Akkadian words of the story, was first published in 1872.[2] The fragments are dated about 650 B.C., but older fragments have been found dating back to about 1000 B.C. Some feel that the story goes back to at least 1700 B.C.

The story was inscribed on seven tablets, the contents of which have been fairly well restored except for tablet number five. There are about one thousand lines in total.

The creation process is filled with more violence among the gods and goddesses than in the Sumerian myths. The basic ideas are much the same.

Briefly, the story is that originally there was a male fresh water ocean and a female salt water ocean that mated and produced a multitude of lesser deities, which were various aspects of nature. Apsu, the fresh water ocean, became angry because of the noises of his offspring and decided to destroy them. Instead, one of them, the god of wisdom, killed Apsu and produced the remarkable storm god, Marduk. The salt water ocean, Tiamat, became angry and mothered a host of dragons to fight Marduk.

Other high gods were frightened and commissioned Marduk as their leader during a huge banquet. The battle was fierce, but Marduk killed the dragon, Tiamat, and split her body in half. The upper half was made into the sky and the lower half into the earth. Out of chaos came order, with stars and the moon, and a calendar was created. The field marshal of Tiamat's army, Kingu, was killed, and some of his blood was mixed with earth to produce man, who was to serve all the needs of the gods and goddesses.

A temple was made to Marduk on top of a huge mound of earth at Babylon, where Marduk was supreme.

All of the indications are that a Sumerian original glorifying not Marduk but Enlil, the air god, lies behind the Akkadian *Enuma Elish.*

In a composition called "Creation of Man by the Mother Goddess," man is depicted as made out of clay mixed with the blood of a slaughtered god and then given birth by the mother earth goddess.

Another famous myth, "The Epic of Adapa," was found at Nineveh in four fragments in the library of Ashurbanipal. It is also dated about 650 B.C. Another fragment was found among the Tell el-Amarna tablets in Egypt and is dated about 1370 B.C.

---

2. J. B. Pritchard, *Ancient Near Eastern Texts* (Princeton: Princeton University Press, 1969). Unless indicated otherwise, all ancient literature mentioned in this chapter can be found in this volume, often called ANET.

The story relates how the god of wisdom gave his priest, Adapa, wisdom, but not eternal life. Adapa cared for the temple at Eridu but liked to go fishing. One day the south wind capsized his boat, and, in anger, Adapa broke the wing of the south wind. This act angered the heaven god, and Adapa was summoned to judgment. Prior to the judgment, the god of wisdom privately instructed Adapa to dress in mourning and to fast. Adapa was not to eat of any food in the presence of the heaven god.

When Adapa arrived at the gates of heaven, he won the favor of the gate keepers, who in turn softened the anger of the heaven god. Instead of judgment, Adapa was offered a banquet with the food of life and the water of life, along with other things. Adapa obeyed the god of wisdom and refused the bread and water of life, for which he was banished back to earth. The man had missed eternal life because he had obeyed his god, and this is the reason mankind suffers disease and death.

The Babylonian-Assyrian version of the flood story is contained in the Epic of Gilgamesh. Fragments were first found at Nineveh in the library of Ashurbanipal in 1853, but they were not recognized as the Flood story until 1872. Four accounts in the Akkadian language have been found, some in Boghazkoy of the Hittite Empire. Fragments of a Hittite translation and a fragment of a Hurrian translation have been found. The oldest Akkadian versions come from about 2000 B.C.

This portion of the Gilgamesh Epic contains a flood story with remarkable parallels to the Genesis account.

There are twelve tablets in the Epic of Gilgamesh. Tablet number eleven contains the description of a flood. The hero of the epic was Gilgamesh, two-thirds god and one-third man, who was King of Erech. Early in the story we are told that the mother goddess made from clay a man who roamed with the beasts, savage and wild. He was tamed and "civilized" through the seductive charms of a harlot and became a close friend of Gilgamesh. His name was Enkidu.

The remainder of the first ten tablets tell of the many adventures of Gilgamesh and Enkidu. Enkidu finally died because he had insulted a goddess. Filled with grief, Gilgamesh roamed the earth and crossed the Waters of Death in a boat looking for immortality. Beyond the Waters of Death, Gilgamesh met Utnapishtim who told him the story of a great flood.

The flood story is essentially like the Sumerian, for Utnapishtim was the Sumerian Ziusudra, but more detail is preserved in the almost perfectly conserved eleventh tablet.

It was the god of wisdom who told Utnapishtim that the gods were sending a flood and that a boat must be built. The boat was 120 cubits each way, a perfect cube, with six stories. It was covered with bitumen and loaded with food, gold, silver, his family, craftsmen, and animals.

The storm lasted six days and nights. The boat touched ground on a mountain; a dove was sent out, then a swallow, and finally a raven. Utnapishtim offered sacrifices to which the gods gathered like flies. When the god's appetites were sated, they began to fight over Utnapishtim's fate. Finally, the air god was blamed by other deities for the flood, and in remorse he conferred on Utnapishtim and his wife the immortality of divinity.

In the Epic of Gilgamesh, an alternate name, Atrahasis, occurs for Gilgamesh. Of great interest is the publication of an English translation in 1969 of a so-called Atrahasis Epic.[3] It was recorded on three clay tablets and written in a mixture of literary Babylonian and northwest Semitic dialects. The script is cuneiform and the tablets indicate they are to be dated to the reign of Ammisaduqa about 1600 B.C. The tablets are copied from older tablets, the age of which is unknown.

The story is a combination of how man was created from the blood of a slain god and from clay, and a flood account. During the thirty-six-hundred-year reign of Atrahasis, mankind became too numerous and too noisy to suit the sleepy sky god. This god tried to exterminate mankind by epidemics of disease and then by famine, but each time he was thwarted by other deities. Finally a flood was sent to wipe out mankind, but the

---

3. W. C. Lambert and A. R. Millard, *Atrahasis: The Babylonian Story of the Flood* (Oxford: The Clarendon Press, 1969).

god Enki told the hero, Atrahasis, to build a reed boat and thus survive with his family and many creatures.

Recently, a specimen of a story about the confusion of tongues has been found among Akkadian tablets (see p. 142).

The Egyptian Myths

The Egyptian creation mythology is, at the same time, more limited and much more complex than that of Mesopotamia. There are a number of short creation myths located in other longer contexts. These short myths show great variation among themselves. A number of common characteristics mark these myths, such as a primordial ocean filling the universe (Nun); a primordial hill appearing in the midst of Nun (in the Memphite theology, Ptah seems to be this hill); the first god, commonly one of the forms of the sun, appears on the hill; the first god brings other gods into being; and the other gods have to do with natural elements and kingship.

Studies in recent years have stressed important similarities of the above with Sumerian mythology.

Essentially, there are four groups of myths in Egypt. These are associated with the four great royal and/or cult centers. The Atum/Re stories relate to Heliopolis; the Ptah stories, to Memphis; the Amon/Re stories, to Thebes; and the Ogdoad stories, to Hermopolis. The latter seems independent of the other three and is for this and other reasons often considered most ancient.

There are two versions of "The Creation by Atum." The oldest comes from an inscription carved inside the pyramids of Mernere and Pepi II, dating about the twenty-fourth century B.C. The first paragraph simply states that Atum 'Kheprer, the sun god, situated above the primeval hill, spit out the air god and the goddess of moisture. The last paragraph says that Atum was also the father of the earth god and the sky goddess, the plant god and the fertility goddess, the desert god and the mother goddess.

The second version is in the seventh chapter of the Book of the Dead, found on coffins dating about 2000 B.C. This version was popular for many centuries. The producer of all things is depicted as Atum, or Re, the sun disk, but also the primal water associated with a primal hill. No indication of how he created the other few gods mentioned is present in this version.

Another composition is "The Theology of Memphis," of which the oldest document is dated back only to about 700 B.C. But it is thought that internal evidence pushes its origin back to about 2700 B.C.

In this myth, Ptah, god of Memphis, is identified as both the father of Atum and Atum himself, the sun god. The creation of the other aspects of nature is depicted as an intellectual process of thinking and speaking rather than as physical action.

One of the many Egyptian funeral texts that are collectively entitled "The Book of the Dead." This panel shows the heart of the deceased being weighed in the balance scale with truth.

From a longer text found in the Papyrus Bremner-Rhind, dated to about 310 B.C., comes a shorter portion entitled "The Repulsing of the Dragon and the Creation," in ANET. The rising sun is presented as the source of the gods and of all things. Since he had no female counterpart, the god was forced to bear the other gods himself. This was accomplished through masturbation as a result of which the gods were conceived within his body and then spat out. Men were created from the sun god's tears, coming from his eye. Other gods and goddesses were born by natural means. There was a dragon enemy who was kept conquered by means of magic.

Among the coffin texts of the Middle Kingdom comes a brief statement about the creation of man. It is dated about 2000 B.C. The "All-Lord," the sun, made the winds so all men might have equal right to breathe; he made the Nile to flood so the poor could gain from it as well as the noble; he did not command evil, but every man devised his own evil; and he gave to every man the task of making sacrifices.

A text carved on the tomb walls of Seti I, Rameses II, and Rameses III (fourteenth-twelfth centuries B.C.) and entitled in ANET as "Deliverance of Mankind from Destruction," tells of a rebellion of man against the sun god. The fertility goddess decided to destroy mankind, but the other high gods prevented her by making a barley beer mixed with red ochre and pouring it on the ground at night. The fertility goddess drank it, became drunk, and forgot about destroying mankind.

The Religious Literature of the Canaanites

The Canaanite myths are preserved only on the tablets discovered at Ugarit (Ras Shamrah) since 1929. There are some poems about Baal, the storm god, and Anath, the fertility goddess in a composition called "The Legend of King Keret," and another entitled "The Tale of Aqhat." El was the father god, but he was overshadowed by his son, the storm god, Baal, who is the center of most of the mythology. The focal interest of the stories is the processes of reproduction found in the soil, crops, and the cattle. Baal's enemy was the god of death, and he had fights with the sea god, or more often, the sea goddess. The creation of the main gods and goddesses is depicted as due to natural procreation. There is no clear

Ugaritic text with the legend of Aqhat.

description of the creation of man, of the fall of man, or of a flood such as in the Sumerian and Akkadian stories. The significance of the Canaanite material is related to the development of Hebrew ritual and cult and will be discussed in later sections.

Myth and Ritual in the Religious Literature

Although much remains to be learned about the nature and function of institutions in the ancient civilizations, broad outlines can be be laid out. The purpose of this section is to relate the literature just discussed with the content of other written documents and with archaeological remains that throw light on ancient practices and institutions, and to summarize the salient features of ancient Near East religions.

Words have a way of carrying a variety of meanings, both technical and popular. The word *myth* is one of those words capable of nuances of emphasis, depending on the outlook of the one who uses it. Broadly, a myth is a fanciful story that seeks to explain some practice of unknown origin, or some belief embodied in a ceremony or institution. It may be concerned with either nature objects or heroes. A myth largely lacks factual basis, but the community that preserves it accepts it as true. Normally, a myth has its roots in a faraway time and often in a faraway place.

In a technical sense, myths center about the activities and interrelations of gods and goddesses. The literature that has been discussed in the previous section is of that sort and is classified as myth because god and goddesses are everywhere present and human beings only rarely present. Those stories that possess one or two humans or semihumans as important characters are classified as epic or hero tales. In these tales divine beings are prominent also. A basic question is: How were these compositions related to life and practice of the ancient peoples of the Near East?

In the ancient Near East, practically all of daily life was tied with religious practice. Some literature, such as proverbs and precepts, scarcely refers to religion, but this is the exception rather than the rule. There is much material of the nature of prayers, hymns, lamentations, liturgies, and texts that instruct the priests on how to perform their duties. Ritual, then, was a very important aspect of the religious activity of people of the ancient Near East.

What is ritual? Ritual is the sum total of the forms employed during the act of worship. The procedures of worship are set up in prescribed order long observed by the worshiping community. The actions performed during worship are rites, and the words uttered are prayers, dedications, and benedictions. Ritual is the systematizing of these actions and words in a fixed order.

In summary, myths seem to be the expression of man's inner thoughts and feelings about his world, about men, and about his own inner experiences; whereas ritual is oriented toward the appeasement and manipulation of powers in the world round about, or powers, such as disease, that may threaten human life.

What myths actually did for the ancient Near East people is not always clear from the inscriptions available. It is known that the Epic of Creation, or *Enuma Elish,* was recited at the annual Babylonian New Year's Festival and probably parts of it were enacted (see ANET, p. 332). Other functions can only be surmised from the content of the myths themselves. Scholars are generally agreed on the following: (a) some myths serve to answer questions about the origins of aspects of nature, peculiar phenomena among animals, human occupations, and mystifying features of human experience or customs; (b) some myths purport to explain the meaning of names of places, tribes, and persons; (c) some myths try to clarify how the world is organized as it is and why society is stratified according to levels of status. This view would understand myths as vehicles of instruction. Whether the people of ancient times actually understood that myths performed these functions in their midst cannot be proved, because their writings, so far, have not recorded their thoughts on the matter.

The ancient literature provides clearer statements concerning the functioning of ritual. The Sumerian and Akkadian myths clearly state that man's task was to care for the needs of the gods and goddesses, and the ritual literature illustrates this reason for man's existence. Still, some purposes for the ritualistic acts and words may be deduced from the general content of the literature itself.

Scholars are generally agreed that the sacrifices, by magical means, were believed to perform these functions: (a) they satisfied the hunger of the divine beings; (b) they represented rent paid the deities for the use of their land; (c) they kept the gods and goddesses in good humor, for failure to provide delicacies for the gods and goddesses could provoke their fierce anger; (d) they could serve as substitutes for a sick person, for by magical means the sickness could be transferred to the animal, which then was sent away or burned; (e) a human being could be sacrificed in a community emergency to take the place of the king or to transfer the young person's vigor to the ailing community deity; (f) a worshiper might eat the flesh or drink the blood of a sacrificed, deified animal, and, by that means, gain strength from the divine realm; and (g) the blood of an animal could be used to rid a temple or house of defilement.

Often the prayers, benedictions, and ritualistic acts served magically to

exorcize evil spirits, to cure diseases, and to protect the worshiper from harm.

It has been stated above that the Epic of Creation was recited in the ritual of the New Year's Festival. This information is found on an inscription dating from about 250 B.C. At the end of the tablet is a note stating that a certain scribe had copied the inscription from an older tablet. How far back the practice of reciting the Epic of Creation goes is unclear, and how many other myths were recited at festivals is likewise unclear. Kramer insists that there is no evidence that the Sumerian myths were ever a part of the Sumerian ritual. This seems to be true of the Hittite and Canaanite myths also. But there is evidence that the Egyptians combined, at least somewhat, their myths with their ritual.

The following observation can be made concerning the interrelationship of ancient myth and ritual. There is no inherent reason why myths need to be a part of ritualistic practice, since in content they are basically self-sufficient. Likewise, there is no inherent reason why ritual needs the myths, since it, too, is basically self-sufficient. On the other hand, there is no inherent reason why at least some of the myths could not be united with ritual. The inward roots of myth in thought, imagination, and experience and outward orientation of ritual in magical power could be fitted together like hand and glove. Thus an integration of thought and action could take place during times of strong city-states or powerful empires. Just as easily, myth and ritual could fall apart during times of weakness; and after the destruction of a civilization, myths could continue simply as stories and ritual fragmented into fetish practice. Or they could be caught up into another civilization and reintegrated, or they could continue as separated aspects of life. Various attempts have been made to elaborate on each of these possibilities, but uncertainty persists.

The Historical Literature Up to 1200 B.C.

A sizeable gap exists between the mythological and ritualistic literature on the one hand, and the records that ANET classifies as "Historical Texts." Because a crucial controversy has raged about the question whether the Pentateuch is basically myth or a reliable account of what happened to the Hebrew people and what they believed, a careful look at the historical texts is necessary.

This section will inquire about the nature of the historical texts of the three main areas of the Near East, the basic concerns of those who composed the texts, how much actual history they reveal, and the relation of the mythological to the historical material.

No one in ancient Sumeria wrote a history of their people in the sense that modern authors write such compositions, nor were their scribes

The Sumerian king list gives the earliest tradition of rulers who reigned before the flood, and of later rulers whose reigns reached to historical times.

reporters of events as are modern journalists. The contents of some of their tablets do have historical value. By 2700 B.C., votive and dedicatory inscriptions about the building, repair, and furnishing of temples were made on clay tablets. There are extant nearly one thousand tablets of this type; they are brief, and the information they provide is scanty.

The earliest tablets containing business records and office memos date to about 2500 B.C. Many of these have date formulae based on naming years according to important events in each year. There are lists of the names of years in the reign of some kings and even a succession of kings. The Sumerian King List (ANET, p. 265) contains lists of royal names, cities, and amazingly long reigns for each king before the Flood. After the Flood, the reigns are shorter, but still hundreds of years in length. Some of the kings figure prominently in mythological stories. The names of some kings have appeared on other tablets containing royal correspondence between cities. The list seems to date from the nineteenth century B.C.

A more sober document is the "Sargon Chronicle," which dates from the seventh or sixth century B.C., but discusses in a brief, generalized manner kings and acts from Sargon I (about 2350 B.C.) until the invasion of the Kassites, going up to about 1500 B.C. Somewhat similar is a large tablet bearing copies of ancient inscriptions on temple objects at Nippur. These mention Sargon I, Naram-Sin, and Gudea.

The Eblaite archives include a host of letters, records, and treaties. Translation and study of these important tablets has just begun.

Kramer mentions treaties, diplomatic letters, the Tummal inscription, a few poems, and epic tales. He admits, however, that when all this material is analyzed, we still fall far short of a real history of the Sumerians.[4] In many instances, the present-day historian finds it difficult to separate fact from fancy in this literature.

Some documents of importance come from the empire of Hammurabi, which began about 1728 B.C. A list of date formulae covering the first forty-three years of Hammurabi and another such list of year names for his son Samsuiluna are found in ANET, pp. 269-270. There are two king lists of the Old Babylonian Empire, which Hammurabi founded. Later, the Assyrians set up a synchronistic chronicle of Babylonian and Assyrian kings. There are other shorter records that come from kings of the second millennium B.C. In many ways these lists are like the genealogies and king lists in the Book of Genesis, but no history of the Babylonian or the Assyrian peoples was produced in the second millennium B.C. In the first millennium B.C., the Assyrian kings kept lengthy annals or record books. These still, however, made no attempt to be objective or to note historical cause and effect relationships.

Because the Egyptians looked upon the universe as static and the kingship as supremely important, they gave little heed in their records to events not directly related to the throne.

Very little comes from the Old Kingdom of Egypt that bears upon events as such. There are only a few snatches, plus a short description of the campaign of Pepi I into Asia. Open to question is just how much of this account is factual and how much is royal bragging. Other royal records are missing. Some tomb and temple inscriptions have titles and refer to functions of office, but this information is limited. The Palermo Stone bears the names of some kings of the Old Kingdom; little more is known.

---

4. S. N. Kramer, *The Sumerians* (Chicago: University of Chicago Press, 1963), pp. 34-39.

During the Middle Kingdom, various short inscriptions in the Levant mention Egyptian officials and the names of some pharaohs. An inscription in Sinai, dated about 1800 B.C., throws some light on the mining activity of the Egyptians, and a stele found at Abydos tells of the achievements of an official. The pharoahs themselves left no record of their administration. No inscription from the Hyksos invasion period has survived.

A few inscriptions of historical value come from the New Kingdom. There are some short documents that refer back to the Hyksos. A strident, triumphant note marks each of these compositions.

Four king lists come from the New Kingdom: The Turin Canon of Kings, the Table of Abydos, the Table of Sakkara, and The Table of Karnak.

Several of the imperialistic pharaohs left behind accounts of campaigns into other lands, mainly Asia. Among these kings were Thutmose III, Amenhotep II, Seti I, and Rameses II. Common in these is a date formula that follows this pattern: "Year x, x month of x season, day x." Thutmose III and eight pharaohs after him have left records of countries that each conquered during his reign. ANET also preserves short documents by officials in the New Kingdom that bear upon events that happened during their lifetime (note also the treaty between Egypt and the Hittites, ANET, pp. 199-201). Some other historical insights can be gleaned from stories, a few letters, and a limited number of legal documents.

As in Mesopotamia, no history of the Egyptians can be found in their literature. Egyptian documents, however, have supplied enough information for scholars to put together a more consistent sequence of kings and dynasties of the Egyptians, with dates within a decade or two of accuracy, than of other peoples of the ancient Near East. Chapter 1 has shown how this chronological framework serves as a reference point for biblical studies. Yet, for all this, the Egyptians had little interest in history as we know it.

Practically all the historical material dealing with the Levant comes from non-Canaanite sources. Some information can be found in Egyptian inscriptions; some references are in Akkadian, Hurrian, Mari, and Hittite documents. The Ugaritic tablets have documents of trade relationships of some significance. Perhaps the Tell el-Amarna letters of the early fourteenth century contain the most material, but it is still very scanty. None of the Canaanite inscriptions prior to 1000 B.C. are very helpful. In short, for the Levant, there is a huge lacuna of knowledge as far as historical literature is concerned. Archaeological artifacts have provided generalized data, but it is not adequate for a true history of the area.

In summary, the ancient people of the Near East made no attempt to relate events with each other in a movement toward a climax, either within a king's reign, within the span of a dynasty, nor over the spread of centuries. There was no searching for underlying reasons as to why events were related to each other, and certainly there was no analyzing of social forces or pressures or of the effects of economic supply and demand.

The ancient archivists and chroniclers engaged in no interpretation of events by means of concepts of progress, or dialectics, nor with a sense of movement toward a climax and its aftermath. They did not present variant points of view; hence their documents are one-sided and loaded with propaganda. They possessed no awareness of the dynamic of personal-interpersonal relationships, no crisis of dilemma, no breathtaking decisions made in freedom—as a deliberate selection of one course of action from among several alternatives.

Stele of Seti I, which was discovered at Beth-Shan, in Palestine.

Remarkably, neither the Sumerians, Babylonians, Assyrians, Egyptians, or Canaanites made any clear effort to tie together their mythological literature and their annals, king lists, or chronicles. In the mythological stories, the political events are vaguely in the background. In the more-or-less historical material, the gods and goddesses are not prominent and are sometimes not mentioned at all. The governor, king, priest, or pharaoh dominates the so-called historical literature; and each document describes, as it were, isolated incidents that have no overarching purpose. The deities were involved somewhat in the incidents, but not to any great extent.

Suggested Books for Further Reading

Driver, G. R. *Canaanite Myths and Legends from Ugarit.* Edinburgh: T & T Clark, 1956.

Gordon, C. H. *Ugaritic Literature.* Roma: Pontificum Institutum Biblicum, 1949.

Gray, J. *The Legacy of Canaan.* Leiden: E. J. Brill, 1965.

Heidel, A. *The Babylonian Genesis.* Chicago: University of Chicago Press, 1967.

Ions, V. *Egyptian Mythology.* London: Hamlyn, 1968.

Kramer, S. N. *Mythologies of the Ancient World.* Garden City: Doubleday & Co., 1961.

————. *Sumerian Mythology.* New York: Harper & Row Publishers, 1961.

————. *History Begins at Sumer.* London: Thames & Hudson, 1958.

————. *The Sumerians.* Chicago: University of Chicago Press, 1963.

Lambert, W. G. and Millard, A. R. *Atrahasis: The Babylonian Story of the Flood.* Oxford: The Clarendon Press, 1969.

Pritchard, J. B. *Ancient Near Eastern Texts.* Princeton: Princeton University Press, 1969. Also available in a paperback edition.

Thomas, D. W., *Documents from Old Testament Times.* New York: Harper & Row Publishers, 1958.

The Ur-Nammu stele depicts the king receiving divine directions for building a ziggurat. In successive register he completes the task assigned to him by his god.

6

Thought and Expression in the Ancient Near East

The volume of inscribed material that has been excavated, deciphered, and translated in the past century is remarkable. Early as much of this literature is, it is certainly not all primitive. The upper classes of the civilizations of the Mesopotamian and Nile were far from illiteracy and simple-mindedness. On the contrary, ideas are presented in this literature that have profoundly affected the thinking of later civilizations. Nor are we free of the grip of many of these concepts today.

An attempt will be made in this chapter to summarize the basic ideas that governed the thinking of the peoples of the ancient Near East and to note how these ideas were expressed in their organized life and practice. As in the previous chapters we will move from the civilizations of the Mesopotamian valley to the Nile valley, and then to the Canaanites, who dwelt along the eastern seaboard of the Mediterranean.

The Sumerians and the Akkadians

Pantheons. The theological views of the Sumerians set the pattern for the later Akkadians and then the Babylonians and Assyrians. Since creativity was associated closely with processes of reproduction, the gods and goddesses were regarded as related to each other after the manner of a family, such as husband-wife, father-mother, or parent-child. These relationships involved wife stealing, partner swapping, incest, and a variety of sex deviations; therefore, an exact genealogy is difficult to construct.

In general terms, the genealogy of the Sumerian pantheon can be laid out as follows: Nammu, the primeval sea goddess; An, the heaven god; and Ki, the earth goddess were conjoined in the form of a mountain. They were the parents of Enlil, the air-god, who pushed An and Ki apart. Enlil forthwith captured his mother, Ki, and mated with her. Ki then became known by three basic names—Ninhursag, Nimmah, and Nintu—and continued to be identified as Mother Earth. From this mating came the gods and goddesses related to the earth. Enlil also paired with Ninlil, an air goddess, and they became parents of Namma, also called Sin, the moon god. Namma-Sin mated with a sky goddess called Ningal, who gave birth to Utu the sun god. Other gods and goddesses of the sky seem to come from this branch of the genealogy.

The gods and goddesses were also understood to be related according to a power status structure. Since these gods and goddesses were tied to temples in specific cities, the place of the deities in the power structure tended to change as the power and prestige of the several cities rose or fell politically during the years. Again, generally speaking, the power arrangement of the Sumerian pantheon can be summarized in this fashion.

The myths speak of a council made up of seven members, in which there was a Big Four. The leader of the council was Enlil, the air god; Enki, the water god or god of wisdom; An, the heaven god, who was the father of Enlil but nevertheless down the power ladder a few rungs; and Ninhursag (Nimmah, Nintu), the Mother Earth.

The remainder of the Council of Seven were three astral deities: Nanna, or Sin, the moon god, who was very important during the Third Dynasty of Ur; Utu, the sun god; and Inanna, his sister, the fertility goddess (who seems to have been identified with the planet Venus).

With lower rank, the fifty Anunnaki are referred to as a group of workers. Whether the seven judges of the nether world and a dozen or more other gods and goddesses named in the literature were members of this group is not clear. Nor it is apparent whether Dumuzi, the shepherd god, was a member of this group. Dumuzi is identified as a king of Erech early in the third millennium B.C. who was then given the status of god. His love affairs and conflicts with Inanna was a favorite theme for the writers of Sumerian mythology.

The Igigi, who seem to have been minor sky gods and goddesses, appear in the myths at times. There were also a multitude of demons of all sorts who were called "the galla." They were completely evil.

When the Akkadians, who spoke a Semitic language, came into the valley and set up an empire under Sargon I, they adopted the Sumerian pantheon with little change. The genealogy of the pantheon was somewhat different, some names were changed, the sex identification of some deities was revised, and a few Semitic deities were introduced. When Hammurabi established the Old Babylonian Empire, a few shifts were made. The

Assyrians did the same when they rose to the heights of power. The kings of the Neo-Babylonian Empire made some changes, but basically the pattern was the same.

The Eblaite tablets name about five hundred deities, many of which appear in both Sumerian and Akkadian literature. A remarkable feature is the occurrence of *Ya(w)*, the equivalent of *Yahweh* in the Old Testament. For additional information on the Ebla tablets, see pages 293–96 in the appendix.

According to the Epic of Creation, the genealogy of the pantheon proceeded as follows: Apsu, the sweet-water ocean and formerly the abode of Enki, mated with Tiamat, the female salt-water ocean. They produced one son, possibly the mist, who had no female counterpart. They also produced two brother-sister pairs: Lahmu (m) and Lahamu (f), and Anshar (m) and Kishar (f). Precisely what nature aspects these represented is not clear, but the last-named couple was especially prolific. Their important offspring were Enlil, the air god, and Anu, the heaven god. Anu produced Ea (Enki), god of wisdom, who paired with Damkina (f) to bring forth Marduk, the storm god. A mass of evil gods came from Tiamat, but many other gods apparently came from one or the other of members of the pantheon listed above. In general, references in other compositions support the genealogy of the Epic of Creation.

The same composition indicates that the power structure of the pantheon was essentially the same as in the Sumerian religion. There was a group of seven gods who made the big decisions, but the make-up of the council was different. It seems to have consisted of Anu, the heaven god, as its early leader; then Enlil, or Ellil, the air god, who took over leadership;

The figure of a Sumerian priest, from Tell Asmar.

107

and Ea, the god of wisdom. These gods made up the Big Three of the pantheon. In the empire of Hammurabi, Marduk (earlier known as Adad), the storm god and a Semitic deity, was elevated to a supreme position in the pantheon. The Assyrians preferred the name Ashur to Marduk, and in the Neo-Babylonian Empire Marduk was called Bel. Another member of the seven was the mother goddess, Aruru (Ninhursag). Then came Sin, the moon god; Shamash, the sun god; and Ishtar, the fertility goddess, who had a lot of influence because she was the wife of the storm god, hence sort of a shadowy eighth member of the high council.

The Epic of Creation mentions a Council of Assembly but does not name its members, except that the Anunnaki and the Igigi seem to be involved. The Anunnaki, the worker deities, are referred to as being numerous. Three hundred were assigned to the heavens and three hundred to the nether world. One line in the epic mentions the fifty great gods but does not name them.

As a summarization, the following list of deity equivalents may be helpful:

Sumerian	Aspect	Akkadian
An	*heaven*	Anu
Enki	*water–wisdom–magic*	Ea
Enlil	*air*	Enlil, Ellil
Ninhursag Nimmah Nintu	*mother goddess*	Aruru
Nanna Sin	*moon*	Sin
Utu	*sun*	Shamash
Inanna	*fertility goddess*	Ishtar
Abzu	*sweet-water ocean*	Apsu
Ishkur	*storm*	Adad Marduk Ashur Bel
Nanshe	*salt-water ocean*	Tiamat
Dumuzi	*shepherd–vegetation*	Tammuz
Ereshkigal (f)	*head of nether world*	Nergal (m)
Ashnan	*grain*	Dagan
Nidaba	*deity of scribes*	Nabu (m)

Cultic Priests. Though the several classes of Sumerian priests are known, very little information is yet available concerning what each class actually

108

did. The kings of Sumer seemed to serve as high priests, at least at the annual New Year's festival and did engage in many of the rituals of worship. The head of each temple was an administrator, who was called the *sanga,* whereas the spiritual leader was the *en.* The *en* would be a priest if the temple was dedicated to a goddess, and a priestess if a god was worshiped.

The lower classes of priests were the *guda* and *mah,* whose duties are unknown; the *ishib,* who seemed to be in charge of the libations; the *gala,* who seemed to be singing poets; and the *mindingir.* Besides these, there were choirs, musicians, eunuchs, and sacred prostitutes. It can be assumed that each group had assigned duties in the temple activities.

The Akkadian (including Assyrian and Babylonian) literature provides much more information about the functions of the priests. Though the king continued to serve important functions in the great festivals, there arose a priest called the *urigallu* who served as a leader of the priests in the great feasts. They were appointees of the king.

These classes of priests and their functions are known: (a) *kalu* priests were chanters of the hymn and liturgies in the festivals; (b) *mashmashu,* or *ashipus,* priests were basically magicians, or perhaps better described as witch doctors, for they specialized in casting out evil spirits and reciting magical incantations, along with providing symbolic acts or amulets to protect the worshipers from harm (in some cases they provided substitution sacrifices for the sick); (c) *baru* priests were diviners who were skilled in observing omens in nature, interpreting dreams and the art of astrology. They were in charge of the calendar. There were also the *qadishtu,* holy women, who served in the temple as sacred prostitutes, plus the choirs and the musicians.

The priesthood was hereditary and the secrets of their profession were not open to those outside the priesthood. Most knew how to write and were experts in Sumerian as well as their native Akkadian. Pictorial representations of priests show that in early days they did their work without wearing clothes, but later their garment was a white linen robe, and on special occasions a red robe. In some rites they wore animal masks. As in other parts of the ancient Near East, priests' heads were normally shaved and no beard was worn.

Sanctuaries. The oldest Sumerian temple to be uncovered was found at Eridu and dates to the late fourth millennium B.C. Enki, the water god, was worshiped there. The building originally was only twelve by fifteen feet in size, but later was enlarged with adjoining rooms. Many other temples have been found, belonging to the third millennium B.C. Two common features

The ziggurat of Ur-Nammu at Ur. A restoration.

are a niche in which were placed the statue of the god or goddess and a flat-topped mound of brick on which offerings were placed.

The earliest temple was built on an earthern platform. Somewhat later, temples rested on platforms, which in turn were placed on artificial mounds. Later temples had platforms and two stages. Finally, the multi-staged ziggurat was built to support the temple. By 2400 B.C., the temples were extensive complexes that dominated each city. The temple at Ur was surrounded by a wall that enclosed an area 600 by 1,200 feet with a ziggurat measuring 150 by 200 feet at its base and rising to a height of 70 feet. The structure was made of bricks, faced with burnt brick set in bitumen.

Complex structures continued down through the Neo-Babylonian Empire, with ziggurats. There were temples on top and around them. All of the temples, which were of different sizes and shapes, had a central courtyard and a small room or a niche in which the image of the deity was placed. The priests and other functionaries lived close by the temple.

At Babylon was found the most elaborate temple, which was established in honor of Marduk. A huge enclosure possessed a ziggurat in one corner and a temple to Marduk with fifty-five chapels at the south side of the court. A processional road led from the main gate of the enclosure to the temple. Sanctuaries to other gods and goddesses were also in the courtyard. The complex was built by the Assyrian emperor, Esarhaddon, about the middle of the seventh century B.C.

The temple was the place where all the ritual of the religion of these people took place, and it was in and about the temple that the great festivals occurred.

The Festivals and Ritual. In the Sumerian literature there is no description of festivals as such, but they can be assumed because of the scores of hymns, lamentations, and incantations and because of passing references to months in which festivals are placed. Mention is made of a feast to the new moon, the feasts on the seventh, fifteenth, and last day of each month. There were surely daily sacrifices and libations. A New Year's Festival is noted as the time when a holy marriage took place between the king, representing the god Dumuzi, and one of the priestesses, who represented Inanna. This act was to affect fertility and prosperity, hence it had a sympathetic magical meaning.

There is no Sumerian document that sets forth the ritual of any worship service or ceremony; there are only individual rites, such as prayers and hymns. Nor are the myths ever specifically tied to ritual.

The early Akkadians, the Babylonians, and the Assyrians carried over the Sumerian religion into their own structure of society in Mesopotamia. They embellished some aspects with innovations, but the form and content of the religion remained essentially the same. The temple complexes were more extensive and the art more sophisticated; the ziggurats were perhaps more impressive and the ritual more complicated. The later literature does provide more detail about the nature of the festivals and the structure of the ritual, at least of the New Year's Festival.

The Mesopotamian peoples believed their divine images needed precise, daily care. After an image was fashioned, it was put into service by means of a "mouth-washing" ceremony. It was then alive. Daily they had to be washed, dressed, and perfumed with proper rites. Food and drink offerings had to be given them; music and dancing had to amuse them. Beds and bed partners had to be provided. Incense and sprinkling purified the temple for their presence.

Being farmers basically, the Babylonians had two main seasonal festivals; one was in the fall and the other in the spring. But the city of Babylon itself observed an eleven-day festival in the spring. This was the New Year's, or Akitu, festival, and its ritual has been preserved in a document from the third century B.C. Indications in other documents show that its contents were ancient.

Briefly, the New Year's festival can be summarized thus: On the first day the high priest bathed in the river two hours before dawn, entered the temple of Enlil, knelt and prayed, and then opened the temple doors to admit priests and singers who carried out the liturgy of the day. This procedure was done for four days. Late on the fourth day the white-robed priests gathered in the main room of the temple; the high priest walked to the center of the room and recited the tale of Enlil's struggle with Tiamat (Epic of Creation). The holiday began.

On the fifth day, at dawn, the temple was purified and the priests washed themselves. The "Golden Sky," a crown, was placed in Nebo's dwelling place, and a golden table of offering was set in his inner chamber. Certain priests brought the king from the palace. He walked to the temple followed by his chariot; his ministers carried his crown, the ring, the sceptre, and the sword. The king took the symbols at the temple door and entered alone. The high priest laid the royal symbols at the feet of Enlil. He then rushed back, hit the king three times on the face and dragged him to the feet of Enlil. The king professed to be innocent of any crime, so the high priest gave him the royal symbols and struck him hard on the face. Outside, the crowd was making a frantic search for Marduk, who was declared lost.

At dawn of the sixth day, the crowds gathered to welcome boats that were bringing the images of various gods from their servant cities. The king, in rags, with unkempt hair and with dirty hands, met them at the bank and together they marched in triumph to the temple. The other gods had arrived to find Marduk.

The seventh day was the "Day of Deliverance." The temple doors were opened at dawn and out marched the high priest, followed by priests carrying torches, the king in full battle dress, and the images of the visiting deities, which were carried on donkeys. They marched to a man-made "mountain" (ziggurat?) and waited. Suddenly, the door of the mountain opened and the god Marduk emerged. The crowds shouted with joy and celebrated Marduk's deliverance.

"The Day of Judgment" was the eighth in the series. At dawn the doors of the temple opened only for the king, who had a rod in his hand. The council of the gods was called to assemble in the Chamber of Destinies. The images were brought in one by one and the heavy copper doors were closed. The city was silent, for everyone's fate was in the hands of the gods and goddesses.

The ninth day was "Army Day." The streets were filled with happy people, for Marduk had defeated Tiamat. Soon a parade with soldiers in full dress passed through the streets, followed by crowds carrying clubs and sticks. At the river, the king, the images, and the royal ministers paraded

A fertility goddess, excavated at Mari.

through the crowd to the boats that took them to the feast house for a victory banquet.

The big celebration was on the tenth and eleventh days. On the tenth, the temple doors opened at dawn only for the priests who carried food for the gods in the temple. The populace celebrated by feasting and merry making. Presumably on this day the king was married to a virgin priestess and their marriage was consummated in the inner chambers of the temple. Wild orgies completed the feast.

The phases of the moon played a part in determining other festival periods. There was a feast on the appearance of the new moon and the seventh, fourteenth, twenty-first, and twenty-eighth were unlucky. The nineteenth was a day of wrath, which was marked by sacrifices and fasts.

113

There were barley harvest, malt harvest, and sheep shearing festivals. Besides these important days, there were incantations against diseases and acts and formulas to cast out demons available any time a worshiper might need help. Divination of coming events was ready for anyone who could pay a fee.

Prophets. When speaking of prophets in the religions of the ancient Near East, one must use the term broadly, as comprising predictions of the future. None of the Sumerian texts now available describe any means of obtaining information about the future except through dreams given to leaders and interpreted by a deity. In one instance, Gudea's dream is explained by the goddess Nanshe, and in another case Dumuzi's dream is unraveled by his sister, goddess Geshtinanna. There is no clue about methods used in the interpretation process. No oracles to men from any of the deities have yet appeared in the Sumerian literature.

As noted previously, the Akkadians, Babylonians, and Assyrians had a class of priests called the *baru,* whose work was part of the regular activities of the temple. The term *baru* means "to see," and the task of the priests was to observe the action of oil and water in a cup, the way in which objects fall, the condition of the entrails of sacrificed animals, the relation of the various heavenly bodies to each other (astrology), the movements of animals and birds, and the symbols of dreams. Hence, the baru priests were highly skilled technicians, and the methods of their work were closely guarded secrets. They did record some of their knowledge on clay tablets, however, and some of these have been recovered.

The baru priests believed that their deities spoke through the natural phenomena mentioned above, and they referred to the conclusions they reached about the nature of coming events as "the word of god." Sumerian literature does not indicate that orgiastic behavior was a trait of these priests.

There are some literary specimens of oracles, attributed to a few deities, to kings, and a few people of lower rank. These oracles are mostly transmitted by women but give no information about how the oracles were received. The date of these samples is the early seventh century B.C. There is one composition that has been called a prophecy; it is regarded as late (see ANET, pp. 449-452).

The most remarkable literary material that bears on Mesopotamian "prophecy" comes from ancient Mari, located on the bank of the upper Euphrates River. In the Eblaite tablets, the *mahhu* and the *nabi'utum* are mentioned as two classes of prophets. As yet, little is known of their character or activity. Over the last twenty years, an increasing number of tablets have been identified as bearing messages of one sort or another from deities to people, mostly the king. To date about thirty tablets have been labeled as this "messenger" type.

One type of person who claimed to receive oracles was the *apilu,* meaning "answerer." Only one tablet bears a message by the man himself; all the others are reported by a third party. There is no statement on how the messages were obtained. The content of the messages was mostly political, sometimes critical, sometimes hortatory, and sometimes bearing a promise. In a few instances, the apilu demanded that offerings be made to the deity. Interestingly, the messages had to be tested by the professional diviners.

The second kind of messenger was the *assinnu,* a male prostitute connected with the temple. The texts bearing these oracles show that the assinnu at times received his oracle in a state of wild, ecstatic behavior. The messages warn of plots against the king and assure him of help, but were tested by divination before being considered valid.

The third class of messenger was the *muhhu.* Some scholars think these men were ecstatic, but others doubt this. Some were connected with the temple, but many were not. Mostly, the messages urged attention to making sacrifices to the deity, or requested information about the king's activity. Dreams have a prominent role in many of these tablets, and in many instances it was a woman who had the dreams. Test by divination was common.

In summary, the "prophets" in the Mari tablets claimed that they had received a message from a local deity and said they were commissioned to send that word to the king, primarily. One must also note, however, that the content of the messages shows that the local deity felt sorely neglected and wanted attention. In practical terms, this would mean that the priests felt neglected; they wanted more offerings and they wanted more information about what the king was up to. These "prophets" spoke in behalf of the ecclesiastical establishment.

Kingship. The statements are scattered and fragmentary, but enough information comes through the Sumerian literature to indicate that early in their history the Sumerians had an assembly of two sections, the "elders" and the "men." In addition, there seems to have been an elected or appointed "city manager" or *ensi.* In times of emergencies, the elders put complete authority in the hands of a military leader (called *lugal*–"big man"), but took it back afterwards. Perhaps it was the demands of united action that irrigation and trade placed upon them that caused the role of the king to become permanent. The picture is not fully clear, though the Epic of Gilgamesh seems to show their early arrangements. The Epic of Creation may reflect the political process of choosing and establishing a young man as a king, instead of being limited to a mythology involving gods and goddesses.

115

Only a few of the early Sumerian rulers are labeled as kings; there were also high priests and ensis. These could be separate men, or a man might have more than one of the titles. The first king to be identified with the determinative sign for divinity was Naram-Sin of Akkad, and all but the first of the kings in the Third Dynasty of Ur were so designated. Some rulers of a few other cities were marked as divine, but Hammurabi never used the sign, though he boasted in his law code that he was both "the devout, god-fearing prince," and "god among kings." The custom of labeling the kings as divine died out with the Kassites.

Lugalzaggesi of the Early Dynastic period was the first to have the title "King of the Land," and Sargon I called himself "he who rules the Four Quarters." This title has been reserved for high gods, so it indicated an assumption of divinity. The Assyrian emperors took the title "King of the Universe," but scholars are divided on whether this meant that they thought they were divine.

In the Sumerian king list, both before and after the Flood, the phrase "kingship was lowered from heaven" appears. This phrase seems to apply to the *office* of kingship rather than to the king, and other passages indicate that divination was at times employed to determine who was to be the king. Many of the kings stated that they were chosen to reign by a deity or deities. There were times when kingship was passed from father to son, but this appears to be the exception rather than the rule. Ancient Mesopotamia was famous for its rapid shifts of power from family to family. In the last Assyrian period, a system of coregency was introduced to smooth the shift of power from father to one of his sons. The death of the aged monarch did not bear directly on the accession of his son to the throne.

The successor to the dead king was enthroned by an act of coronation. When he received the royal insignia, he was endued with the qualities of kingship. Several tablets describe a coronation ceremony.[1] As ruler, he must find guidance from the gods mainly through dreams, through omens, and through oracles.

The tasks of the king were threefold. His first task was to interpret the will of the gods to man, and in this role he must be a diviner himself and/or he must have as his counselors a group of expert diviners. Secondly, the king was to represent his people before the gods, hence he was the high priest of all the temple cults. He made sacrifices to the gods in time of crisis and during the major festivals of the year. His place in the New Year's Festival illustrates this aspect. His third task was the administration of the affairs of state, in times of both peace and war.

---

1. H. Frankfort, *Kingship and the Gods* (Chicago: University of Chicago Press, 1958), pp. 245-47.

The Egyptians

Pantheon. The four main Egyptian cosmogonies were based at four main cult centers: Heliopolis, Memphis, Hermopolis, and Thebes. The pantheon that was the core of the cosmogony of Heliopolis basically continued on into the theologies of the other three cult centers.

The pantheon of Heliopolis is sometimes called the *Ennead*, which was made up of genealogy of the high gods. The Pyramid texts of the Fifth Dynasty are the basic source of information about this Ennead.

This genealogy is described briefly as follows. The god Nun, primeval watery wastes, gave rise to the primeval earth hill upon which was Atum, later associated with the sun. Atum fathered from his own body Shu, the air god; and Tefnut, the dew and moisture goddess; Geb, the earth god; and Nut, the sky goddess; Osiris, the vegetation and nether-world god; and Isis, the fertility and mother goddess; Seth, the red desert and war god; and Nephthys, another mother goddess. From the union of Osiris and Isis came Horus, the falcon, sun-god, and the living pharaoh. Very early, Ra (Re), the father sun-god, became identified with Atum and was often confused with Horus.

Step pyramid of Djoser, first king of Egypt's Third Dynasty. The pyramid was designed by Imhotep, vizier to the king.

In Egypt the structure of the pantheon was quite different from that in the Mesopotamian pantheon in which Enlil was a leader among peers, or Marduk a leader chosen by the council of gods and goddesses. In Egypt the sun was the dominant factor of every day, for storms in the delta were infrequent, and, south of the delta, rain was a rare occurrence. It is not surprising then that Ra, the sun-god, and Horus, another aspect of the sun-god, should dominate all other members of the pantheon. Since the pharaoh was the human counterpart of the sun, he, true to the parallel, saw his greatest glory in being the absolute ruler of the land.

Across the Nile River and a bit south was the rival of Heliopolis, the political and cultic city of Memphis. The priests of Memphis did not deny the validity of the Ennead of Heliopolis; they simply insisted that their high god, Ptah, was Atum, who was both the watery wastes and the land. Therefore, all the members of the Ennead were but manifestations of Ptah as parts of his body. For example. Atum was the mind, Shu his heart, and Tefnut his tongue. It was not a monotheism, nor was it really a monism or a pantheism. It seemed to be more of an ordering of all the gods and goddesses under an absolute rule. Horus (Ra) was, as the sun, the most prominent nature object in this organization, and, further, was identified with the pharaoh. Thus he soon replaced Shu as the heart of Ptah. The moon was also a most dominate feature of the night sky, so he, Thoth, replaced Tefnut as the tongue of Ptah and became his constant companion.

The Ogdoad of Hermopolis, a city of Upper (southern) Egypt, was composed of four pairs of gods and goddesses. Each pair represented an aspect of chaos. Nun and his wife were primeval ocean; Huh and his consort symbolized infinitude; Kuk and mate connoted the phenomena of darkness; and Amon with his spouse were the atmosphere or perhaps, space. In graphic and sculptured art, the gods of this group were shown with frog heads, whereas the goddesses were depicted with serpent heads.

Together, the Ogdoad originally created and ruled the world, then died and became deities of the nether world. This view did not become dominant in Egypt by itself; rather it rose to high influence because its god, Amon, was placed at the head of the Theban cosmogony.

Thebes was the capital of Egypt from the middle of the sixteenth to early in the eleventh century B.C. Because it was in Upper Egypt it was influenced by Hermopolis. Since Amon was an air god, it was not difficult for the Theban priests to transform him into the creator of all else. More thoroughly than Atum or Ptah, Amon incorporated all other deities as phases of himself. This procedure did not mean that the temples, images, or rituals of the other deities were destroyed. The Ogdoad was one expression of Amon and the primeval mound of Memphis was another expression.

The sun-god Ra was Amon's eye, and the deity came to be known as Amon-Ra. Amon was also Thoth, the moon, and Horus, the falcon sun-god.

As a broadscale takeover of all Egyptian thought, Amon was declared the organizer of the Ennead and of the Ogdoad. He made the mother goddess, Tefnut, the concubine of the pharaoh.

Because Thebes was a rival of Memphis, Thebes claimed that it was the primeval hill in the midst of the primeval waters. Thebes allowed Memphis to continue to say that Osiris—the vegetation, funerary god—died and came alive again at Memphis. But Thebes simply topped the claim by saying that it was the city of Osiris's birth. Eventually, this proved to be the undoing of Amon, for Osiris was the far more popular deity and moved up to be the supreme god of Egypt.

For a short period, early in the fourteenth century B.C., there was a revolt against Amon-Ra and the power of his priestly caste at Thebes. The man who openly broke with Amon-Ra was Amenhotep IV, who repudiated this throne name and took another title, Akhnaton or Ikhnaton.

This heretic king built a new city between Thebes and Memphis and made it into both a political capital and a cult center in honor of Aton, an ancient title for the sun disk. Worship in all other temples was forbidden, and Aton was declared supreme. Some scholars have called this variant religion a form of montheism, but it was probably more of a monism. Aton was purely a nature entity and, curiously, the pharaoh continued to regard himself as a god, too.

When Ikhnaton died, his capital, known to us as Amarna, was abandoned and the supremacy of Amon-Ra at Thebes was firmly reestablished. Atonism was too esoteric to be popular; it had no mythology and, worst of all, it tried to upset long-rooted power structures.

The Egyptian, as did the Mesopotamian, worshiped a multitude of nature objects, plants, and animals as visible deities and treated them with great reverence. But, perhaps of more interest, is a comparison of the Egyptian pantheon with the Mesopotamian pantheon. Such a task cannot be performed easily, for the traits and functions of the deities were distributed differently, and sex identification was often reversed. The following parallelism may give some idea of a possible matching arrangement.

The Sumerian and the Egyptian pantheons were more nearly alike, so they will be related according to this format: the Sumerian deity/deities will be named, the nature aspect will be stated, and then the Egyptian counterparts will be given.

119

Sumerian	Aspect	Egyptian
Nammu (f)	*primeval water*	Nun (m)
An (m)	*heaven, sky*	Nut (f)
Ki (f)	*primeval earth hill*	Atum (m)
Enlil (m)	*air*	Shu (m)
Dumuzi (m)	*vegetation*	Osiris (m)
Ereshkigal (f)	*head of nether world*	Osiris (m)
Ninhursag Nimmah Nintu	*mother goddess*	Tefnut Hathor Nephthys
Enki (m)	*wisdom*	Thoth (m)
Nanna-Sin (m)	*moon*	Thoth (m)
Nidaba (m)	*deity of scribes*	Thoth (m)
Inanna (f)	*fertility goddess*	Isis (f)
Utu (m)	*sun*	Ra, Horus (m)
Ishkur (m)	*wind, war*	Seth (m)

(Caution: Don't be too precise in this parallelism, yet one point is clear. The deification of the same basic phenomena of nature is common to both religions.)

Cultic Priests. At the head of all Egyptian cults was the pharaoh. He was the embodiment of the sun-god, the essence of the state, and the supreme symbol of the practical side of Egypt's religion—the cult itself. The pharaoh functioned at the most important festivals, but he appointed high priests at each cult center to represent him; often the succession of high priests remained in the same family. The high priest had scribes to aid him and a more or less complex retinue of priests, depending on the size of the temple. There were many priestesses at each temple to serve as the concubines of the deity. These women also seemed to be musicians and dancers.

Little is known about the classes of priests or their duties before the New Kingdom, but the abundance of prayers, hymns, incantations, and lamentations in the pyramid and the coffin texts (a few are reproduced in ANET) would suggest a fairly large group of priests even in early times. Most of the early priests were of royal blood but were aided by lay officials. The literature would indicate that their duties were very similar to those in Mesopotamia.

During the New Kingdom the priests became powerful at Memphis, Heliopolis, and Thebes and owned sizeable sections of land. At times they seemed to rival the pharaoh in practical power. Indeed, at the end of the New Kingdom, the high priests of Amon-Ra reigned as pharaoh for a century or more.

The god Horus guards the entrance to the Horus temple at Edfu.

Sanctuaries. Knowledge about the early temples of Egypt is largely limited to the funerary temples near the pyramids, and these are mainly temples to Ra. There were also temples near the royal palaces. The impressive structures that awe the modern traveler to Egypt are mostly from the New Kingdom and later. The complex at Luxor (ancient Karnak and Thebes) is overwhelming.

Huge pylons guarded the gateways, and within the courtyard stood one or more shafts of stone, topped by a miniature pyramid, known to us as obelisks. The obelisk was sacred to the sun-god, Ra, and represented a ray of sunlight. Almost every available wall and column surface was decorated with carvings of figures and hieroglyphs. Many temples seemed to be tied more closely to funerary practices than to worship services in which personal piety was expressed. Great festivals did center in the important temples, too.

The Festivals and Ritual. As in Mesopotamia, the literature of Egypt provides a variety of separate rites but only a limited amount of ritual as an ordered sequence of rites that constitutes a service. Most of the rites are limited to royal activities and throw but meager light upon how the common people worshiped.

The temple of Amun.

Magical qualities were part and parcel of the rites, which dealt with diseases, enemies, decision-making, and death. Incantations were directed toward enemies, and mechanical divination probed the divine secrets to gain guidance for the future.

The festivals that are described have to do mainly with the death of the old pharaoh and the enthronement of the new ruler. When the pharaoh died, a series of rites connected with the embalming of his body lasted for seventy days. The so-called Book of the Dead contains rites that were supposed to aid the pharaoh to pass through the Judgment Hall successfully. A ceremony of transfiguration of the dead pharaoh took place the day before the coronation of the new pharaoh.

While the dead pharaoh was being embalmed, the new ruler enacted at various shrines the "Mystery Play of the Succession," of which there is a papyrus copy dating about 2000 B.C. The coronation festival normally lasted five days and was related to one of the several New Years of the Egyptian calendar.

Another royal festival was the jubilee called the *Sed*. It had no set time for its observance but was commonly related to one of the three "seasons" of the calendar year. Much like the enthronement ceremony, the Sed festival sought to renew the king's vitality. Often the festival was celebrated at the consecration of new temples. (See ANET pp. 325-330 for a few of Egypt's rituals and pp. 365-381 for some hymns and prayers.)

122

Prophets. In a sense, the pharaoh was the supreme prophet of Egypt. Through dreams and divination he was supposed to convey to the nation the will of the gods, especially the will of sun-god Ra. In several instances the oracle had to do with the selection of a new pharaoh. In several inscriptions, prophets are mentioned, but no description of their activities is given.

Two compositions in ANET, which are classified as prophecies, can only be called such by confining the word prophet to mean critic, or flatterer. Neither the "Admonition of Ipu-wer" nor "The Prophecy of Nefer-rohu" carries a claim that a message from the divine realm has been received or is being conveyed. The piece laments that the nobles were losing their power and wealth, whereas the second is concerned with humoring the pharaoh with a tall tale about a future time of joy in contrast to a present time of grief and hunger. That Nefer-rohu was a priest with skills of divination is quite clear; but it is difficult to see that he possessed other skills.

The Egyptian tale "The Journey of Wen-Amon to Phoenicia" has within it a scene of a young man who uttered a short oracle when he was seized with a spirit. But since this fellow was not an Egyptian and the episode happened in Phoenicia, it will be discussed in connection with the Canaanites.

Kingship. In Egypt, the first pharaoh of the very first dynasty was regarded as a god, and this conviction did not die out until Christianity became dominant. The living ruler was called Horus, the son of Ra. The pharaoh was not merely divine while he was ruling; he was god before birth and during his childhood. The pharaoh never died; he simply became the god Osiris, the vegetation god, and continued to influence life in many respects.

The Egyptians understood the essence of the universe as static. The ever-reliable sun punctuated this belief, and, since the pharaoh was the sun in flesh, he was identified with the cosmos. When the pharaoh was crowned, he did not become a god; he was simply unveiled as a god. In the cult, the Pharaoh was high priest; in the government, his rule was absolute; in war, he was the army; in art, he symbolized Egypt. The pharaoh could delegate his powers to others, and at times his underlings may have seemed more powerful than he; but his power was repeatedly reemphasized. There is no clear evidence that a real revolt of the people was ever mounted against him. Even invaders were absorbed into the concept of the pharaoh's supremacy and ejected as soon as possible.

Egypt never produced any real law codes; the word of the pharaoh became law immediately. Yet he was not so much a tyrant as the one who maintained the fitness and order of things. The pharaoh was not merely a leader among men; he was a leader without human peers. The pharaoh, as the Egyptians believed, had the qualities of the high god—the sun. Like the gods he could be depicted with both human and animal features. In art he towered above all earthly creatures, but he was the same size as the gods. Sacrifices were offered to the pharaoh, and he was worshiped in temples dedicated to him.

The pharaoh was the lord of Upper and Lower Egypt, but he was the single monarch of all Egypt. Here a basic Egyptian concept shines through. To the Egyptians, two opposites must be held in balance in order to have totality. Therefore, the pharaoh was both Horus (Lower Egypt) and Seth (Upper Egypt); he was both Ra, the sun, and Osiris, the god of vegetation. The pharaoh was the bond between heaven and earth, between the divine realm and man.

The pharaoh was believed to fulfill several human and natural needs. He was thought to dominate and motivate the natural processes of crops, cattle reproduction, and even the flooding of the Nile. The pharaoh was the being who distributed the harvest to the people; it was his power that kept society operating smoothly and that kept his subjects vigorous.

The foregoing doctrine about the pharaoh was the ideal, but in real life there were many contradictions to this belief. Serpents and fierce

The Deir el-Bahari temple of Queen Hatshepsut.

enemies threatened the land, and disease endangered the people. Nonetheless, the Egyptians bent every effort to exalt the pharaoh as the victor over all foes.

The Levant

Within the Levant, the views of the Canaanites are of the utmost importance to the student of the Pentateuch. Here the information is almost totally limited to the tables found at the ancient ruins of Ugarit (Ras Shamrah). Some snatches of data concerning the beliefs of the Canaanites can be found in the Pentateuch, and more can be found in the rest of the Old Testament; but when summed up, the picture is inadequate. At present, the Ugaritic literature remains the best source for our knowledge of the Canaanites.

Pantheon. The composition of the Canaanite pantheon was basically patterned after the Mesopotamian religion, but a few of the gods were much more like some of the Egyptian deities. The pantheon was not nearly as tightly organized as those in the Mesopotamian or Nile valleys. Also the individual deities were much more rowdy and violent.

The genealogy of the gods of Canaan is not as explicitly laid out as in the Akkadian and Egyptian religions. Statements in the Ugaritic literature and in a group of magical collections from the Nineteenth Dynasty of Egypt do suggest some family-type relationships.

The father of the gods was known as El, who was also creator and the heavenly "Bull." In the Ugaritic epics, El is a remote heaven-god and quite inactive. His name seems to have meant "Lofty One," or "Strong One." Asherah was El's wife and the mother goddess. One of her titles was "Holiness," but she was also revered as the patroness of diviners. It is not clear whether Baal (Hadad) was the son of El; he is called also the "son of Dagon." Baal was the combined fertility and storm god and so was called "King of Heaven and Earth." His home was at Mount Casius of Zaphon.

Paired with Baal were two goddesses, Anath and Astarte (another form of the name Ishtar). Both were listed as sisters and wives of Baal. Anath was depicted as a woman dressed like a man in battle array. One of her titles was "Queen of Heaven," and she was known as both a protectress and a destroyer and as both a lover and a cruel killer. Astarte is the goddess best known in the Bible. She was pictured in pagan art as a naked girl riding a stallion and carrying weapons. Like her sister, she represented both fertility and war. The evening star (Venus) was her heavenly emblem. Other deities are not described as directly related to this "family."

The structure of the Canaanite pantheon is vague. El was supposed to

Astarte figurine mold with modern cast.

be the leader, but Baal was by far the most active god, so far as the epics are concerned. There seems to have been a council of the gods, but there is no clear data on the make-up of the council. Probably the cosmic deities listed above would have been prominent. Other deities that could have been members were (a) Koshar, the god of craftsmanship, magic, and music; (b) Horan, a war god; (c) Resheph, a god of war, of disease, and the nether world and his wife Adum, the red earth; (d) Dagon, the grain god; (e) Sin, the moon god; (f) Yam, the sea goddess; and (g) Shamash, the sun god. There were many other deities of cities and clans. Some animals were considered to be divine.

The writers of the epics realized that their gods and goddesses were like the deities of their Mesopotamian and Egyptian neighbors. Correlations between them can be found in the literature of the time. In the following sequence the name of the Canaanite deity will be first, then the nature aspect they represent, then the Akkadian deity, and finally the Egyptian deity. The equivalents could only be set up in general terms as differences did exist. Note the following:

Canaanite	Aspect	Akkadian	Egyptian
El	*heaven*	Anu	Ra
Asherah	*mother earth*	Aruru	Tefnut
Baal	*storm*	Marduk	Seth
Anath	*fertility*	Ishtar	Hathor
Astarte	*fertility*	Ishtar	Isis
Koshar	*wisdom*	Ea	Ptah
Resheph	*nether world*	Nergal	Osiris
Dagon	*grain*	Tammuz	Osiris

Cultic Priests. As in the other ancient Near Eastern religions, the king was the high priest of the cult. In both the "Legend of King Keret" and "The Tale of Aqhat," the king acted as priest in making sacrifices. In each case the sacrifices were made for their own benefit, but this does not exclude a probable role of the king as priest of the community.

There are several priestly groups mentioned in the epics. The *khnm* (Hebrew: *kohenim*) were priests, but nothing is said about their duties. The same is true of the *ngdm* (Akkadian: *nagidu*), though in Mesopotamia these priests were diviners. The third group were the *qdsm* (Hebrew: *qedeshim),* who had a place in the cult, but again there is nothing to show that they were the same as the cultic prostitutes condemned in the Old Testament and common in both Mesopotamia and in Egypt. The tablets list twelve priestly families, which suggests that priests had a prominent place in Ugaritic society.

It can only be assumed that the priests offered sacrifices and prayers, that they divined the future by means of dreams and other techniques, that they carried out the ritual of the festivals, and that they performed magical acts to promote healing and fertility. But these duties are nowhere tied to the priests in the literature. A few administrative texts at Ugarit connect priests with the army, but what they did in the army is not known.

Sanctuaries. Canaanite temples have been excavated at several cities in the Levant. A temple that goes back to early in the second millennium B.C. and up to about 1200 B.C. has been found at Ugarit. It was dedicated to Baal. Near it was a temple to Dagon. They had three divisions, an open court with altar, an outer temple room, and an inner shrine. Several temples were found at Byblos with marked Egyptian influences. The three sections were not in a straight-line axis as were others that have been found at Megiddo, Beth-Shan, Shechem, Lachish, and Alalakh. The temple at Hazor had two pillar bases at the entrance of the main hall. A number of stone plaques, or stelae, along with sacred vessels have been found at many of these temples. A few open-air high places with round altars have been identified. None of these sanctuaries were as elaborate or as complex as those in Mesopotamia or in Egypt.

The Festivals and Ritual. The Ugaritic literature, so far published, provides little information about the festivals of the Canaanite people. Old Testament references indicate that the Canaanites had autumn and spring solstice feasts and new moon feasts, but the nature of these feast events are not fully described. Weeping, singing, dancing, and the offering of animal, even infant sacrifices, seem to fit into the ceremonies in some fashion. There are no literary documents yet available that have preserved the ritualistic patterns of the celebration. Albright mentions some unpublished ritual texts found at Ugarit. In the near future, perhaps, this gap in our knowledge will be filled.

Prophets. Apart from references to prophets of Baal in I and II Kings, there are only two references to the receiving and giving of oracles. One incident is embedded in the Egyptian tale "The Journey of Wen-Amon to Phoenicia." While Wen-Amon was at the port of Byblos, he was engaged in a series of negotiations with the local prince. On one occasion, while the local prince was making an offering, a young man was possessed by the god and delivered a message to the prince. The youth, however, did not claim to speak in the name of the god (ANET, p. 26).

On the stone inscription of Zakir and Lu'ath, there is a notation that the king received messages from his god Be'elshamayn through the seers and diviners. The messages received were promises of aid in military activities. How the seers and diviners obtained their oracles is not described (see ANET, pp. 501-502).

Kingship. Here, again, the passages that describe who the king was in relation to the city or national god are scarce. Many scholars utilize the models of the Mesopotamian or the Nile valleys to organize a composite picture of the kingship among the Canaanites. This procedure is criticized by others as improper, for it tends to superimpose explanations current in countries A or B upon generalized statements in country C.

There are a few references to the king as "son of god X," but whether this indicated a cultic relationship in which the king was the chief worshiper of a certain god is not clear. Nor is it apparent whether or not the term refers to the Egyptian idea that the king was born as an incarnate god and was always a god in essence. A few statements suggest that the king was worshiped by his followers. It is much clearer that the ruler was the high priest of the cult, made offerings, and participated in the annual festivals; but even this information is meager. In short, the Canaanite literature of Ugarit lacks an organized ideology of kingship, but does have scattered statements that tie the king closely with the gods, and combine the offices of kingship, priesthood, and, to a limited extent, prophet together in the royal person. The fact that the position of king was hereditary gave a measure of stability to the office.

Summary

In spite of the individual differences between the cultures of the ancient Near East, certain salient features are common to all. This summary endeavors to highlight these characteristics.

The Nature Circle Is All-inclusive. Each of the religious systems discussed on the previous pages encompasses all realms of reality—divine, natural, and human—within natural phenomena. The lines of demarcation between the divine, natural, and human were understood as porous, that is, there was easy movement and cross identification between them. The divine

Relics of the temple at Hazor on display at Haifa Museum.

A god of Ugarit, wearing a high crown of Upper Egypt. The figure is made of bronze, covered with gold and silver, and dates from the fifteenth or fourteenth century B.C.

could be a natural object and vice versa; the human could be a divine being or become a divine being and vice versa. Through magic a human could become an animal-like creature or an animal could take on human personality traits. The interrelationship was fluid, and though the gods and goddesses were personified, their relationship with humans was impersonal and mediated through the cult.

A Primeval Simplicity Lay Behind All Things. At the beginning of all things was a primordial darkness, water, earth, or sky. Mostly, the primordial was thought of as a combination of darkness and water, in Sumerian theology as a female principle and in Egyptian cosmogony as a male principle. Out of the primal stuff come all gods, goddesses, creatures, and humans, either by procreation or by magical utterance.

After all things came into existence, there remained a force—a fate that was beyond the individual deities and that regulated them. This would be particularly evident in the orderly movements of the sun, moon, stars, and planets. The seasonal sequence of wet and dry weather in the Mesopotamian valley and in the Levant, or the sequence of the flooding of the Nile, the sprouting of seed, and the harvest points to this primal power beyond the deities. The arts of divination and magic were rooted in the mysterious force that seemed impersonal, awesome, and potent.

The High Gods Were Cosmic in Character. Each of the high gods had the traits of having a history of being born, of being parents, and some, of having died or repeatedly dying. Yet they were understood to be immortal. The high gods were identified with the sky, air, earth, and water. Also high on the list were the sun, moon, the evening star (Venus), and vegetation. The mythological stories major on the tensions that are observable in daily life between these aspects of nature and also on the forces that limit their powers.

The traders, diplomats, and migrants of the ancient Near East were quite aware that the features of nature, which the high gods represented, were present wherever they traveled. Hence, ancient man both tied their high gods to specific images at localized temples and saw that the high gods of other nations were like their own. This phenomena made it easy for Akkadians to adopt the religion of the Sumerians, or the Egyptians to absorb foreign deities into their pantheon.

The Divine Realm Was Subservient. The deities were subject to restraints of various sorts. Enlil, or Marduk, might be leader of the pantheon, and Atum, Ra, Amon, or Aton might be the major god of Egypt, although none were truly sovereign. Even the highest gods were endangered by an almost coequal demonic power whom they were able to control only by the barest margin. On the practical level, the superiority of the high-god theology within royal circles was offset by the popularity of the lesser fertility deities among the common people. The essence of the high gods was always endangered by the tendency to distribute it among an almost endless multiplication of provincial, tribal, urban, clan, and family deities. Neither the effort to combine all these deities in Ptah, or Amon, nor the attempt to abolish them in Atonism could do away with the popular polytheism.

The gods and goddesses were subject to all the needs, weaknesses, and woes of mankind. They made mistakes of judgment and committed grievous moral wrongs. Some were killed; some were banished to the nether world. They were dependent on the human cultic system for food and drink. They could be manipulated by magicians, and their secrets ferreted out by skilled diviners. Vile passions were prone to govern many of their actions.

Though the gods and goddesses were personified, they were never really persons. They were not truly free, nor could they enter into meaningful personal relationships with the primordial stuff, with each other, or with human beings. They were really only aspects, or objects, of nature.

The Popular Fertility Cult Was Grossly Immoral. The exact history of the origin of the fertility cult is unknown, but it is generally agreed that it became visible in the Dumuzi (later Tammuz) cult of the Mesopotamian valley. Some significant mythological stories center about the amorous relations of Dumuzi with Inanna and Tammuz with Ishtar. Artifacts of fertility and phallic import have been found in abundance all through the ancient Near Eastern ruins. The major festivals, especially the New Year's feast, focused on sexual activity. Prominent in each of the ancient religions were hosts of male and female prostitutes who were an integral part of the temple personnel.

The fertility cult was grounded in male and female reproductive functions, which were considered inherent in the universe and nature. Naturally, this emphasis was important to the herdsman and the farmer, and the fertility cult was particularly popular with them.

Many details about the fertility cult are unclear, but the spring and the fall festivals marked by weeping and joy seemed to be especially important. Many scholars believe that the sacred marriage of the king at the New Year's feast and the orgiastic revelings of the masses at the conclusion of the festivals were essential parts of the fertility cult ritual. The activities of the cult prostitutes may also have been basic to the fertility emphasis.

The main aspects of nature were central in the fertility cult such as rain with its thunder and lightning in the upper Mesopotamian valley and the Levant, the flooding Nile in Egypt, the fertile soil, the staple crop of the region, the important domestic animals—especially the bull and the ram and their female counterparts, and the period between harvest and the sprouting of the seed.

The function of the fertility cult seemed to focus on the idea that its feasts and rites could break the power of the dry season or a period of drought by assisting the deities to mate, thus "triggering" the wet season, sowing, and sprouting seed, finally guaranteeing a fruitful harvest and a goodly number of calves, lambs, and kids.

The Mythological Stories Provided a Rationale for the Status Quo. The myths of the ancient Near East present the only witnesses we have of the pagan thought patterns about the world in which they lived. It was a kind of thought that was partly based on observation of the natural world, but mostly grounded in imagination. The mysterious movements and interrelationships of the heavenly bodies were viewed dynamically, as were also the phenomena of weather and of reproduction. Even the ebb and flow of politics was tied in with the astral bodies, the climate, and cycle of life and death. Apparently, mythology was the ancient's endeavor to construct a unified world view that correlated with life as he experienced it.

The Cultic Rites Sought to Maintain the Status Quo. There are enough explicit statements in the cultic literature to indicate the intentions of the priests and worshipers as they participated in the temple rituals. Their aim was to secure and guarantee the continuance of the prosperity of the community and the individual and to check the power of evil that threatened on every hand. For the individual there were rites of passages dealing with birth, puberty, marriage, and death to assure safe arrival through times of crisis. For the community, the festivals were to assure the welfare of the group by conquering drought, starting the rains, sprouting the seeds, gathering a bountiful harvest, and increasing the cattle.

Rites of intensification sought magically to strengthen man's relationship with the spirit world. The power of the king must be renewed regularly. The potency of the images must be kept virile by proper care and regular meals of food and drink. The evils of impurity, sickness, and curse must be

Baal, the storm god, holds a club in his right hand and a lance in his left hand. The lance extends upward in the form of a tree or stylized lightning. The figure was found at Ras Shamrah in 1932.

133

counteracted. Sacred objects must be charged with power. The rites were to initiate and bring into being a course of events congenial to man and in accord with the cycles of nature.

Myth and Ritual Unified the Pagan's World. Most of the clear evidence of the combination of myth and ritual is in the late Assyrian and Neo-Babylonian periods and in the funerary-coronation cycle in Egypt. Some scholars have concluded that myth and ritual were closely tied together in the Sumerian and Canaanite cultures or in the daily life of Egypt, but no clear evidence yet supports this theory. Presumably, when kings were strong and aggressive in building their empires, myth and ritual were most closely interrelated. The possibility was there for the pagan to bind his universe into a functioning whole by combining myth and ritual; the measure of his success is yet to be assessed fully.

Divination Oriented the Pagan Toward the Future. The peoples of the ancient Near East had a deep-seated interest in the intentions of fate. Their gods and goddesses were also gripped with this concern. A significant percentage of the literature they produced revolved about astrology, the reading of omens, and the techniques and skills necessary to ferret out the secrets of the unknown. This type of knowledge was not distributed widely among the people, but was restricted to the priests and priestesses or a limited lay group. The wise in these arts were powerful, and their influence reached to the throne itself.

Mostly, the diviner of the ancient Near East was a shrewd observer and an expert in shrouding his predictions in ambiguities. He or she was normally a member of the temple personnel, but the cult was not necessary to his art; he or she could work quite independently. Both the prestige and the fees of the trade were adequate to boost the diviner to wealth and power. Skill fed itself on the hopes of the people for a better life and on their fears of calamity.

Magic Was at the "Control Board" of Power. If it may be said that the ancient diviners were at the "radar towers" searching for signs of coming events; the magician was the "control board" seeking to control the future by use of proper word formulae and by potent, symbolic acts. Magic, per se, is not religious, yet the temple cults of all sections of the ancient Near East had wedded their rituals with the concept that certain words and certain acts are in themselves potent. Properly recited or acted out, the rituals would renew the potency of the king, reactivate the reproductive cycles of nature, assure the welfare of the community, and stay the power of evil. It was an effort to find security in a dangerous world.

*Stele of the Hittite storm
god Teshub.*

135

The gods as well as men must rely on magical activity. The mythological stories are replete with instances in which the god of wisdom (magic) was influential because he possessed skills in magic. The contest between Marduk and Tiamat centered on the magical potency of their weapons. Thoth, the moon god and magician of the Egyptian pantheon, was indispensable to Ra, the sun god. Baal, the storm god of the Canaanites, had his potent, magic-charged clubs. In each case, magic pointed to a power beyond, or above, the deities themselves. The god or the human who knew how to concentrate power within himself or how to manipulate the power resident in certain objects or animals occupied a key place in the power structure of any community. For a fee, and according to his whim, the magician could focus blessing upon those he favored and pour curses upon those he hated.

Since it was mainly the priestly caste that knew the arts of magic, the masses were slavishly dependent on the amulets the priests sold and the potency of the incantations and benedictions they pronounced. No force protected the interests of the status quo more than did the magical vitality of the temple ritual.

Suggested Books for Further Study

The bibliography of the previous chapter is appropriate for this chapter as well. For several sections of this chapter these books and articles will be helpful.

Engnell, J. *Studies in Divine Kingship in the Ancient Near East.* Oxford: Blackwell, 1967.

Frankfort, H. *Kingship and the Gods.* Chicago: University of Chicago Press, 1948.

Hooke, S. H. *Myth, Ritual and Kingship.* Oxford: Clarendon Press, 1958.

Huffmon, H. B. "Prophecy in the Mari Letters." *Biblical Archaeologist* 31 (1968): 101-124.

Jacobsen, Thorkild. *The Treasures of Darkness.* New Haven: The Yale Press, 1976.

Montet, P. *Eternal Egypt.* New York: New American Library, 1964.

Roberts, J. J. "Antecedents to Biblical Prophecy from the Mari Archives." *The Restoration Quarterly* 10 (1967): 121-133.

Ross, J. "Prophecy in Hamath, Israel and Mari." *Harvard Theological Review* 63 (1970): 1-28.

Walters, S. D. "Prophecy in Mari and Israel." *Journal of Biblical Literature* 89 (1970): 78-81.

*An ancient Mesopotamian
statue of a worshiper kneeling
before his god. This relic was
recovered at Larsa, which was
a Sumerian town in southern
Mesopotamia.*

7

The Ancient Literature Compared with the Pentateuch

A storm center of controversy within Old Testament studies has been the extent of interrelation and dependence that existed between the Pentateuch and the literature of the ancient Near Eastern civilizations. Hopefully, the content of the previous chapters has helped to build some concept of what the non-Hebrew literature is like.

The literature of the ancient Near East should be related in some manner to the Pentateuch, and that is the purpose of this chapter. It is especially important to relate the first eleven chapters of Genesis to this body of literature and evaluate claims that Genesis is heavily dependent on the mythology of Mesopotamia and Egypt. An effort will be made to tie the Patriarchs, Moses, and the migrating Israelites to the world in which they lived and moved.

The distinctives of the Pentateuch in terms of theological and historical values will be probed, especially in those areas in which the Pentateuch differs from mythology and the thought environment of its day. Since chronology is valued by the Western mind, possible segments of ancient history will be compared with events mentioned in the Pentateuch and points of correlation will be weighed in the balances of judgment.

Genesis 1-11 Related to Its Background

Even scholars such as H. Gunkel and O. Eissfeldt, who make much of the presence of myths in Genesis, admit that neither this book nor the remainder of the Old Testament contains erotic myths. Nor is the material in Genesis 1-11 mythological in the sense that this type of literature is centered on the interactions of gods and goddesses who are aspects or objects of nature.

Ever since the publication of the Akkadian creation and flood stories a century ago, scholars have wrestled with the problems of actual and/or possible ties between those stories and the biblical accounts. Many have held that Israelites simply rewrote, according to their late theological views, the pagan stories they had become acquainted with during the Exile. Others have insisted that the biblical material had a separate literary history.

Perhaps the matter can be clarified somewhat by taking each biblical story and comparing it with the pagan myths.

An outstanding feature of the creation account is prominence of one God and one only. He was prior to all aspects of nature and at no time is God identified with nature except as its Creator and Lord. There are no sexual processes nor material emanations from a primordial darkness or sea. To be sure, there is an abyss, there is darkness and a sea in the account, but they are not personified nor are they deities.

Much has been made of a similarity of sound between the Hebrew word for "deep" or "abyss," *tehom,* and the sea goddess, *Tiamat,* of the Akkadian Epic of Creation. Though the two words may have come from the same root, *tehom* is masculine and denotes inanimate, watery matter, whereas *Tiamat* is feminine and designates salt water as a personified, active deity.

A remarkable feature of Genesis 1:16-18 is the writer's omission of the names of the "greater light" and the "lesser light" and his mention of the stars as though an afterthought. Though these astral bodies were important gods in the religions of the ancient Near East, especially in Egypt, and the stars were vital to astrology, the biblical account simply says that God put them in place and assigned them tasks, and that was that.

In Genesis 1:26 occurs a plural pronoun in a divine speech "Let us make man in our image . . ." and a singular pronoun in 1:27, "his image. . . ." Some scholars have suggested this is a vestige of polytheism and infers a divine council in which Elohim is chief, hence contrary to the monotheism of 1:27 and the rest of the chapter. Others have suggested a verbal plural of majesty, or a council of angels. Many in the traditional Christian approach have seen here an oblique reference to the Trinity. The plural pronoun appears in divine speeches also in Genesis 3:22 and 11:7. Given the strong antipolytheistic and antimythical nature of the rest of the passages in context, it is not likely that these plural pronouns are vestiges of paganism. If the Trinity is in fact eternal, it is also difficult to see how these plural pronouns must be ruled out as not being oblique references to the triune character of the Godhead. The statement is vague enough, though an openness must be maintained for further light.

The idea of "image of God" appears in some of the Mesopotamian literature, but it seems to be either related to the kingship or to idols that represented the deities and in which some of the power of the deities was concentrated. But in Genesis 1:26, 27, the image of God cannot be limited to either royalty or idols. The image of God can be only in man and seems to denote his special place at the apex of God's creative acts. Only man can communicate with God, have a personal relationship with God, or be God's agent in ruling nature.

In the Babylonian Epic of Creation, the deities relaxed after the creative events and had a huge feast, but in Genesis 2:1-3, God's rest simply sets an order to life for man and the Sabbath is made holy. The pagans often made holy certain places, people, or things; but God selected a segment of time for worship and made it holy. The Babylonians had a word *shabattu* but it designated certain days that were ominous with danger; the biblical Sabbath was freighted with blessing.

One cannot find in the pagan literature an answer to the meaning of the word "day" in Genesis 1. True, seven clay tablets bear the Epic of Creation myth, but this doesn't help much. A study of the Hebrew word for day, *yom,* does not aid the search for meaning. For centuries, scholars in the traditional stream of thought have split between an understanding of "day" as twenty-four hours or as indefinite periods of time. The Hebrew word for "day" is broad in its meaning, and in Genesis 1:5, 1:16, 1:17 and 2:4, several different meanings are apparent. The phrase "evening and morning" is an unusual sequence in Hebrew and may simply designate the totality of the act.

There are loose literary parallels in the arrangement of the days. Days 1 and 4 deal with day and night; day 1 divides them and day 4 lists three categories. Days 2 and 5 do the same thing, only the waters are divided and the three groups are creatures. Days 3 and 6 are concerned with the earth. In day 1 the earth is separated from the sea and three kinds of plants are listed; and in day 6 three types of beasts are mentioned, along with man, the crowning act of creation, the seventh in the series. There is a seventh day to cap the six days, and God does three things on that day. A parallelism of other details on these days, however, does not work out well.

The literary structure of the material treated under the category of a day is similar. Each day has one to four declarations of God's decision to do something; then there is a statement concerning the carrying out of God's decision; and, finally, a notation of divine approval. Within this structure there is some freedom of phrasing and syntax. Pagan literature that includes creation does not possess this type of structure.

That the author intended some type of sequence in the steps of making the earth habitable for man seems evident. What is not so evident is data by which we can set up time spans for each divine act, or the precise methods by which each aspect of nature came into being.

Some recent scholars, notably S. H. Hooke, have promoted the idea that the division of the creation account into days was the result of liturgical usage of the material in a New Year's festival. But no New Year's festival has been established for ancient Israel and there is no evidence that Genesis 1:1–2:3 was ever a part of Israelite liturgy.

There have been extensive efforts during the past century to show that Genesis 2:4b–3:24 is a second account of creation, having a desert as a chaos and a different order of events. Actually, the creation of Adam and then Eve are only segments of a setting for the climatic events of chapter 3.

The creation of man is depicted in the pagan accounts as man mixed with a combination of earth and divine stuff, or as made of the tears of a god. In Genesis 2:7, God made man of the earth, but no more than breath was transferred from God to man. Nor was man produced to provide for the physical needs of God; man's work had to do only with cultivation of the land. The God-man relationship is presented in purely personal terms.

Kramer equates Eden with the Dilmun of Sumerian mythology.[1] But Eden was simply a home for man, whereas Dilmun represented both a home for man and a mysterious divine home for the deities somewhere to the east. In Sumerian economic texts, ships of trade plied between Sumerian docks and Dilmun. Possibly, Dilmun was the homeland of the Sumerians who had worshiped ancestral gods there.

In Eden were two trees of special importance. The tree of life shows up in ancient art and in the literature to some extent. In paganism the tree of life seemed to symbolize the natural powers of reproduction in plants, animals, and man. These sacred trees were in divine abodes, and deities ate of them. Very few humans were allowed access to them, and these were reigning kings. As priest, the king might dispense the powers of the tree through cultic ritual. In Genesis 2, man was not forbidden to eat of the tree of life until after he was judged for sin. The tree seemed to point to spiritual life sustained as a gift of God, but which could be withheld. Loss of access to the tree of life exposed man to physical death.

The tree of knowledge of good and evil has no parallel in pagan litera-

---

1. S. N. Kramer, *The Sumerians* (Chicago: The University of Chicago Press, 1963), pp. 148-49.

ture, but in Genesis 2 and 3 it is intimately related to obedience or disobedience to God's authoritative command. When God's command (2:17) was disobeyed, the harmony of the God-man, the man-woman, and the man-nature relationships was shattered.

Nowhere in the first two chapters of Genesis is there a demonic force challenging the Creator and the stability of creation. By contrast, a cosmic demonic force of an array of demons are common to the pagan creation stories. In Genesis 1-3, evil comes into the picture in a different context than from the creation, *per se.*

The serpent is referred to in 3:1, 14 as merely an animal, but he was more than that; he could speak and reason. The adjective "subtle," is elsewhere applied to man, mostly in a bad sense, in the Old Testament. The serpent could seduce Eve and challenge God, yet he is not presented as a cosmic power in nature, as in pagan mythology. In the Babylonian Epic of Creation, reptiles are associated with evil cosmic power; and in the fertility-cult, serpents seemed to have phallic significance. In Egypt, the serpent was commonly identified with the anarchic powers that the pharaoh must always keep under control.

In Genesis 3:24, cherubim appear to be somewhat similar to the guardian images of pagan temples and palaces, but the biblical creatures bear no hint of divinity.

As a literary production, Genesis 2 and 3 have no parallel in ancient Near Eastern literature. The Epic of Adapa, often presented as a parallel, is not really so, either in literary structure, in moral emphasis, or in theological content.

Kramer suggests that an old myth called "Emesh and Enten: Enlil Chooses the Farmer God" is somewhat like the Cain and Abel story.[2] Such a comparison must be very loose at best. Emesh and Enten were personified gods, both claiming the right to represent herd and crop fertility. They quarreled loudly and finally Enlil chose Enten. There was no violence and no rejection of a divine warning.

Considerable argument has boiled about the meaning of "sons of God" in Genesis 6:1-4. Some scholars have declared that this section is a vestige of an old polytheistic myth; thus the sons of god were deities who engaged in illicit relations with humans. But there is also evidence that pagan kings were called "sons of god" in ancient times. There is no way to prove or disprove that either of the above two meanings was attached to the biblical text by the Hebrews. One can only note that the inclusion of a pagan literary segment in the text is totally contrary to the anti-

---

2. S. N. Kramer. *Sumerian Mythology* (New York: Harper and Row, Publishers, 1961), pp. 49-51.

mythical emphasis of Genesis 1-11. Also, there are two other possible meanings, as follows.

Elsewhere in the Old Testament (cf. Job 1:6; 2:1; 38:7; Ps. 29:1; 89:6; Dan. 3:25), angels are designated as sons of God, and some commentators in the traditional camp have suggested that fallen angels married women and corrupted mankind. However, Jesus said that a married state did not apply to angels (Matt. 22:30).

Other traditional scholars have held that the *ha' elohim* of the phrase "sons of God" elsewhere in the Old Testament regularly means "the one true God," hence pagan deities and pagan rulers are ruled out. It is also argued that the idea of worshipers of God being regarded as His children or sons is not unknown in the Old Testament (see Deut. 32:5; Ps. 73:15; Hos. 1:10 and 11:1), and the phrase appears several times in the New Testament (see John 1:12; Rom. 8:14; Phil. 2:15; I John 3:1; and Rev. 21:7). The "sons of God" would represent descendents of Seth, and the "daughters of men" would come from those who did not worship the one true God. But whether or not this is the true interpretation is open for more study.

Though the story of the tower of Babel comes after the flood, it is mentioned here because remarks about it are brief. Recently, S. N. Kramer has published the content of a fragment from ancient Sumerian.[3] This fragment states, "Enki . . . Changed the speech in their mouths/ (brought (?)) contention into it/ Into the speech of man that (until then) had been one."

No reason is given for this act of confusing human language. The biblical story does provide a reason—a divine reaction of judgment.

In the previous chapter, which discussed the mythological literature of Mesopotamia, the Sumerian flood story and the Babylonian Epic of Gilgamesh were summarized. There are closer parallels between these two stories and the biblical story of the flood than between the pagan creation stories and the biblical creation account. In these accounts, a hero is warned of the flood and told to build a boat. In each case the flood was world-wide and the destruction total. The boat rested on a mountain, each hero worshiped after disembarkment, and each received a blessing. The Sumerian account does not speak of birds being released, nor do the earliest fragments of the Epic of Gilgamesh, though the specimens found in the seventh century B.C. at Nineveh have birds going out from the ark. The differences in many other details and in theology are vast, however.

The pagan flood accounts have only a one-week flood, but the Bible

---

3. S. N. Kramer, "The 'Babel of Tongues': A Sumerian Version," *Journal of American Oriental Society* 88 (1968): 108-11.

CHRONOLOGY OF THE FLOOD
Genesis 7 and 8

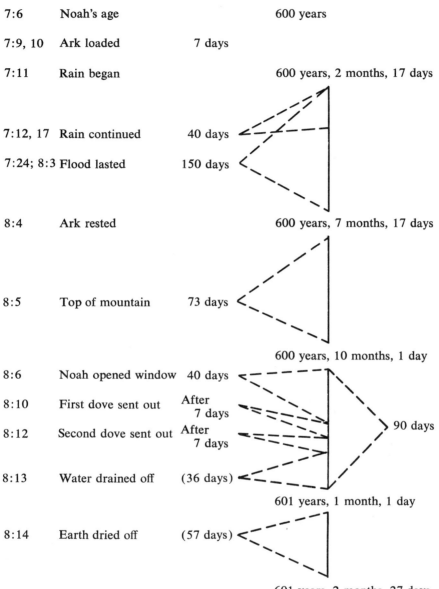

7:6	Noah's age		600 years
7:9, 10	Ark loaded	7 days	
7:11	Rain began		600 years, 2 months, 17 days
7:12, 17	Rain continued	40 days	
7:24; 8:3	Flood lasted	150 days	
8:4	Ark rested		600 years, 7 months, 17 days
8:5	Top of mountain	73 days	
			600 years, 10 months, 1 day
8:6	Noah opened window	40 days	
8:10	First dove sent out	After 7 days	
8:12	Second dove sent out	After 7 days	90 days
8:13	Water drained off	(36 days)	
			601 years, 1 month, 1 day
8:14	Earth dried off	(57 days)	
			601 years, 2 months, 27 days

Note: The Hebrew calendar had months of thirty days each. A thirteenth month was added after the last month every third year, giving a total of four extra months every eleven years.

has a lengthy flood. Some scholars have insisted that the dating formulae in the biblical account contain material from two variant sources and contain contradictions also. It is possible to harmonize the dating data in the biblical story. The chart on page 143 lays out the sequence of this data, yet the information provided does not help us to place the flood in a chronological slot according to our calendar. To do that we need much more than is now available from the Bible or from geology.

The Understanding of Man Is Vastly Different. Man is an "image of God," but he is not partially divine nor can he become divine as in paganism. Man is made of earth and can relate with God on a personal level; but he cannot be God. Attempts to crash the limitations of being human result only in disaster. Man does not simply take over divine menial tasks; he is commissioned by God to a high destiny of dominion in the world and is gifted with powers of freedom of choice before God. Man is not inherently immortal, but he can experience grace and mercy and life as gifts from God. Man can also reject them.

The Understanding of Sin Is Vastly Different. In the Bible (Gen. 1-11), man knows nothing of the rigid cause and effect structure of the universe that haunts man in the ancient pagan stories or ritualistic poems, prayers, and lamentations. Pagan man knew of "good" deities who were capricious and deities who were vicious, but the biblical man knew a God who is a just yet compassionate Judge, granting mercy and deliverance to those who submit to Him. Man knew a tempter who is clever and seductive, and he also knew himself as the one who freely chooses to disobey God, hence he is responsible for the evil that comes into his life.

The pagan man felt compelled to wrestle with nature and the gods by means of divination and magic, but he never really won the contest. The biblical man of trust and submission to the one God experienced release from sin's power and corruption and had fellowship with his Master. The pagan had a limited sense of what ought to be in the areas of justice, truth, and concern, but his low ethical practice constantly nullified them. God's commands, exhortations, and promises showed biblical man what is lofty in moral behavior and, though he failed, often he also, by God's help, rose much higher in practice than did the pagan.

The question remains: What do the similarities and differences mean in terms of the literary dependence and the literary history of these two bodies of material? No definite answer can be given to this question, hence several theories have gained the approval of various groups of scholars. These theories are as follows: (1) Genesis 1-11 was written during the Exile after the Jews had become acquainted with the Mesopotamian literature and had radically rewritten it to fit their own needs; (2) the Sumerians and Babylonians took the ancient prototypes of the biblical stories and embellished them fantastically; (3) the Patriarchs brought the Mesopotamian stories with them to Palestine and many generations of Hebrews gradually remolded them till they reached their present form; (4) both the biblical and the Mesopotamian literature hark back to events that were common knowledge in the ancient world, and each developed its own literary account and interpretation of those events. The biblical account, however, preserved the true interpretation of the events and the Mesopotamians corrupted its memory with polytheistic views of life.

Theory No. 1 has been the favorite of the Wellhausen school, and theory No. 3 has been suggested by some recent exponents of the "Salvation History" view. Both reject any possibility that God revealed the basic contents of Genesis 1-11 (especially Genesis 1 and 2) to any man, or that any transmission of early sources could have remained uncorrupted by later generations.

Theories No. 2 and No. 4 have been common among scholars of the traditional viewpoint. These scholars admit lack of direct evidence for their theories, but do insist on the reality of divine revelation and inspiration and the possibility of careful transmission, even through oral transmission, because of continuous divine concern about the truth and because of the sacredness of the content of the material to worshipers of the one true God.

Genesis 1-11 as History

During the nineteenth century, an increasing chorus of disapproval arose against the long-held belief of Jews and Christians that Genesis 1-11 spoke of things that actually had happened. The new view held that Genesis 1-11 was in fact a mixture of "folklorish" myth or legend and late Israelitish theology; theological statements of strong monotheistic tone would be the latest in date. The amount of historical material in Genesis 1-11 would be extremely limited.

With the rise of the form-critical method in this century, there has been a tendency to grant the presence of more and more ancient memory in Genesis 1-11. Parallel with form criticism there has been a tendency to split the values in Genesis 1-11 between (a) the meaning of the content and (b) the concrete factualness of the content. Extremely low value has been given to the latter, though there has been a growing admission that the author of Genesis 1-11 believed that what he wrote was an account of what actually happened. So did writers of other Old Testament books and so did the New Testament writers who referred to Genesis 1-11.

Part of the problem in the controversy has been ambiguity in Western scholarly minds as to the true nature of history. An unabridged English dictionary lists a number of words that come from the basic word *history,* and many of these words have variant meanings. A reading of literature on what history is indicates that the dictionary has not exhausted all the nuances of meaning that scholars hold about the nature of history.

The question of how divine revelation has been and is related to history has long been vital to biblical scholars and theologians. There will be no attempt here to plumb the depths of opinion on the subject; only a few items will be discussed.

The simplest definition of history is that it denotes events that have actually happened; hence, history would be the opposite of myth, legend, or fiction, which would have a minimal interest, or no interest at all, in what actually happened. Also, history is commonly understood to be a written narrative of those past events that happened to some people or peoples. This history may be concerned with aspects of human culture and may attempt some explanation or interpretation of those events. Of central concern to this kind of history are people, places, time, and cause-effect relationships.

Early in the nineteenth century, a deep concern developed in regard to "brute facts." Scholars desired precise accuracy. As many facts as possible must be gathered about people, especially leaders, about cultural institutions and practices, and about geographical environment in volume of encyclopedic proportions. This data must be arranged about a chronological timetable that is as complete and exact as possible. Methods were developed to validate the statements found in sources, to ferret out discrepancies, to separate fact from fancy, and to determine the true participants, the precise places, and the exact time of each event.

The scholars' concern for facts and proper methods is highly commendable; they made great contributions to human knowledge, but it was soon seen that more than "brute facts" were needed to have a full picture of "what actually happened." In spite of the historian's aim to be a neutral observer and to be objective in dealing with facts, he could not really live up to his goal. Many scholars arbitrarily ruled out the activity of either the supernatural or the demonic in human affairs and soon enlisted some current philosophical system to aid in understanding history.

Historicism became dominant in Europe, and its influence spread to other parts of the world. Historicism sought factual connectors between a series of cause and effect elements. But the factual was wedded to a network of rigid natural laws whose chief trait was a dynamic movement toward ever higher stages of achievement. The views of Comte, father of logical positivism, and Hegel, champion of logical progression after the pattern of a thesis-antithesis-synthesis sequence, were particularly influential among Old Testament scholars. Later the principles of Darwin's biological evolution were applied by some to the Old Testament. In the last several decades, a neo-Kantian split between secular history and theological or existential meaning has been a trait of some scholars.

Late in the nineteenth century, the Wellhausen school, taking their clue from Hegel, declared that monotheism and a complex priestly system did not appear in Israel until the Exile of the sixth century B.C. This meant that all monotheistic views and ritualistic practices in Genesis 1-11 must of necessity be dated to the sixth and fifth centuries B.C. The rest of Genesis 1-11 was considerd to be much more primitive and assigned to no earlier a date than the late tenth century B.C. Very little of the content of Genesis 1-11 was thought to be actual facts of ancient history.

A combination of studies—archaeology, history of religions, and form criticism—has altered the Wellhausen view. Gradually it was seen that monotheism had to be taken back at least to Moses, and that the creation, fall of man, and flood narratives had to come into the Hebrew community with the patriarchs since an antimythical and an antipagan attitude had long been a part of the Hebrew heritage. More and more it has been recognized that the author of Genesis 1-11 believed that the events he wrote about had actually happened. He also wanted his readers to believe that they had happened. Form criticism has done much to stress this attitude of the Hebrews toward Genesis 1-11. Nevertheless, such scholars stoutly insist that the biblical writer was wrong—that the events in Genesis 1-11 never happened, but the meaning they gave to "history" is so valuable we need to extract it and apply it to present life situations. Here one cannot but pose a question: If the meaning the biblical writer proposed for history led him to construct, intentionally or naively, a past that never happened, may not this same "meaning" lead later writers to abuse the past by talking about "events" that never happened? And if we adopt the meaning of history found in Genesis 1-11, or any other part of the Bible are we not likely to build a totally incorrect picture of events happening today?

As mentioned at the close of the previous section of this chapter, neither the Sumerians, the Babylonians, the Assyrians, nor the Egyptians really tried to tie their mythology with their annals, chronicles, or other reports of trade and war. Yet the mythological literature may be termed historic because it had great impact on government and common people. Dream interpretation and divination entered into the making of many a decision, and ritualistic magic was part of many a power play.

Genesis 1-11 may also be classified as historic because its content had impact on other Old Testament writers (check reference column in Bible), especially Job, Psalms, and Isaiah. The same cross reference check will reveal how deeply the New Testament writers were impressed by Genesis 1-11. The same is true of Jewish and Christian theology.

To hold that Genesis 1-11 is more than historic (as per the above paragraph), that it really contains accounts of events that really happened, traditional scholars have been faced with several problems. The first problem is that there were no human eye witnesses present to behold and record the creation events in Genesis 1 up to man's own creation by God, nor in Genesis 2 up to the moment God breathed into Adam's nostrils. Then there was the span of time between Adam's creation and the invention of writing, plus another span of time up to the actual writing down of the contents of Genesis 1-11.

Traditional scholars approach this problem on the basis of the validity of divine revelation. Admittedly, the Pentateuch does not have an explicit statement saying that God related to someone the content of Genesis 1:1-27 or Genesis 2:1-7. However, the text (Gen. 1:28-30; 2:16-17; 3:9-19) states that God spoke directly to the first man and woman in terms of command, instruction, interrogation, and judgment. Scholars not in the traditional stream flatly reject a concept of a speaking God who communicated directly with man; this attitude holds true of the entire Bible, not just Genesis 1-11. Traditional scholars firmly hold to the doctrine of a speaking God, thus, they affirm that God had revealed the creation account to someone. Presumably, Moses was that someone, but some earlier recipient of revelation is not ruled out.

The second problem that faces traditional scholars is the fact that Genesis 1-11 is not an encyclopedia of data about people, places, and chronology. And historians are hungry for this kind of information. Apart from the genealogies, only a few people are mentioned by name: Adam, Eve, Cain, Abel, Lamech, Adah, Zillah, Seth, Noah, Shem, Ham, Japheth, and Canaan. Only a few geographical places can be positively identified: the Tigris (Hiddekel) and Euphrates rivers, Assyria, mountains of Ararat many of the nations, coupled with geographical areas in chapter 10, Ur of Chaldees, land of Canaan, and Haran. Outside of Genesis 1, the only date formulae in Genesis 1-11 are in the genealogies of Genesis 5:1-32; 11:10-32 and in the flood story (Gen. 6:9–9:28). Archbishop Ussher notwithstanding, this is exceedingly meager data with which to construct a chronology prior to Abraham, and few are the traditional scholars who now attempt to do so.

Few modern written histories attempt to record *all* events that have occurred. Even histories that extend into multiple volumes try to do no more than to focus on those events that the historian considers to be significant. And there are few that do not endeavor to tie events together into some kind of narrative, or some type of movement toward a goal.

The material in Genesis 1-11 centers on what were regarded as significant events, which were put together in a fairly consistent movement from the creation to the time of Abraham. Even the genealogies were made to play their part; they either served to sidetrack those who rebelled against God (Cain, Japheth, Ham, Canaan) or to connect the believers in a straight line from Adam to Abraham. Quite the opposite of the pagans, who made no attempt to fit their mythology with their king lists and annals, the Hebrews skillfully blended that which they believed to be truly human events with their theology of a Creator God who is Lord of nature and history, and Judge and Redeemer of mankind. This procedure is true of their treatment of the past in Genesis 1-11; it is true of all the Scripture.

James Barr has noted that he has observed no real difference between the four "narratives: the creation, the flood, the Exodus and the destruction of Jerusalem by Nebuchadnezzer," at the level of presenting God as speaking and acting in the affairs of men. According to Barr, none of these stories are "history" (presumably secular) as we commonly use the term, but they do present their contents as events of which God was an integral part.[4]

To the biblical writer, an event was not simply factual data (he had no quarrel with facts of person, place, or time); he believed an event was a happening on earth, among men but involving God. This understanding is as true of Genesis 1-11 as it is of the rest of the Bible.[5] To the biblical writer, the events he recorded were unusual and unique, and they created precedents for later events; he did not see a process or a set of rigid natural laws. The biblical writer met a speaking and acting God on a person-to-person basis, and he believed this to be true from the first created couple onward. In the events he recorded, there was a God who decided to turn to the world by creating it, to turn to selected people to reveal His will concerning them and all mankind. In those events were people who obeyed or disobeyed Him, with good or bad consequences. These events were the initial patterns for all subsequent encounters of God with men. They were not simply events, but they were unique events.

Within this framework of biblical event, there is no reason why a student

---

4. James Barr, "Revelation Through History in the Old Testament and in Modern Theology," in *New Theology*, ed. M. E. Marty, no. 1 (New York: Macmillan Co., 1964).

5. A. J. Heschel, *The Prophets* (New York: Harper and Row, Publishers, 1962), pp. 426-446. What this author says about the prophets' understanding of event is true of Genesis 1-11 also.

cannot welcome and utilize all facts that research may bring forth about all aspects of nature, about all artifacts of man and his culture, or about details of ancient chronology.

Genesis 1-11 as a Religious Document

The biblical writer evidences no embarrassment as he blended together his belief that the events in Genesis 1-11 had actually happened with a clear-cut theological point of view. There need be no hesitancy in declaring that this part of the Old Testament is a religious document. Genesis 1-11 is the bearer of religious beliefs that extend forward into the rest of the Bible.

Whether Genesis 1-11 was incorporated into the liturgy of the worshiping Israelites is unknown; it is clear that parts of it influenced certain Psalms, which were a part of their worship (see Ps. 8, 19, 33, 74, 78, 104, 136). That Genesis 1-11 was part of the instructional material of Israel's teachers seems to be increasingly clear. Form criticism has been successful in pointing out didactic characteristics in the units that make up Genesis 1-11.

Since this body of material is religious, one must be careful not to be too literal in regard to each and every word in it. Undoubtedly, there are symbolisms, metaphors, and theological nuances in many passages. And it is not easy to detect the difference between literal statements and symbols, or metaphors, or idioms that may have a theological thrust. On this matter scholars will disagree, but this should challenge us to diligent research. It should not, however, paralyze us so that we miss the clear messages of Genesis 1-11.

The Patriarchs and Moses

The ancient mythological literature of the Mesopotamian, Egyptian, and Canaanite peoples do not bear directly upon the patriarchal narratives or the life and work of Moses. One could read Genesis 12 on through the Pentateuch and not be aware that ancient mythological literature existed.

The varied artifacts of ancient cultures and the nonmythological literature of the second millennium B.C. have thrown startling light on this section of the Pentateuch. Not that the Pentateuch explicitly says that these non-Hebrew sources existed. The "knowledge explosion" of the last century, and especially of the last several decades, has mostly been unexpected, though highly appreciated.

The aims of this section are (a) to bring together and summarize pertinent materials that parallel the content of Genesis 12 through the remainder of the Pentateuch; (b) to discuss briefly the basic features of the religious thought and practice of the Patriarchs in terms of the world in which they lived; (c) to carry this procedure on into the life, faith, and practice of Moses, together with the people whom he led from Egypt to the east bank of the Jordan River; and (d) to evaluate how much the Israelites culturally depended on their neighbors and how much they adapted some cultural features common to the ancient Near East to be vehicles of expression for their faith in God.

Scholars have long recognized that the Patriarchs lived during the first half of the second millennium B.C. Some exponents of the Wellhausen viewpoint had serious doubts whether the Patriarchs were real men, and a few, notably Cyrus Gordon, have suggested that they lived nearer the middle, perhaps even after the middle, of the millennium. He has also suggested that Abraham did not come from Ur of Chaldees in the southern part of the Mesopotamian valley, but, rather, from the highlands to the northeast of the Tigris River. There is large agreement that the Nuzi tablets from the Tigris valley and the Mari tablets from the Euphrates valley, plus clay tablets from Alalakh in northern Syria have illuminated remarkably the cultural environment of the Patriarchs.

Archaeologically, the time of the Patriarchs is designated as the Middle Bronze Age. The period, approximately the first half of the second millennium B.C., began with extensive movements of people. Some moved from the highlands to the north and east into the same valley, and some moved out of the valley into the Levant area. Some moved on into Egypt. Violence accompanied the migrations of these people and many old-city centers were left in utter ruins. After the migrations settled down, new fortified cities arose on the old ruins, and extensive trade, utilizing numerous donkey caravans, developed all across the ancient Near East. W. F. Albright has been the leading scholar in highlighting the value of relating archaeological findings from the Middle Bronze Age with the Patriarchs.

The economic, domestic, legal, and political literature of the Middle Bronze Age have been especially helpful in aiding us to understand the customs of the Patriarchs. These same tablets, however, have also helped us to better understand the religious thinking of the Patriarchs.

The clay tablets of the Middle Bronze Age reveal that the names of some of Abraham's close relatives became names of cities in the land between the Tigris and Euphrates rivers. Names, such as Serug, Terah, and Nahor, belonged to cities close to Haran.

Names very much like the biblical names Abraham and Jacob appear in the texts, as well as the name of a tribe called the Banu-Yamina. This name has much the same meaning as Benjamin, namely, "son/s of the right (south)."

Some of the Nuzi tablets reveal a practice not to sell land directly. Instead, a man, often a slave, was legally adopted so that a couple's inheritance could be transferred to him. In return, the adopted son would care for the couple's needs. But there was a restriction: if the couple should bear a son themselves, the adoption was no longer binding. Though the text does not explicitly state that Eliezer had been adopted by Abraham (Gen. 15:2 ff.) or that Jacob had been adopted by Laban (Gen. 29-31), many recent scholars believe this had been the case.

Some of the Nuzi marriage contracts provided that in the case the wife could not produce a child, she was obligated to provide the husband with a substitute wife whose offspring would become legal heirs. Again, there was a restriction. If the couple still bore children, he/they took precedence over the children of the substitute wife. The Bible is explicit that Hagar was given as a substitute wife (Gen. 16), and that the handmaids of Leah and Rachel were given as substitute wives solely for the purpose of obtaining children (Gen. 30).

Another aspect of the Mesopotamian law bears upon the expulsion of Hagar (Gen. 21). The Nuzi tablets state that a substitute wife cannot be expelled from the household after the first wife bears a child. This explains why Abraham hesitated to send Hagar away and did so only after God overruled the custom (Gen. 21). The Code of Lipit-Ishtar (see ANET, pp. 159-161) does say that freedom should be granted a substitute wife who was expelled, and this is what Hagar obtained.

The birthright incident between Jacob and Esau (Gen. 25:31 ff.) puzzled many Bible students until a Nuzi tablet was translated that relates the agreement of the man Tupkitilla who transferred his birthright to another man in exchange for three sheep. Other examples on Nuzi tablets have also appeared.

The Nuzi law recognized household gods as evidences of the inheritance of a family. Whoever possessed the gods had primary claim on that inheritance. The "teraphim" of Genesis 31:19 seemed to have had that kind of importance to Laban.

The blessing pronounced by the leader of a family or other social unit was of great significance to the people of Nuzi as well as to the Patriarchs. An oral blessing was as binding as one written. Court cases recorded on Nuzi tablets preserve decisions that upheld such oral blessings as the final will of the leader who had just died.

Some 450 texts found at Alalakh parallel the Mari and Nuzi tablets. They show that the first-born son had special rights over his brothers or half-brothers born of substitute wives. Still, they also demonstrate that the father could choose a son other than first-born for leadership if he so desired. The Patriarchs did this several times, usually under divine guidance (see especially Gen. 48).

Carvings and paintings in Egypt show Asiatic people coming to Egypt for various purposes. The most significant for illustrating the Patriarchal period come from the tombs at Beni-Hasan. The customs of Joseph's experiences in Egypt have been related often to the Hyksos control of Egypt. The chariot, the ring, and ways of treating the pharaoh are much like Hyksos customs. The embalming of Jacob's and Joseph's bodies were distinctly Egyptian customs. Other parallels can be gleaned from books listed in the bibliography below.

Covenant Forms

For centuries, traditional scholars have written volumes about the covenant as a biblical doctrine. Nonbiblical knowledge about covenants was limited and did not extend back before the first millennium B.C. It was popular to use modern Bedouin agreements as analogies, if nonbiblical illustrations were utilized at all. Wellhausen and his followers insisted that the biblical covenant was not known by Noah, or Abraham, or Joshua, or David, but was a very late kingdom, most likely exilic, invention. This view has been promoted even into the middle of this century.[6]

The "knowledge explosion" in the area of ancient Near Eastern literature has radically changed all that during the past two decades. Scholars saw on the old Sumerian "Vulture Stele" a treaty that stated what was to be done, plus an oath to seal the agreement. Several other treaties have the same format, all from the third millennium B.C. The Mari tablets do not have treaties as such; diplomatic texts employ covenant terms (ANET, p. 482). One tablet comes from Alalakh (northern Syria) with a treaty, or covenant, between a "great king" and his vassals in which he binds himself with an oath and kills a sheep to seal the oath. Most pertinent specimens of covenants come from the Hittite archives. These covenants are mostly between the "great king" and vassals and are quite detailed.

The format of the Hittite covenants have all or most of these components: (1) a preamble in which the initiator is identified; (2) a historical prologue; (3) stipulations; (4) the deposit of the text in a temple and provision for a yearly reading in public; (5) a list of divine witnesses, and in a few cases human witnesses, to the treaty; and (6) blessings and curses, with an emphasis on the curses.

---

6. Georg Fohrer, *History of Israelite Religion* (New York: Abingdon Press), pp. 80-81, 144, 186.

This format is true of the suzerainty treaties mentioned above, but is also true of parity treaties between equal partners. An example of a parity treaty is one made between Egypt and the Hittite king early in the thirteenth century B.C. (see ANET, pp. 199-206). A few covenant treaties come from the Assyrian royal archives of the ninth and eighth centuries B.C., but these are more of the suzerainty type.

The new knowledge about the covenants current in the ancient Near East during the patriarchal and Mosaic time span has aided our understanding of the Scriptures. Scholars of all theological persuasions have admitted their debt to this new information, for it is not too strong to say that the religious faith and life of the Old Testament men and women cannot be understood apart from a careful study of the covenant relationship in the Old Testament.

The first occurrence of the word *covenant* in Scripture is in Genesis 6:18-21 and again in 9:9-17. The covenant is prominent next in the patriarchal stories about Abraham (Gen. 12:1-3; 12:7; 13:14-17; 15 and 17), about Isaac (Gen. 26:24); and about Jacob (Gen. 28:13-15). The covenant was central at Sinai (Exod. 19-24) under the leadership of Moses, then at Shechem under Joshua (Josh. 8:30-35 and 24). David also entered into a covenant with God (II Sam. 7).

There are a few illustrations of parity covenants (not the texts of the agreement, but descriptions of covenant making) in Genesis 21:22-32, between Abraham and Abimelech; in Genesis 26:26-33, between Isaac and Abimelech; and in Genesis 31:44-54, between Jacob and Laban. Note also the covenant between Jonathan and David (I Sam. 18:3; 20:8-17; 23:18). The format of the parity treaty was very similar to the format of the suzerainty treaty.

The treaties, or covenants, between God and Noah, the Patriarchs, and Israel at Sinai are similar in that they were between God and man, with God taking the initiative, and are binding for all ages. In the covenants with Noah and the Patriarchs, God bound Himself with an oath, but there is no record of such an oath either in the Sinai account or in Joshua 24.

By taking the several components of the suzerainty treaties made by the Hittites (see above), several facets of how the covenant form was adapted to the God-man relationship in the Pentateuch can be seen. It is well to remember that we are dealing with descriptions of covenant-making events, not with the covenant texts themselves. Hence all the components do not show up in each instance.

Preamble. The Scripture simply identified the initiator of the covenant in briefest fashion:

156

"I am thy shield, and exceeding great reward" (Gen. 15:1).
"I am the Lord God of Abraham thy father, and God of Isaac" (Gen. 28:13).
"I am the God of Bethel" (Gen. 31:13).
"I am God Almighty" (Gen. 35:11).
"I am the God of thy father, the God of Abraham, the God of Isaac, and the God of Jacob" (Exod. 3:6; cf. 3:15, 16; 6:3, 8, 29; 34:6).
"I am the Lord thy God" (Exod. 20:2; cf. Deut. 5:6).
"Thus saith the Lord God of Israel" (Josh. 24:2).

These references stress the fact that the covenant-maker was God Himself, who is almighty, yet personally related to the person spoken to. He is not many gods, but the same God to all generations and to the group as well as the individual whom God selected as recipient of the covenant. God is fixed in His identity.

Historical Prologue. Apart from Joshua 24, the references to the past acts of God are brief. In Genesis 15:7 there is the simple declaration "I . . . brought thee out of Ur of the Chaldees, to give thee this land to inherit it." In Exodus 6:3-5 is a statement that God had made a covenant with the fathers and had heard the cries of His people, and in 19:4, the reference is to the escape from Egypt, as is 20:2 (cf. Deut. 5:6; 32:6-7).

The pagan rulers based their demand that their vassals obey them on past treaties and on an account of the relation between the covenant parties for several generations. It was important this account be essentially accurate. In the Pentateuch, man's relationship with God is not based on nature or natural law, but on an act of God in the historical, concrete relationships of man. God is not automatically bound to help man upon request. He alone makes the decision when to act, though He is concerned about man's predicament. God's call of Abraham from Mesopotamia and then the Exodus from Egypt were the major acts of God that overshadowed the narratives of God's relationship with the Patriarchs and with Israel.

Stipulations. Not many stipulations are found in Genesis. Mainly they are limited to the following references: "Walk before me and be thou perfect" (Gen. 17:1); "Every man child among you shall be circumcised" (Gen. 17:10); "Sojourn in this land" (Gen. 26:3); "Return to the land of thy fathers, and to thy kindred" (Gen. 31:3); and "Be fruitful and multiply" (Gen. 35:11). God gave a command to Moses (Exod. 3:16) and then the Ten Commandments plus the Book of the Covenant (Exod. 20:2–23:33) and worship regulations (Exod. 34:11-26). There are stipulations scattered through Numbers and almost throughout all of Leviticus and Deuteronomy.

Many of these stipulations are given in an imperative mood (sometimes Hebrew imperative and sometimes imperfect) and in the second person. This type of command is found in the Hittite political treaties, but not in the religious literature.

As far as the Pentateuch is concerned, God, as sovereign, has the right to lay down the rules and regulations of the relationship. Some of these stipulations were concerned with movements from one place to another, some with the quality of the personal relationship between God and man, some with ethical conduct, some with cultic ritual, and some with domestic, social, and economic situations. All were laid down by God Himself.

Deposited in Sanctuary and Read Publicly. Exodus 25:21 contains a strong implication that the stipulations were to be put in the ark of testimony, or covenant (cf. I Kings 8:9). Deuteronomy 6:7-9 has a command that parts of the covenant were to be placed on the hand and on the forehead, as well as on the doorposts of the house, and 27:8 speaks of writing it on stone (cf. Josh. 24:26). Hearing the law is mentioned in Deuteronomy 31:9-13 (cf. II Kings 23:1-2 and Neh. 8:1-8).

By placing the stipulations of the covenant, especially the Ten Commandments, in the sanctuary, the leaders emphasized the holiness and authority that God had given to the law. When the people heard them read, every individual and each generation were made aware of covenant requirements. This was not always strictly carried out, and the people were often unaware of the foundations of their religious heritage.

Witness and Tokens. The gods of the pagans were excluded. In the case of Noah, the token was the rainbow, but circumcision was the token given to Abraham and his descendents. At Sinai, the people witnessed by committing themselves to obedience: "All that the Lord hath spoken we will do" (Exod. 19:8; 24:3, 7; cf. Deut. 5:27 and Josh. 24:22). The clearest statement of relationship of token, decision, and witness is found in Joshua 24:22-27 (cf. Hos. 2:21-22; Isa. 1:2).

Blessings and Curses. God set alternatives before individuals and Israel as a nation. In some cases the curses and blessings are implicit rather than listed. Genesis 17:12-14 states that the circumcised will be in the covenant and the uncircumcised will not, and 18:19 suggests that the fulfillment of God's promises was related to man's performance of justice. Alternatives stated in Exodus 19:5-6, and 19:12-24 warn of the dangers of trifling with God. Exodus 20:5-6 has both a warning of danger and a promise of mercy, and 20:20 has a warning. Exodus 23:20-31 has both warning and promise. An explicit list of curses and blessings occurs in Deuteronomy 27 and 28 (cf. Josh. 24:17-20).

Covenant-making Rites. Four rites are mentioned as parts of the covenant-making event. They are the setting of a stone or a group of stones, the taking of an oath, the sacrifice of animals, and/or a communal meal.

A number of standing stones are mentioned in ancient literature, and many have been found by archaeologists all over the ancient Near East, including Palestine. In the Pentateuch, some narratives mention stones in relation to covenants. A heap of stones and a single stone are mentioned in the covenant between Jacob and Laban (Gen. 31:46-49). Moses set twelve pillars by an altar as part of a covenant-making ceremony (Exod. 24:4). Moses also is said to have commanded that plastered large stones with inscriptions be set up after crossing the Jordan River (Deut. 27:1-8).

The taking of an oath is mentioned in Isaac's covenant with Abimelech (Gen. 26:26-31) and in Jacob's covenant with Laban. A meal is mentioned in connection with both of these covenants and also in Moses' covenant with Israel (Exod. 24:11), except in the latter instance the chief men represented the community (cf. Deut. 27:7).

The sacrifice of animals is mentioned in Genesis 15:9-11, in Genesis 31:54, and in Exodus 24:5-8 where the sprinkling of the blood of the covenant is a key part of the ceremony.

Salt is mentioned in connection with covenant making in at least one passage (Num. 18:19; cf. II Chron. 13:5).

The covenant relationship between God and the Patriarchs and later between God and Israel bore significant implications for the religious life and practice of the Israelites. These implications were not limited to the Pentateuch, but extended throughout the Old Testament and formed the foundation for the New Testament. A few of these implications are discussed below.

The original decision was God's; therefore, whomever He chose or whatever He promised originated within Himself. Thus whatever revelations He made of Himself to man through word or event were His own revelations. The covenant relationship itself was "established," "made," or "remembered" by Him. This fact was a constant external point of reference; God was the Judge of the people's desires.

The actualization of election was in the act of calling an individual for a task or in the deliverance of the people from slavery to become a nation. God was not under compulsion to choose this one or that one. Each act of choosing was an act of mercy. Noah "found grace in the eyes of the Lord" (Gen. 6:8). Lot escaped Sodom due to God's mercy (19:19). God's gifts to Jacob were not based upon the patriarch's worthiness, but on God's mercy (33:10). God delivered Israel from Egypt because of their needy situation and their cries of supplication (Exod. 3:7, 9; 6:5), and His response was one of mercy (15:13). The best statement of this truth is in Deuteronomy 4:32-40 and in 7:6-8. The tie between the love of God and the acts of deliverance served as the key to the meaning of the election of Israel. What they were and would become was wholly due to God's purposes (see also Ps. 103:8-13; 106:45).

The counterpart of mercy in the covenant was God's jealousy, which is clearly stated in such passages as Exodus 20:5; 34:14; Deuteronomy 4:24; 5:9; 6:15; Joshua 24:19, and in many other instances. The covenant insists that the emotional involvement of the worshiper be centered in the God of Israel alone. This is the stress of the first of the Ten Commandments and of Deuteronomy 6:5. Idolatry was the threat to this exclusive devotion and the most dangerous enemy of the covenant relationship. When applied to God, the concept of jealousy does not carry the connotation of a warped emotion, but, rather, of an insistence on the singleness of worship of Jehovah.

The Ten Commandments were unique in Old Testament times because they posssesed prohibitions in the second person singular and because they stressed both man's exclusive worship of one God and man's honoring the other person's body, rights, and possessions. Breaking these commandments would result in spiritual confusion and in human exploitation.

The father-son relationship was one of the early metaphors taken from personal and social life to describe the covenant between God and Israel or individuals. Authority was centered in the father, whereas the son was dependent upon the father for all that he possessed or whatever he would receive as a religious heritage. A few references to this in the Old Testament are Exodus 4:22; Deuteronomy 1:31; 8:5; 14:1; Hosea 11:2; Jeremiah 31:20 and 3:19-20. There are many more in the New Testament; and the most telling application is the story of the prodigal son (Luke 15:11-32).

Although it was more formal and awesome, the king-subject relationship was also popular from the days of Sinai. In this relationship, the authority of the superior party and the dependence of the subject was even more clearly apparent. Such passages as Numbers 23:21 and Deuteronomy 33:5 emphasize the power of the king. But there is a personal touch in many of the references to God as King (see Ps. 5:2; 74:12; 84:3; 149:2; Isa. 6:5; 33:22; Jer. 10:10; 23:5).

A man-creature relationship was pressed into service as a powerful and moving example of the covenant tie between God and man. This is the shepherd-sheep metaphor. A remarkable amount of personal content is poured into this form of expression. The compassion of the greater party and the dependence of the lesser is dynamically portrayed. The term appears mostly in the Prophets, the Psalms, and the New Testament (see Isa. 40:11; 49:9-10; Jer. 23:3; 31:10; Ezek. 34:7-24; 37:24; Mic. 2:12; 4:6-7; Zech. 11:7-9). The gem of all is Psalm 23, but other passages are 95:7 and 100:3.

The most effective of the metaphors was the husband-wife relationship. The husband represented the superior partner and the wife, the dependent partner; but more dominant was the depth of intimate concern and compassion that could enrich this relationship. The breach of this relationship was more tragic in its consequences and the cost of restoration was more heartrending. Hosea's domestic tragedy gave to the metaphor peculiar force (Hos. 1-3) and the metaphor became popular with other prophets (Isa. 50:1; 54:6-7; Jer. 2:2; 3:1, 12; Ezek. 16:8-22). The metaphor retained its popularity within the Christian community.

These metaphors were forceful because they were, on the whole, taken from the realm of personal relationships (the shepherd-sheep metaphor was lifted to a personal level). Their structure in biblical times was such that the partners in the relationship were not truly equal. The father, king, shepherd, and husband had a higher status of authority, whereas their opposite numbers were dependents. In each case the parties who possessed authority initiated the relationship and controlled it. Though on the human level these parties could be unfaithful, God was never unfaithful. Hence the fact, as well as the possibility, of unfaithfulness in the dependents is stressed in the application of these metaphors to Israel, and later to the church. The relationship could only be restored by an act of mercy by the superior party. These metaphors were also capable of conveying the deep emotional overtones of the covenant relationship, summarized as "your God—my people."

On man's part, the response was to be one of gratitude coupled with a sense of obligation. An abundance of blessings was available to the obedient: land, its fruits, posterity, security from enemies, the presence of the Lord, and a great future. When Israel sincerely accepted the Lordship of her God and committed herself to His ways, she experienced these blessings in a very real way. At the same time, however, she placed herself under a heavy claim.

Embedded in the privilege of freely choosing Jehovah as a personal God, was the prodding of a sharp set of alternatives. The promises of the Lord could not be treated lightly, nor could they be regarded as guaranteed apart from Israel's attitude toward God. The demand for an exclusive devotion to God set Israel apart from other nations. The standard of morality enjoined, though in many respects below New Testament standards, was so markedly different from that of paganism that social relations were well-nigh impossible without compromise. The dark side of the covenant relationship was the danger of divine displeasure expressed by a removal of God's presence, a lifting of God's protection from enemies, famine, pestilence, and an ejection from the land.

The promises of God were grounded in His redemptive purposes but were not fixed upon any particular person or generation. A concept of being a "chosen people" based upon egotism could boast that, since the Lord had chosen them, all others ought to grovel at Israel's feet. But the declaration of Amos is more truly based on the covenant sense of obligation: "You only have I known of all the families of the earth: therefore I will punish you for all your iniquities" (Amos 3:2). Hence the true adherent to the covenant knew that Israel was not only overshadowed by the special love of God, but that she also was overshadowed by the knowledge that sin would not be tolerated.

The story of Israel contains not only the establishment of a covenant that set Israel apart in the world, but also contains narratives of repeated breaches of the covenant, of punishment, and of restoration to the covenant relationship (see Jer. 3:1, 12; Ezek. 16:8-22; Mal. 1:2-3; concerning God's freedom to reject Israel, see Exod. 32:10, 26-29; Num. 14:12; 17:6 ff; 25:1 f; in the New Testament see Matt. 21:33). When the covenant finds its response, election has completed its function.

The responses of God within the covenant relationship are related to the responses of man to His claims upon him. Undergirding the covenant is the deep love of God, but there is also God's great abhorrence of sin. The people—the object of His love—had sinned, but to destroy them completely would blot out the ones He loved and shut off the channel of revelation to the world. Consequently, throughout the prophets, there is the concept of the remnant, the called-out ones, who respond to Him and become the nucleus of a new covenant community.

Society was altered by the application of the covenant demands. The fact that a poor, enslaved people in Egypt was the object of God's concern and was delivered by Him to become a nation, also had significance for the poor and the defenseless ones within the Israelite community. Actually the first expression of this interest is found in the institution of the rite of circumcision (Gen. 17:12), for those "bought with money of any stranger" were to enjoy the privilege of the covenant on the same basis as the freeborn. In the Book of the Covenant (Exod. 21:1-11, 20, 26-27), the Hebrew slaves had definite rights, and the widow and orphan were protected (Exod. 22:22-23; see also Lev. 25:39-55; Deut. 10:17-19; 15:7-

15). The prophets stressed the same point; Isaiah 1:17; Jeremiah 34:14; Ezekiel 22:7 are but a few examples.

The government of the nation was affected by the claims of the covenant relation. Moses, Joshua, and the judges were God-called and God-endowed men. God was the leader of the people, and the story of the period between the Conquest and the Kings was an alternation of breaking the covenant by forgetting God and the restoration of the relation through repentance, deliverance, and restoration of the covenant.

The establishment of the kingship in Israel was affected by the covenant restrictions, bringing about a radical departure from the despotism of the contemporary monarchies. Samuel laid down a definite limitation upon the power of the king by laying on him the obligation of facing alternatives before God (I Sam. 12:12-15). David made a covenant with the elders of Israel before the Lord that definitely limited his powers (II Sam. 5:1-3). The kings who followed him were evaluated on the basis of their adherence or departure from the norm of David's religious life and administration of kingly power (cf. I Kings 15:3-5).

The emphasis upon loyalty, goodness, righteousness, and kindness led to an intensification of these aspects of the covenant relationship, causing a shift from the outward rites of worship to a deepening of an inner fellowship and communion with God. Out of this came the Psalms and the new covenant of Jeremiah 31:31-34; 32:37-40 and of Ezekiel 16:60-63. These express a depth of fellowship that was above the purely legalistic and liturgical and that exposed the core of the covenant doctrine of election.

The redemptive purpose of God's love for man has been clarified by the coming of Christ, His life of service, His death on Calvary, His resurrection, His ascension, and His high-priestly function of intercession. The entire Book of Hebrews is devoted to bringing out this truth of the gospel.

The Christian concern for the distressed peoples of society is an extension of the covenant concern from the Jewish people to the entire world, as well as the acknowledgement of Christ's admonition that the Christian's function in the world is that of a servant and not of a master (John 13:1-20). The tie between fellowship with God and love for man is so close that James could declare, "Pure religion and undefiled before God and the Father is this, To visit the fatherless and widows in their affliction, and to keep himself unspotted from the world" (James 1:27). Thus every Christian effort to cure the ills and needs of humanity has its roots in the consciousness that their calling and election are to be channels of divine blessings in the world.

Many features of the covenant relationship carry over into the inclusion of Gentiles within the redemptive program. The parallels are quite clear in Romans 9-11. The priority of divine sovereignty, and God's right to choose whom and how He will, is strongly stressed in Romans 9. The fact that the choosing is an act of God's grace is also brought out in that same chapter. The response of man as one of faith and obedience through hearing the claims and provisions of the gospel is expounded in chapter 10, and the fact that a chosen people may be set aside and another brought into His purpose of world redemption is elaborated upon in chapter 11. The alternatives of the covenant are sharply defined here, along with an emphasis on the remnant.

Monotheism

When reading the Pentateuch in any of the manuscripts, including the earliest of the Dead Sea Scrolls, it is difficult to see where any doctrine other than monotheism is present in the text. This did not, however, deter the followers of Wellhausen from insisting that monotheism was a theological product of the Exile and was never known prior to that time. Their conclusion drawn from this belief was that the pervading presence of monotheism in the Pentateuch had been written into the traditions by the priests living during the Exile.

W. F. Albright led a revolt against this tenet of the Wellhausen position,[7] and his argument has gained growing support among scholars in the "History of Salvation" point of view. Albright has contended that Moses' theology contained an implicit monotheism that was the base for a later explicit monotheism. Y. Kaufmann has reinforced this position. He has claimed that Moses arrived at a monotheistic doctrine through intuition. The Scripture presents a "One God" doctrine from its very beginning and makes no essential difference between the God who spoke to Abraham or any other man in the Pentateuch. The doctrine is expanded and enriched, but not essentially changed.[8]

Though there is a variety in the names associated with God, the text is careful to show that the God of the covenant was always the same God. Neither the Patriarchs nor Moses confused their God with the pagan gods and goddesses, after God had initially revealed Himself to them. They found it a bit more difficult to comprehend that some practices and customs in their pagan environment were not compatible with a doctrine of one God. It took a series of encounters with God to clear up some of these points of contrast.

---

7. W. F. Albright, *From the Stone Age to Christianity* (Garden City, New York: Doubleday, 1957).
8. Y. Kaufmann, *The Religion of Israel* (Chicago: University of Chicago Press, 1960).

Essentially, the men in the Pentateuch understood deity to be the source of being, the Creator, and one distinct from nature. There is no hint that they believed that God emerged from some preexistent nature-stuff; none of the narratives contain references to a mythologically oriented fight between God and other deities. There are no dramas of God's inner life, beyond expressions of God's deep concern for people, their sins and corruptions. In a restrained manner, God's reactions to man's condition, and His decision to do something about it are depicted deftly with a remarkable economy of words.

The God of the Patriarchs and Moses was self-sufficient; He did not beg for food and drink, or for personal attention for selfish reasons. God is everywhere presented as majestic and holy, moved by anger against sin, but more deeply moved by merciful love. God is portrayed as present anywhere any man may be located. There is no clear indication that He must be worshiped at one fixed geographical spot, and none other. Universal knowledge of God was regarded as possible, although, at a given time, only a few might believe in Him. He revealed Himself in majestic power to any and all through nature, but He never hesitated to select an individual or a group as witnesses to His reality in a pagan world.

The Patriarchs themselves worshiped God in a simple fashion; they seemed to have little of the complicated cultic procedures of the Mosaic and later periods. The covenant, dealt with above, provided a framework of interpersonal relations between them and their God. Prayer seems to have been spontaneous and filled with dialogue; many are intercessions, and a sense of dependence is prominent.

What the Patriarchs and Moses experienced as the revelation and leadership of God was grounded in the rugged situations of life. God's initial contact with each one produced awe and a measure of fear, and called each one to a decision that radically changed the course of his life. The crucial moments of faith in Abraham's life centered in the delayed promise of a son, and then the command to give up that son. The religious experience of Jacob occurred in a down-to-earth context of parental strife, trickery, malice, and fear between brothers, wives, father-in-law and son-in-law, between sons, and between the family and its neighbors. The experiences of Joseph took place in a context of jealousy, slavery, lust, false accusations, imprisonment, and high levels of government power. Through every misfortune, Joseph kept his faith in God's providence and concern steadfast and unsullied. The experiences of Moses centered about a passion that led to murder, exile, confrontation with the god-king of Egypt, a narrow escape, and a long series of trials and hardships in the desert with a people difficult to lead.

Mosaic Prophecy and Pagan Divination

There has been considerable discussion about the phenomena of prophecy in the ancient Near East and in the Old Testament, with varying views prevalent among scholars. Most of this discussion has centered in the Books of I and II Samuel, I and II Kings, and the so-called Major and Minor Prophets, since most of the biblical literature concerning prophets is in these books. Only limited material is found in the Pentateuch concerning prophets, but there is enough to warrant an evaluation of what the biblical writers thought prophecy to be like. As noted in a previous section of this chapter, literature among the pagans concerning their prophets is also limited, prior to 1200 B.C.

Earnest efforts have been made to determine from the Hebrew and other Semitic languages what the word *prophet* meant to them. The Hebrew word *nabi',* according to Gesenius' Lexicon, probably meant "to bubble up, to pour forth"; but there are others who declare that a better meaning is "to speak for another" and cite Exodus 4:14-16, which reports the arrangement God made so that Aaron would be a spokesman (Exod. 7:1-2 uses the word "prophet") for Moses. This meaning would be in line with an Arabic word *naba'a,* said to mean "to proclaim or announce." But Albright insists that an Akkadian word, *nabu,* meaning "call" in the sense of being given a task, was the proper parent. Others say the same word means "to call or speak," hence the noun "speaker or spokesman."[9] Interestingly, the word *prophet* is first applied to Abraham (Gen. 20:7), who was to be an intercessor, a spokesman, before God in Abimelech's behalf.

Moses is designated a prophet (Deut. 34:10), and many times in Exodus, Leviticus, and Numbers God is depicted as speaking to Moses and then commanding him to take the message to an individual such as Pharaoh or to the people as a group. This happens about forty-seven times in Exodus, twenty-four times in Leviticus, and thirty-five times in Numbers.

In Deuteronomy 34:10, the word *prophet* is closely related to the phrase "Whom the Lord knew face to face," and to this statement may be brought such passages as Exodus 25:22; 33:9 and Numbers 7:89; 12:6-8. Examples of this "face-to-face" relationship can be seen in Exodus 3:1–4:17; 15:22-27; 16:1-36; 17:1-7; and Numbers 11; 21:1-3, 4-9, 21-35. These stories have a tone of tense emotion, but no hint of the kind of phenomena alluded to in Numbers 11:24-29. On a special occasion at the tabernacle, the Spirit of the Lord prompted the seventy elders to proph-

---

9. Theophile J. Meek, *Hebrew Origins* (Gloucester, Mass.: Peter Smith, 1960), p. 150.

esy; and then two others, Eldad and Medad, prophesied in the camp. In reaction to this unusual behavior, a young man and Joshua asked Moses to forbid the activity. Moses replied, "Would God that all the Lord's people were prophets, and the Lord would put his Spirit upon them." Many scholars have assumed that more than messages were spoken; to them it would seem evident that uncontrolled physical activity was involved. This kind of activity is often termed "ecstasy." Some scholars have suggested that Moses' condition when he came down from the mount after receiving the Ten Commandments the second time was, in fact, a state of ecstasy. No description is given, however, except that Moses' skin shone and the people were afraid of him (Exod. 34:27-35).

What is ecstasy? One cannot discuss the matter without noting the wide range of meaning of the term in the English language or without including the many other prophets mentioned in the Old Testament. Nothing more will be attempted here than to summarize definitions of ecstasy and to compare one kind of ecstasy with what the Old Testament provides us concerning the prophetic experience before God.

Broadly, ecstasy can be any intense emotional experience, which may range from constant emotional change to a sense of rapture—to violent, uncontrolled agitations of the body. Among Old Testament scholars, H. W. Robinson has led the way to a limitation of meaning to the Greek word *ekstasis,* which denotes a removal or displacement of the soul from the body, somewhat similar to the English phrase "out of his senses."[10] This suggestion is akin to A. J. Heschel's distinctions between pagan prophecy and Hebrew prophecy, which was really prompted by God.[11]

An example of uncontrolled behavior may be seen in Saul (I Sam. 19:24); another example is the activity of the prophets of Baal on Mount Carmel (I Kings 18:20-29). No true Hebrew prophet acted like that as far as biblical evidence goes.

In a broad way, the uncontrollable kind of ecstasy can be compared with the Hebrew prophetic experience. The ecstatic prophet sought suspension of his normal consciousness and a release of his soul from the limitations of the body, by means of learned techniques. The resultant experience was an end in itself, remote from the concrete life of this world. Its content was essentially secret and noncommunicable. In contrast, the true Hebrew prophet did not seek to disengage his inner being from his body; there is no clear evidence that techniques were important or ever used. He was aware of a command to declare an important message to other people. Always he remained historically and concretely oriented.

---

10. H. W. Robinson, *Inspiration and Revelation in the Old Testament* (Oxford: The Clarendon Press, 1946), pp. 134-135.
11. Heschel, *The Prophets,* vol. 2, pp. 104–14.

To the ecstatic prophet, the divine realm was a fluid, suprapersonal, and all-pervasive force that either invaded him overwhelmingly or quietly absorbed him into its essence. In this kind of experience the dividing line between the divine and human would be obliterated. But the true Hebrew prophet sensed a profound moral separation from God; he was repelled by, and often deeply feared the Almighty. Yet he viewed his relationship with God in personal terms and spoke of Him anthropomorphically. To Him God is one who acts on His own, and since God is spirit and man is flesh, with a soul integral to his body, there can only be interaction between God and man, never absorption or a violent takeover. In summary, the ecstatic understood the divine as active subject and man as passive object, but the true Hebrew prophet believed that both God and himself were distinct, active subjects.

Prediction of the future has been an activity that has long been associated with prophecy. As indicated in an earlier section of this chapter, the neighbors of the Hebrew people had devised ways of divining the future by watching the stars, plants, animals, and many other aspects of nature. The ecstatic experience was associated by some people with prediction.

Prediction of the future occurs often in the Old Testament and to some extent in the Pentateuch. Many of the encounters of God with men, from Adam and Eve to Moses, are recorded as containing statements about the future. Promises and predictions of the future are integral to the covenants with Noah, Abraham, Isaac, Jacob, and with Israel at Sinai. Joseph is famous as one who could interpret dreams, though he stoutly insisted that all interpretation was from God and not from himself (Gen. 41:8, 16). The predictive element is prominent in Jacob's blessing on his sons (Gen. 49).

Since divination and magic are related, i.e., divination ascertains the future and magic seeks to control it, a comparison of divination with the kind of prediction found in the Pentateuch is important to make.

Mosaic Miracles and Pagan Magic

There has been a tendency among Old Testament scholars to assume that all events that have a supernatural element are tied up with magical activity, even though the one true God is involved. Not that these scholars believe in magic; rather, they hold that the pagans believed in and practiced magic, and so did the Hebrews who naively ascribed unusual happenings to divine interventions.

The literature of the ancient Near East makes it clear that all pagan priests were in some way tied up with magic, and that cultic ritual was basically magical in purpose. Besides the many incantations inscribed on stone or clay, magic is prominent in several of the mythological stories. Specimens are "The Epic of Creation," "Inanna's Descent to the Nether World," "The Baal Epic," and "The Repulsing of the Dragon and the Creation."

These pagan stories tell of deities who appealed to some kind of fate or power that was beyond themselves, sometimes to seek nullification of decrees, sometimes for their own protection. The god who possessed the most knowledge about magical practice was Enki (Ea), and his priests were reputed to be skilled in the magical arts also. But other gods and goddesses could perform magic; for example, Tiamat and Marduk. Pagan incantations usually had three components: a brief account of the past, a statement of desire, and a command. Ritual was capable of bringing to pass the content of the incantation, or, on the positive side, to reactivate the nature cycle of fertility. Note Kaufman's point that magic is a realm apart from deity over which deity has no control.

In Genesis 30:37-43 is an incident that has struck some as having over-tones of sympathetic magic. Jacob cut strips of bark from rods taken from the poplar, hazel, and chestnut trees and laid them in front of the sheep and goats during the mating seasons. The purpose was to obtain lambs and kids of unusual color patterns, for he had agreed with Laban that he would take as his wages this kind of offspring. But Jacob also told his wives that God had revealed to him how to obtain the off-colored sheep and goats (Gen. 31:4-13). The emphasis was on the off-colored traits of the rams, an indication that selective breeding was being practiced.

No doubt Jacob was influenced in his actions (making striped rods) by current thought, but came to understand that the result of obtaining the off-colored lambs and goats was through an act of God rather than by a magical phenomenon.

The confrontation of Moses and Pharaoh during the ten plagues has more of the characteristics of a miracle, i.e., the direct action of God in each event. According to Exodus 4, the changing of the rod into a snake and back into a rod was an act of God, which would be a sign that the God of Abraham, Isaac, and Jacob had appeared to Moses. It was not a tech-nique that Moses had learned from another, or had discovered. In each instance of its occurrence, the sign would be an act of God and no other.

In the account of the ten plagues, the rod figured prominently in five of the ten plagues (Exod. 7:14–12:32). The Egyptian wise men, sorcerers, and magicians challenged Moses during the first three plagues and were successful in duplicating the first two plagues. They failed to produce lice and admitted defeat by saying, "This is the finger of God" (Exod. 8:19).

Pharaoh continued to resist the power of God up to the death of his first-born in the tenth plague, then he let Israel depart from Egypt.

The ten plagues were essentially a contest of power between the living God and the greatly feared and powerful magicians of Egypt, and finally between the pharaoh and God. The biblical text makes no mention of the fact that magic was the special province of Thoth the moon-god and his devotees, who were mostly scribes and priests. Nor does the text hint that Egyptian theology held that the pharaoh was the physical expression of the sun-god, that the first-born was the god Horus in youthful flesh. But the text does make it clear that the bearer of power was not the rod itself, or Moses, or Aaron, but the one true God and Him only.

The rod is important in the stories about crossing the Red Sea (Exod. 14); changing bitter water to sweet water (15:22-25), in this case with a tree; bringing water from the rock at Rephidim (17:1-7); defeating the

Bronze statuette of King Ur-Nammu, depicting the king as a humble basket carrier during the building of a temple. The figure dates from around 2100 B.C.

Amalekites (17:8-13); bringing water from the rock, this time at the desert of Zin (Num. 20:1-13). In each instance, the act was the result of divine command or divine approval. During the second miracle of bringing water from the rock, however, Moses emphasized himself rather than God; for this act, very similar to the self-seeking of magicians, Moses was punished. He could not enter the land of Canaan.

There were other miracles during Moses' lifetime with which the rod was not associated. The burning bush (Exod. 3:2), Moses' leprosy (4:5, 6), the pillar of cloud and fire (13:21, 22; 14:19, 20), the giving of manna (16:4-31) and of quails (Num. 11:31-32), and many others, are all ascribed to the power of God who acts on His own and is not manipulated by man. Even the use of Urim and Thummin was regarded as God's acting through them and not as techniques of divinations.

It was mentioned above that in many respects diviners shared similar views, hence they will be grouped together in the following comparisons with the miracles associated with Moses and with many of the latter prophets.

The diviner-magician and the Hebrew prophet shared some similar beliefs. Both used acts of drama in which they sought to mimic or symbolically represent what they felt would be the course of the future. The magician believed he could control the future, whereas the prophet of Israel believed the future was in God's hands. Both closely paired word and deed, almost as a unit. Among Semitic peoples there was no sharp distinction between the thing said and the thing accomplished. In Hebrew, the term *dabar* not only represented speech, it stood for "affair" or "happening," too. But the pagan believed that the word and deed had power in themselves, whereas the Hebrew prophet held that power was within God who fulfilled His word.

Both the diviner-magician and the Hebrew prophet identified word and deed with ultimate reality; they believed that what man thought, said, and did had some relationship to universal powers, or power, which had something to do with his destiny. The magician believed that his magical acts brought about a change of status or quality, concentrated a curse or blessing on a person or a group, or reconstituted the reproductive cycles of nature. The diviner believed that his divinatory techniques caused the cosmic powers to reveal events yet to come. The true Hebrew prophet believed that the one true God revealed Himself to whomever He would choose. To that person, God gave an understanding, sometimes only a partial understanding, of His purposes and of His estimate of the situation at hand. This revelation of God's will often dealt with the meaning of the past and of the future as well as the present event. The prophet must then give this message to the people.

In further contrast, the diviner-magician exercised techniques and skills that were not necessarily tied to any religious experience; they could be quite indifferent to the will of the divine realm, if they wished. The Hebrew prophet, or the texts that relate his experiences, stressed the commands of God and His power to do whatever He wished. The acted sign was a pledge of the prophet's loving self-identification with his God.

The magicians' mimetic acts were private or institutional manipulations of reality to gain selfish ends. The diviner had the same selfish goal as he plied his trade. Hebrew prophecy sprang from a response to a divine initiative that was greater than he. Material things had divine meanings, but only as these meanings were pointed out by God.

In ancient pagan literature there is mention of a demonic companion, or a patron deity, who spoke through dreams or through omens. To the Hebrew prophet, God's voice was personal and demanded obedience. He was a prophet, not because he had learned a technique from a master, but because God had called him to serve as a messenger.

Basically, the work of the diviner was sustained by a combination of hope and fear about the future, both in himself and in his clients. Both the diviner and the magician lacked an adequate remedy for the dread that his words and acts produced. For a fee, blessings might be pronounced or amulets provided, but the diviner and magician knew how to utilize fear as a coercive power to keep his victims under his control. The Hebrew prophet's life, word, and work was rooted in trust in the goodness of God. He did not hesitate to point out the awesomeness of the Almighty, nor the fearsomeness of sin and its consequences; yet, he personally experienced the remedy for fear and proclaimed that remedy to his people. They were to put away idolatry and submit themselves completely to the mercies of God.

The work of both the diviner and the magician could not but produce maladjustment with this life and with reality, as they capitalized on their clients' fear of fate, of the mysterious, of aloneness, and of death. The lamentations preserved in pagan literature illustrate this point abundantly. The Hebrew prophets, however, sought to lead their people into a positive adjustment with reality, which included the down-to-earthness of this life as well as God. The prophets did not accomplish this goal without heartache and often experienced outright failure. Moses was able to lead his people into high moments of experiencing the miraculous salvation of God, but he also was bitterly vexed by their rebellions and unbelief. Many perished along the way; others responded and served God faithfully.

The clients of the diviners and magicians lost something of personal dignity and responsibility through association with them. They were robbed of the power of decision; they were helpless in the hands of the diviners and the magicians. But the work of the prophets, and here our interest is mainly centered in Moses, enhanced personal dignity and responsibility. Repeatedly the people were called upon to make their own decisions. It was up to them whether they believed Moses, such as whether they observed the Passover and prepared to march out of Egypt, whether they would commit themselves to the covenant at Sinai, or whether they would look at the brazen serpent and live. They had to bear the consequences for wrong decisions, but the act of deciding was theirs and not someone else's act. When they decided in favor of God, they found that He would graciously work miracles in their behalf.

Mosaic Leadership and Pagan Kingship

According to the covenant statements made by God to Abraham and to Jacob, at some indefinite time in the future kings would be among their descendents (Gen. 17:6, 16; 35:11). In Balaam's prophecy about Israel (Num. 24:7), Israel would have a superior type of king. Deuteronomy 17:14-20 has a set of instructions and limitations in regard to a king and his kingdom in Israel.

There is no reference to Moses as a king; he was a leader and a prophet but not royalty. In contrast to the practice in Egypt where the king was regarded as deity, and to the tendency in the upper Levant and in Mesopotamia where some of the kings were deified, Israelites refused to regard their leaders as more than human beings. No attempt was made to deify the Patriarchs, Moses, or any of their other judges or kings. A leader was appointed by God; Moses was called to his task, and Joshua was designated as Moses' successor (Num. 27:18-23). One wonders if the studious avoidance of mention of Moses' son is not the result of Moses' denial of the right of hereditary rule.

Neither was Moses a priest; that office was given to his brother Aaron. Thus, in Israel, the common unification of kingship, prophet, and priest in the person of pagan rulers was broken up and never brought together in one person until the Maccabean Commonwealth during the second and first centuries B.C.

Mosaic Law and Pagan Law

Before the middle of the nineteenth century, biblical scholars could only evaluate Mosaic law on the basis of modern law, which went back through the Middle Ages to Roman Law. With the "cracking" of the cuneiform and hieroglyphic scripts in the first half of the nineteenth century, vast

Shamshi-Adad V stands under the symbols of his gods. This relief was discovered at Nimrod.

literatures were made available to biblical scholars. Very little legal material has come from Egypt, but thousands of clay tablets have come from Mesopotamia, some from the territory now known as Turkey, and a few from the Levant, mostly from Ugarit.

The reason the Egyptians have left us little legal literature before the Persian period can be traced to their understanding of who the pharaoh was (see pages 121-123 on kingship in Egypt). The customary law was the word of the pharaoh at any particular time. Since the pharaoh was the human form of the sun-god, Ra, legal decisions of the past had little meaning (at least officially), hence written legal documents were of little value. The result was an authoritarian government with no check on the pharaoh's declarations, for he was not accountable to any higher power, not even to the gods.

The situation was vastly different in Mesopotamia and in the nations that were associated with that area. Though there was some tendency to deify the king (see pages 113-114 on kingship in Mesopotamia), fundamentally he was subject to the decrees of the gods and goddesses and must have the approval of the council of elders in the city or state before he could make major decisions. Religiously,, the king was under the sanctions of omens and divine curses; on the civil side he was obligated to pay heed to the tradition of legal decisions made by courts in cities and regions for centuries past. Early in the third millennium B.C., written documents became commonplace in trade, politics, domestic life, and court verdicts. Literally thousands of clay tablets illustrate legal practice in Sumeria, Babylon, and Assyria, and among the Hurrians, Amorites, and Hittites.

A Frenchman, J. Oppert, began to study the ancient legal tablets toward the end of the nineteenth century, but general interest was not really quickened until the discovery of the so-called Code of Hammurabi in A.D. 1901. Since then, three older "codes" or compilations of laws have been found, plus the many tablets of legal content. Other codes and legal tablets have been found, all of which date before the time of Moses.

A chronology of ancient law materials may be set up in this fashion: (a) legal documents of individuals, families, palace, and temple in Sumeria, third millennium B.C.; (b) fragmentary laws of King Urukagina of Lagash

Limestone relief with a figure representing Hammurabi, king of Babylon. The monument was dedicated to a goddess for the king's life.

(about 2380 B.C.) in Sumerian also; (c) the Ur-Nammu code by King Ur-Nammu, founder of the Third Dynasty of Ur in twenty-first century B.C. in Sumerian; (d) code of Bilalama of Eshnunna, about 1925 B.C. and written in Akkadian; (e) code of Lipit-Ishtar by Lipit of Isin, about 1900 B.C. in Sumerian; (f) legal tablets from Mari and dated in nineteenth-eighteenth centuries B.C. in cuneiform Akkadian; (g) code of Hammurabi, founder of the Old Babylonian empire, about 1728 B.C., in cuneiform Akkadian; (h) legal tablets from Alalakh, in the eighteenth century and in cuneiform Akkadian; (i) laws from the Hittites in Anatolia and from the fifteenth century B.C. also in cuneiform Akkadian; (j) legal tablets from Nuzu in the late fifteenth century B.C. in cuneiform Akkadian; (k) Middle Assyrian laws from the fourteenth century B.C. in cuneiform Akkadian; and (l) some legal tablets from Ugarit in cuneiform Akkadian and dating from the fourteenth-thirteenth centuries B.C.

The Eblaite archives contain many legal tablets and possibly some codes. Details concerning these tablets have not yet been published.

Wall carvings and inscriptions show Rameses II storming Ashkelon. A soldier is hacking at a door with an axe. This limestone relief is from the south wall of the Great Hall in the Karnak temple.

Many of these laws can be found in ANET, pp. 159-198 and pp. 217-223. They are well worth reading.

Three features are common to most of the legal literature listed above. This literature was written in the cuneiform script predominantly (apart from the Sumerian, practically all the laws were in the Akkadian language), and as a whole it illustrates the strong emphasis in the Mesopotamian culture on the written document.

One of the functions of the kings in this area was to administer the law as equitably as possible, though they never succeeded due to the stratification of their urban society into upper or noble class, artisan class, and slave class. The penalties for breaking laws varied with these classes. Yet the laws handed down by tradition served to limit the power of the kings and allow a measure of democracy. Law was regarded as being an aspect of the cosmic order, as being impersonal, and as backed by terror-ridden oaths and curses. The law was the major unifying force that bound the various ethnic groups of the Fertile Crescent area into a common culture. In that culture, the possession of proper legal documents seemed to be a matter of life and death. The major codes seemed to have been put together at the beginning of empires and thus helped to establish them on a more or less stable base.

Since practically all of the legal literature listed above is older than the time of Moses, and some statements, especially in the Code of Hammurabi, are much like a few of the laws of Moses, it is apparent that Mosaic law had an ancient rootage as well as a divine origin. The following discussion will seek to trace both the cultural and the divine elements in the Mosaic law.

Exponents of the Wellhausen understanding of the Old Testament proposed that the greater part of the laws in the Pentateuch were products of the Israelite kingdom and exilic periods. There are few who hold to that position now. Many nontraditional scholars recognize the prekingdom character of the laws in the Pentateuch. The biblical picture of Moses as a lawgiver is no longer scorned. Some even trace laws back to the Patriarchs themselves, for, as noted above, many of the customs of these men were set in the legal practices of Mesopotamia.

Not only was the covenant at Sinai the basis for establishing Israel as a nation before God, its core of stipulations—the Ten Commandments—set the basic policies for future judicial decisions. The Book of the Covenant (Exod. 21-23) reflects most of the Ten Commandments; and the regulations in Leviticus, Numbers, and Deuteronomy follow the same path.

Several decades ago, a German scholar, A. Alt, made a major contribution to biblical studies by separating two types of law: apodictic law and casuistic law. Apodictic laws are declarations that are prohibitions with

177

A fragment of the code of Lipit-Ishtar.

the force of categorical imperatives or positive commands. The Ten Commandments are the best biblical examples of this type, though apodictic laws are found throughout the rest of the Pentateuch, too. These laws are in the second person and therefore represent direct speech focused on individuals and families. The nearest parallels to this kind of law are in the Hittite covenants that are political in nature, whereas the biblical apodictic law is the set of obligations that the one true God laid upon Israel. Very few of the biblical apodictic laws provide for community sanctions; God was the one who punished the offender. See example of Dathan and Abiram in Numbers 16:1-53 and the somewhat similar type of punishment in Leviticus 24:10-23.

The prohibition of apodictic law may be regarded as universal since they exclude certain acts and certain relationships from the covenant bond with God. The positive commands are more specific, but at the same time they exclude any alternative attitude or action.

Casuistic, or case law, is amply illustrated in the pagan legal documents. It customarily has the formula, "If a . . . (does so and so), then . . . (definite penalty)." The case law in the Pentateuch is often mixed with apodictic law and is mostly concerned with homicide, slavery, pastoral conflicts, marriage, immorality, and cultic rules of purity or ritual. The "eye for an eye" legal policy found in Exodus 21:23-25 is paralleled in the Code of Hammurabi, but there it operated only in the same social class. For a slave to put out a noble's eye meant death. For a noble to put out a slave's eye involved a fine. In Israel its basic purpose was to uphold equal justice for all and a punishment that would fit the crime. This so-called law of retaliation was intended to curb excessive revenge due to passion and to serve as a block against terror tactics. Case law was closely related to the court decisions of the community elders, and also to the work of the seventy elders who aided Moses in administering the law in Israel (Exod. 18:13-27; Deut. 1:9-18). Case law was open-ended; it could be changed, or replaced by later, more improved law.

In spite of some Mesopotamian rootage in the background of Mosaic law, it was different from Mesopotamian legal practice in many respects. The Mosaic law was definitely monotheistic in tone and constantly claimed to be God's will for His people. Whereas pagan law was impersonal and lacking in compassion, for the most part, the Mosaic law was instilled with a concern for the kind of justice that is an act of love, an act that involved God. The justice proclaimed in the Pentateuch was not mechanical or coldly strict; rather, it was an interpersonal relationship that implied both a divine claim and a human responsibility.

Mosaic law was more concerned with human life—with the honor of womanhood and with the plight of the widow, the orphan, the slave, and the stranger—than any other law in the ancient Near East. Its expression of divine concern for man and its lofty moral tone have had a powerful impact on the long history of Jewish people, on the New Testament, and on Christian law through the ages.

Mosaic Cult and Pagan Cult

In the previous section of this chapter, it was noted that throughout the ancient Near East the king served as high priest. The priestly class was a professional group subdivided into several classes of both men and women; the temple was the dominant institutional complex in many cities; the ritual was burdened with divination, magic, and sacred prostitution; and the annual festivals served as renewing agents in society.

As far as the biblical witness goes, there was no priestly class among the Patriarchs; the head of the family served as its priest. Nor did these men have holy places beyond temporary altars here and there, though there may be some question about Bethel and Shechem. Their ritual was a combination of simple animal sacrifices and spontaneous prayer.

Under divine guidance the Mosaic organization of Israel provided for a high priest, a priestly class, and assistants to the priestly class made up of the men of the tribe of Levi. An elaborate, expensive tabernacle was built and moved from place to place. A group of sacrifices was ordained for daily and other specified times for worship at the tabernacle; annual festivals were established for stated seasons of the year.

The duties of Aaron and his descendents were to carry on the daily round of sacrifices at the tabernacle, care for furniture of the sanctuary, keep the seven-branched lamp burning, and replace the shewbread. The priests were supposed to be the instructors of the people in the law and traditions of the nation and be their personal counselors in time of trouble. They were also the sanitation and health officers of the community.

Besides being the chief administrator of the priests, the high priest was the prime participant in the annual Day of Atonement, at which time he entered the holy of holies of the sanctuary.

The tabernacle and its furniture are described in Exodus 25-40; it was a tent and all its parts and furniture were so constructed that they could be taken apart, or connected with carrying poles so they could be moved from place to place. There are ruins of a few Canaanite temples: Tell Beit Mirsim, Hazor, Megiddo, Lachish, and Shechem; but other than having three sections in a straight line axis, they are not clear analogies for the tabernacle. Some pagan altars had horns much like the horns on the corners of the Mosaic altars.

In Exodus 33:7-11, there is mention of a tent of meeting. But this tent of meeting was a purely provisional tent, before the building of the tabernacle. After the sin of making the golden calf, it was moved outside the camp, Moses went to it to communicate with God, Joshua guarded it. It had no ritual and no priesthood. It may be that Numbers 11:16, 26-27 refers to the tabernacle, which was temporarily outside the camp.

Some scholars have regarded the references to the tent of meeting as part of the traditions of the kingdom of Judah, and the tabernacle as associated with the northern kingdom of Israel and then idealized by post-exilic priestly editors. Others hold that the tabernacle was truly Mosaic in construction and served all Israel until the building of the Solomonic temple.

The tabernacle was built on a ratio of 2:1 and on a radiating decrease of value of metal: gold, silver, bronze, from the center to the outer edges. It was oriented directly east and had a descending value of holiness from the holy of holies to the camp itself. The tabernacle was located in the center of the encampment and was built of materials and labor voluntarily provided by the people.

At the tabernacle, the approach to God was patterned on the approach to God at Sinai. People gathered near the altar at the foot of Mount Sinai (Exod. 19:17); the people (a few) could visit the court of the tabernacle where the large altar was located, but most had to wait just outside the gate. Priests and elders of the people could go up to the mountain part way and worship afar off; the priests could enter the holy place. Moses alone could go up to the top of Mount Sinai; only the high priest could enter the holy of holies.

Various passages in the Pentateuch indicate something of the function and meaning of the tabernacle for the Israelite community. It proclaimed the presence of God and His purposes for them, and it guided them on their journeys. The services held at the tabernacle provided atonement for sin; they revealed how God could be approached and how the people could have fellowship with God. The tabernacle gave the Israelites a sense of unity and a center of government.

Like the pagans, the tabernacle cult had a sacrificial system that utilized animals and food and drink; but unlike the pagans, humans were never offered in sacrifice. The pagans regarded their sacrifices as providing either a means of binding the worshiper to his deities by sharing the body of the sacrificial animal in a holy meal, a gift to induce the gods to act in the offerer's favor, or a means to release vital power from the sacrificial victim to strengthen their weary gods.

In the Mosaic system, wholly new meanings were given to the sacrifices retained. But this system combats, indeed prohibits, any idea that the sacrifices carried automatic power. The sacrifices must be the organ of the spirit; intention rather than act validated the offering. Restitution, confession, and humble repentance were required before the sacrifices were offered. There were no sacrifices for murder, adultery, or blasphemy.

The burnt offering sought to express devotion to God through the worshiper's intimate association with the victim by laying hands on the sacrifice and by confession. The burnt offering pointed to atonement through the sprinkling of blood on the altar; peaceful relations with God were renewed. The offering expressed a general dedication of the self to God with sincerity.

The peace offering was used to celebrate family anniversaries, and hence was a family worship service. Before the offering, the worshiper dedicated himself to God. Only a token of the animal was burned; the priests were given the breast and thigh and the remainder was eaten by the family. The worshipers had to be ceremonially clean. The offering served as an atonement, as did the burnt offering, and expressed fellowship with God and man.

The meal offering was a gift that accompanied the burnt and peace offerings; it indicated acceptance of mercy from God. The offering was made up of ingredients made in the home or shop. They were (a) the finest flour, (b) oil, (c) salt, (d) frankincense, but no honey or leaven.

The sin and guilt offerings were based on the premise that sin barred access to God and could be removed by sacrificial blood. The offerer laid his hand on the head of the animal and confessed his sins; the animal was a substitute in death for the sinner. Some of the animal's blood was sprinkled seven times with the priest's finger before the inner veil; on the Day of Atonement the sprinkling was done by the high priest in the holy of holies. Some of the blood was sprinkled on the horns of the altar of incense, and the remainder was poured out at the base of the great altar. The fat and entrails were burnt on the great altar, whereas the rest of the carcass was taken outside the camp and burnt. The sin offering took away the sins of negligence, accident, and ignorance (Lev. 4; Num. 15:22-31). The guilt offering followed the sin offering and was for offenses that could be assessed for monetary compensation.

The sacrifices symbolized the doctrine that atonement for sin was at the cost of life; they were a means of restoring fellowship with God and had no connotation of feeding God. God was the initiator of the system, for it was He who provided the means to approach Him. The sacrifices stressed the fact that God's standard is perfection and that human sin is beyond human control or cure. The serious sins were beyond the sacrificial system, hence the worshiper could never be complacent, except at his own peril. By its limitations, the system pointed beyond itself to a more adequate sacrifice. That sacrifice was Christ.

Many of the sacrifices were offered at the annual festivals. The Passover with the Feast of Unleavened Bread took place after the spring equinox. The Passover itself was a family affair that extended over two Sabbaths. The animal was slain by the priest, but roasted and eaten at home. The Exodus story was retold during the meal. The next day a sheaf of new grain was dedicated. The Passover commemorated the Exodus as a day of deliverance, of liberty, and of thanksgiving. The sheaf of grain was a dedication of crops to God.

The Feast of Pentecost was fifty days after the Passover and was observed by a presentation of two loaves of bread to the Lord, then an offering of a burnt, a sin, and a peace offering. It celebrated the end of the grain harvest, and in later Judaism, the giving of the law on Mount Sinai.

The Feast of Trumpets was the civil New Years Day and was connected with the autumnal equinox. The Day of Atonement came ten days later, preceded by fasting, almsgiving, and prayer. This was the day the high priest entered the holy of holies with the blood of the sin offering to atone for the sins of the people. He must confess the sins of the people as well as his own sins. A scapegoat was turned loose in the wilderness. The Feast of Tabernacles began five days later and lasted for eight days. Booths of saplings and branches were constructed by families to symbolize the wanderings in the wilderness. It was a thanksgiving occasion at the end of the fruit harvest.

The Sabbath was the seventh day of each week, and, according to Exodus 20:11, it commemorated the original creation of the world and God's rest at the end of it; but according to Deuteronomy 5:15, it commemorated the Exodus. Originally, man had been commanded to subdue all things related to space, but the Sabbath was established by God. It is a segment of time independent of the seasons or any human methods of fixing a date by the moons or stars. Contrary to the Babylonian *shabattu,* which was a day of fear, haunted by demons, the Hebrew Sabbath was blessed by God and was a day in which man thankfully recognized the majesty of God and yielded himself as a servant before his Lord. On this day man admitted that he had a special relationship to God.

At the time of the new moon, the first of each month, extra offerings were made to commemorate a new period of time.

In summary, it may be said that the pagan neighbors of Israel had elaborate cult rites and festivals lorded over by an autocratic priesthood. The Hebrews had a less complex system administered by a servant priesthood. The pagan cult was burdened with an immoral fertility emphasis, with divination, and with magic; the worshiper must be content with the whims of selfish deities and must often resort to bargaining. The Hebrew cult prohibited immorality, divination, and magic; the Hebrew had to honestly face God as a sinner and humbly be willing to meet the demands of a just God. The Hebrew was called to faith, hope, love, and a desire to live a holy life. To the pagan, sin was mainly a breach of ritual, a negligence of providing sacrifices, all within an impersonal relationship. To the Hebrew, sin was a violation of the stipulations of the covenant, a breach of moral law, a fracturing of an interpersonal relationship.

Cultural Dependence Compared with Cultural Adaptation

In the past several decades there has been extensive discussion concerning the cultural and theological dependence of the Hebrew people upon her neighbors. After the cuneiform script had been deciphered toward the middle of the nineteenth century and a mass of Akkadian literature became known, some European scholars were inclined to view all or most of Hebrew thought and practice as directly dependent on Babylonia. These scholars were labeled by others as a Pan-Babylonian school. The nearly contemporary decipherment and translation of Egyptian literature led some Egyptologists to view much of the Old Testament as dependent on Egypt; naturally they were called the Pan-Egyptian school.

Within this century, archaeology in Palestine has brought to light many

Canaanite artifacts but few inscriptions; nevertheless, a group of scholars began to view much of the Old Testament as directly dependent on Canaanite culture. The discovery of Canaanite literature at Ugarit accentuated this emphasis, and a Pan-Canaanite school has pushed its viewpoints. More recently these "schools" have broken up and many scholars are more inclined to view the Hebrews in the light of their total ancient Near Eastern milieu.

The questions remain: How deeply were the Hebrews dependent on their neighbors for their ideas, cult, and style of living? To what extent did the Hebrews creatively remold their environment and add their own unique contributions to the thought patterns and life-style of their own community?

Scholars who have rejected the biblical witness that God revealed to Moses much of that which is contained in the Pentateuch have tended to stress Hebrew dependence on, and borrowing from, her neighbors. Scholars who have accepted the concept of divine revelation have been more cautious concerning the extent of cultural dependence, yet they have recognized that the Hebrews were not isolated and were influenced by the thought world that surrounded them.

The procedures by which the general cultural environment was adapted to bear the revealed truth that God deposited with Israel may be summed up under the following headings.

Spiritual Personalization. Names of God in the Old Testament (i.e., El, El Elyon, El Shaddai)—and most of them are found in the Pentateuch—were taken from the common Semitic culture, with the possible exception of *Yahweh*. It is now known that the old Semitic equivalent for *Yahweh* occurs on tablets from Ebla that are dated 2400–2250 B.C. See pages 293–96 in the appendix. These names were rid of their pagan polytheism and naturism and given a strong personal content while at the same time stressing the majesty, holiness, oneness, and uniqueness of deity. All these names became part of the covenant, for they represented the superior partner in this form of interpersonal relationship.

The covenant structure was taken from a common set of domestic, social, commercial, and political relationships in Mesopotamia and Anatolia. The covenant forms and the covenant vocabulary were instilled with profound religious meaning. Since the covenant was interpersonal, it was capable of dealing with life in its most rugged, down-to-earth aspects and still bear thoroughgoing spiritual and moral content.

The Akkadian *shabattu* was taken over as a basic term and, lifting it up from demonism, the Hebrews related it to God's work as creator and deliverer. A term that had a negative connotation was given a positive function, as the name of a day in which man worships his God.

Radical Displacement. By divine command, Israel was instructed to reject from its midst any attachment to pagan deities, for there is only one God. Image production or worship was prohibited. So were divinations of all kinds, magical practices of every sort, sex perversions, and human sacrifice ruled out. Practices contrary to the nature and will of a God of holy love and contrary to healthy, moral living among men were to be shunned by Israel.

Theological Displacement. Under divine direction, items, terms, and practices were taken from the common Semitic culture, rid of pagan meanings and overtones, and replaced with meanings and overtones that were consonant with a communication of God's will to man with a commensurate faith and practice among His followers. These items would include features like the structure of the tabernacle, its furniture, the sacrificial system, the festivals, and holy days.

Historical Displacement. This procedure is similar to theological displacement, but has a different emphasis. Historical displacement applies mainly to the Passover and the Feast of Tabernacles. The Passover was observed at about the same time as pagan spring festivals, but was based on the historical event of the Exodus from Egypt. Also, the Feast of Tabernacles, which was observed at about the same time as the fall pagan festivals, was based on the wilderness wanderings in Sinai.

Some scholars have used the term "historicization" to describe this phenomena. This argument is that mythology, or a pagan ritual, was retained in basic form, perhaps with some basic meanings, but oriented to an ancient event in human affairs that the community believed had actually happened, but, in fact, had not really taken place. Practically all the stories in Genesis 1-11, or even the stories about the Patriarchs and the Exodus could be understood by modern scholars in this manner. For the Hebrew, the result would be a pseudohistory that could never be verified by any kind of modern scientific research.

The implication of this understanding of "historicization" would be that the Hebrew people, the writers of biblical books, Jesus Himself, the apostles, a host of Christians through the centuries and a host of orthodox Jews have been deluded into thinking that God had actually acted in the affairs of men in ancient times. The result of such a conviction that the Pentateuch and other parts of the Bible are make-believe history is a credibility gap of great proportions. To maintain a position that the doctrines of the Bible are true but its presentation of, say the Exodus, is false, engenders a tension that is difficult to endure.

Surely it is possible for bona fide history to be understood theologically

185

and celebrated in religious festivals without its validity as history being compromised.

Secularization. Like our use of names of gods and goddesses for the names of days of the week, the months of the year, the planets, and modern space vehicles, so in the Pentateuch and the remainder of the Old Testament, names of gods and goddesses were secularized. In each of these instances polytheistic meanings are completely missing.

As illustrations, the Phoenician god for grain, Dagon, became the Hebrew word *dagan,* which means "grain." The god Tirsu, the Canaanite god for wine, became the Hebrew word *tiros,* which means "wine." Neither of the above has connotations of deity in the Hebrew. The goddess Ashtaroth, who was the phenomenon of sexual reproduction, was changed into the Hebrew *'ashterot tson,* which means "sheep breeding." The god of disease, Resheph, meant "disease" and no more to the Hebrew. In like manner, the god of healing, Eshmun, was made into a Hebrew plural, *'eshmunim* and meant no more than "health"; the Canaanites had seven divine midwives called kosharot, but in Hebrew, *kosharot* stood for nothing more than "the birth process." The Canaanite god of skill, Koshar, became the Hebrew *kishor,* the word for "skill."

Depersonalization. This word is intended to designate the act of labeling a nature object as no more than what it is, minus any divine attributions. Thus, in Genesis 1, the heavens, the earth, the deep, the sea, the darkness, the waters, plants, animals (including the sea monsters) have no pagan identification as divine beings. This refusal to regard any aspect of the natural realm as divine continues throughout the Pentateuch and the rest of the Bible.

Vocational Reorientation. Pagan priests made up an autocratic class and were deeply involved in divination and magic. The Israelite priests were subject to God's laws and were to be the servants of the people. They were not to practice the pagan arts of divination and magic.

In Egypt, the pharaoh was a divine king-priest with autocratic powers; in Mesopotamia there was much less tendency to deify the king, and laws restricted his powers, but it was still not difficult for the king to be autocratic and cruel. In Israel, the leader was legitimate if he was chosen by God and had subjected himself to the stipulations of the covenant relationship. He was to be no more than a purely human servant of God and the people.

In paganism, prophets practiced divination and magic, but seemed to be under control of the major institutions of society. A person was a true prophet or prophetess in Israel only if he or she was called of God, truly received God's Word, and faithfully communicated that Word to the people, regardless of cost.

Legal Moralization. Israel's laws were much more humane than the Mesopotamian or Hittite laws: a greater value was placed on human life. There was a deeper concern for the oppressed classes and for animals in Israel than in paganism. The laws of purity in Israel were much more related to cleanliness and good health. The Ten Commandments tower above all pagan law as an expression of rejection of polytheism, of idolatry, of blasphemy, of dishonesty, of exploitation of the human person and his property. Positively it upheld joyous worship on a regular basis and the honor of parenthood.

In summary, one may state three principles that guided the divine-human adventure in setting up a religious faith and practice that challenged the validity of paganism. First, one may observe that those customs, institutions, rites, and laws that could be adapted to the ways of pure worship within the covenant relationship were retained. Mainly, the adaptation centered in the realm of meaning, the significance of the act as it related to the covenant. Secondly, those customs, institutions, rites, and laws that were contrary to the covenant obligations were prohibited. Thirdly, any of these adapted customs, institutions, rites, and laws could be added to or diminished or rejected when they became obsolete.

Cultural items that were adapted to the new faith were transient elements in the new order of life. Because they were of a transient nature, they also posed dangers for the Israelites. Incidents in the Pentateuch and in the remainder of the Old Testament illustrate the fact that when Israel became spiritually indifferent to the covenant relationship with God, she was in trouble. Those customs, institutions, rites, and laws that had been adapted, and which was thus similar to pagan ways, could be corrupted with pagan theology and practice. The stories of the golden calf (Exod. 32), the offering of strange fire (Lev. 10), an act of blasphemy (Lev. 24:10-23), and the fiery serpents (Num. 21:4-9; II Kings 18:4) are a few examples. The later prophets wrestled with this problem constantly.

Another danger was that obsolete customs, institutions, rites, and laws could become so "sacred" that they could not easily be set aside, and so could become a burden on future generations. Within the Pentateuch, there is evidence that case laws were changed as need demanded, and the historical books show that case law was largely open to change as situations varied from time to time and from place to place. The life of Samuel shows that Mosaic institutions were not absolutely essential to his spiritual leadership. It was not until the intertestamental period that Jews really began to make rigid the Mosaic case law, and it has been a problem in Judaism ever since. The apodictic law in the Pentateuch was less subject to change, though even the basis for the observance of the Sabbath could be shifted from the creation to the Exodus.

The matter of cultural adaptation and change came to a crisis level in the early Christian church in the Council of Jerusalem (Acts 15), and the issue was decided in favor of change.

The problems of cultural adaptation have been crucial for the Christian church in its missionary activities and as it has faced new situations on every level from age to age. In our present age of rapid change, it may be that a new study of how God revealed Himself to the Hebrew people and how He led them to build a new society with new ways of religious practice would provide insights that could serve as guidelines.

Suggested Books for Further Study

Albright, W. F. *Yahweh and the Gods of Canaan.* Garden City, New York: Doubleday & Co., 1968.

Gordon, C. H. *The Ancient Near East.* New York: W. W. Norton & Co., 1965.

Guillaume, A. *Prophecy and Divination.* London: Hodder and Stoughton, 1938.

Hamilton, Victor P. *Handbook on the Pentateuch.* Grand Rapids: Baker Book House, 1982.

Harrison, R. K. *Old Testament Times.* Grand Rapids: Wm. B. Eerdmans Publishing Co., 1970.

Heschel, Abraham J. *The Prophets,* 2 vols. New York: Harper & Row, 1962.

Hillers, D. R. *The Covenant.* Baltimore: Johns Hopkins Press, 1969.

Kaufmann, Y. *The Religion of Israel.* Chicago: The University of Chicago Press, 1960.

Kidner, D. *Sacrifice in the Old Testament.* London: Tyndale Press, 1952.

Lindblom, J. *Prophecy in Ancient Israel.* Oxford: Basil Blackwell, 1962.

McCarthy, D. J. *Old Testament Covenant.* Richmond: John Knox Press, 1972.

———. *Treaty and Covenant.* Rome: Pontifical Biblical Institute, 1963.

Mendenhall, G. E. *Law and Covenant in the Ancient Near East.* Pittsburgh: Biblical Colloquium, 1955.

Montet, P. *Egypt and the Bible.* Philadelphia: Fortress Press, 1968.

Speiser, E. A. *Oriental and Biblical Studies.* Philadelphia: University of Pennsylvania Press, 1967.

Vaux, R. de. *Ancient Israel.* New York: McGraw-Hill Book Co., 1961.

Part Three

ASSUMPTIONS, CRITICAL METHODS, AND THEORIES

The monastery of St. Catherine, nestled on the eastern slope of Mount Sinai.

8

Ways of Looking
at the Pentateuch

When we study the Bible, we come to it with a conditioned mind and a complex of attitudes. Consciously or unconsciously, family and church teachings, or lack of them, combine with social and academic environment to create a way of looking at life. We evaluate nature and people from the vantage point of this conditioning. Not only are the Scriptures as a whole evaluated in this way, but, also, the Pentateuch is so perceived. Since the content of each of our lives is different, we tend to interpret the Pentateuch differently.

No less than other scholars, students of the Pentateuch are influenced by their background, training, and the quality of their spiritual experiences. Consequently, their understanding of the Pentateuch has varied, much to the confusion of less well-educated believers.

The purpose of this chapter is to survey in a cursory manner several ways of looking at the Pentateuch that have been characteristic of biblical scholars. It would be easy to expand this task into a book or even several volumes, for the variety of views is great. This temptation will be resisted and, at the risk of over simplification, only traits common to large groups of scholars will be presented.

A secondary purpose is to condense concisely several philosophical viewpoints in Western culture that have had special impact on biblical studies. To be aware of these philosophies will aid those interested in the Pentateuch to see why various scholars have developed certain methods of study and have proposed certain theories of interpretation.

The major approaches to the Pentateuch, and this can be applied to the entire Old Testament, may be classed as traditional, liberal, and neo-orthodox. Each of these will be preceded by a brief summary of ways of thinking that undergird these approaches. Where necessary, the categories will be subdivided.

The System of Thought in the Bible

When one speaks of a biblical system of thought, one must recognize the fact that no organized framework of logic is present in the Bible, though there may be some basis for holding that Paul was systematic in the arguments found in Romans or Galatians. In the third and fourth centuries after Christ, leaders in the church became more systematic, but they grounded their thinking basically on biblical concepts, though increasingly influenced by Greek philosophy. In their own way, Jewish leaders followed the same pattern of being guided by biblical ideas, but mixing them more and more with Greek logical processes. Through the Middle Ages up till the eighteenth century, both products of the Old Testament—Judaism and Christianity—remained grounded in the Bible but incorporated Western philosophies in various blends.

Briefly stated, the biblical complex of ideas built its foundation on the doctrine that the living God is Creator; all else is the product of His power. Both mind and matter are "real," but only as they are the creation of the living God in whom alone is Reality. Nature is not "Mother Nature"; perhaps it could be addressed as "sister nature" for it owes its existence to God, as does man.

As an ultimate goal, God's revealed will binds all things together. In the beginning all was harmony in the presence of the creating God, but not presently. Now there is alienation and conflict; in the future, unity and peace will be restored under God's sovereignty.

The mind is a functional aspect of man's self, capable of truth reception, of analysis, and of application of data. Functioning properly, it is subordinate to the will of God.

Facts are an integral part of total truth. This being so, the world about us can be observed and evaluated by man to gain knowledge about God's creation. Thus, whereas facts do have significance in themselves, their final meaning resides in Him to whom they point.

God's desire is that man should move from rebellion to faith in God, to cleansing, to maturity, to social betterment, to glorification. When God's will is rejected, man moves in the opposite direction, into ruin.

By nature, man is a creature originally created good in the sight of God. Through rebellion to God's command, however, man is a sinner and no person is born other than as separated from God. As a sinner, a person cannot become good except God creatively touches his inner being and makes him one of the people of God.

The ideal is that man should be the companion and servant of God here and now, a steward of God's creation; or, he is the servant of sin and Satan.

Man can have fellowship with God on earth and eternal life in His presence hereafter; or he can be a slave to sin and suffer punishment hereafter. In the Old Testament, the "land of the living" is the main locale of attention, but the afterlife is touched upon occasionally. It is the New Testament that provides a full doctrine of life after death, solidly rooted in the resurrection of Christ from the dead.

The matrix of uniqueness is in God's word and action in history, matched by man's God-given powers of creativity. God is free to interfere in the processes of nature and in the affairs of men and nations. When God acts, something new does take place.

The Traditional Approach

This point of view has been dominant in orthodox Jewish communities, in the Roman Catholic church, and in Protestantism at least up till the nineteenth century. It is still the view of the vast majority of believers in each of these religious communities.

The source of authority has been recognized as rooted in God, who has revealed Himself through men charged with recording and preserving His will in the Scriptures. Also, a more or less important place has been accorded to tradition.

Generally, biblical scholars within these communities have been polemic in their attitudes, that is, they have argued in favor of the Scriptures in opposition to those who would attack them. They have been defensive, but they have also been free to use the Bible as an evangelistic and a missionary tool, especially within the Christian faith. This attitude is interpretive rather than critical.

Because traditional scholars have regarded their Scriptures as a unit, they have been irenic in seeking solutions to problems in understanding the Bible. They have sought to harmonize all parts of the Scriptures, believing that obscure passages could be clarified by other passages.

The major methods of these scholars have centered around exegesis (understanding what the text says), exposition (explaining what it says), typology (showing how people and events in the Old Testament are types of Christ and the church), allegorization (spiritualization of Old Testament accounts, e.g., Song of Solomon as an allegory of Christ's love for the church), and prophetic fulfillment that is an understanding of Old Testament predictions in terms of New Testament events and in world events till the end of the age.

The traditional view has often been labeled as supernaturalistic. It has regarded God as One and distinct from nature or man. God reveals Himself to specific people, giving them an intelligible message. He also acts in the affairs of men through miracles. God is viewed as the Lord of history, working His purposes in the affairs of men with or without their consent.

The key to understanding the Scriptures may be held to be God's election of Israel, in the narrow sense, or, as God's full revelation through Jesus Christ.

Each of the traditional approaches—Jewish, Roman Catholic, and Protestant—have concepts that are peculiar to themselves, and have been expressed in literature. A closer look at each approach may clarify some differences.

Beginning in the intertestamental period (400 B.C. to Christ) an attitude began to develop among Jews that though the Old Testament is the Word of God, and thus the source of all true knowledge, its laws must be interpreted for new situations. These interpretations were recorded and collected in a growing body of literature, dating from about 200 B.C. on into the Middle Ages. This literature has been known as the Midrash, the Mishnah, and the Gemara.

The word *midrash* means commentary and refers to a body of literature that began about A.D. 300. It is subdivided into the Halachah (loosely meaning "legal decisions"), which is a collection of judicial exegesis on the 613 laws of the Pentateuch, and the Haggadah (meaning "narration"), which is more practical and devotional in its exposition of the text.

The Mishnah, which means "repetition," uses the topical method of presenting the basic teachings of the Old Testament and is a compilation of important opinions of various rabbis. It began about 200 B.C. and continued to grow in size until about A.D. 200.

Meaning "completion," the Gemara began as the Tosefta about A.D. 200 by the Amoraim (expositors) and was finished about A.D. 400. This collection is mainly made up of discussions and speeches of the learned rabbis who lived in the Mesopotamian valley.

In time, these three collections were put together into the Talmud, meaning "learning," which is a set of volumes in two editions: the Palestinian and the Babylonian. The Talmud is the honored tradition of orthodox Judaism. It matches the Old Testament, but does not have any formally declared authority, though among the faithful it ranks very high indeed.

The Roman Catholic church has traditionally held that the Scriptures are the inspired, reliable Word of God, but has included the eleven books of the Apocrypha accepted by the Council of Trent in A.D. 1546. It has further declared that revelation is to be found in two sources: the Scriptures and the tradition. The tradition is made up mainly of pronouncements of synods, councils, and the pope given *ex cathedra.* Both the Scriptures and the tradition derive their authority from the church itself, which roots its claim in the mission of the church as the voice of God in the world.

During the nineteenth century, the Roman Catholic church rebuked the few adherents who accepted the new trend to find sources in the Pentateuch and/or denied Mosaic authorship. Yet, in 1943, a papal encyclical, *Divino Afflante Spiritu,* moderately opened the door for the use of the methods of literary and historical criticism. The church quickly found that the door had been opened too widely. In 1961, a warning letter, the *Monitum,* stated that liberalism had gone too far and should slow down. A hot debate flared up in the Vatican Council II in 1962, and it has become more intense since then. Presently, many Catholic scholars have turned to the *Heilsgeschichte,* "Salvation History," point of view because it emphasizes tradition strongly.

Historically, Protestant churches have declared the Scriptures to be the Word of God, possessing intrinsic authority, because God through the Holy Spirit had revealed Himself and superintended the writing of Scripture. But Protestantism has also been the center of a rejection of this view.

In contrast to Judaism, Protestants have held up the New Testament as the supreme revelation and, in contrast to Roman Catholicism, they have rejected the Apocrypha and tradition as containing any revelation that goes beyond Scripture.

During a fierce controversy in America in the 1920s, much of traditional Protestantism hardened into what is known as fundamentalism. Since the early 1940s, a growing group of traditionally oriented scholars has sprung up. They prefer to be called conservatives and are more open to the best in biblical scholarship, though strongly rooted in the authority of the Scriptures.

The System of Thought Called Idealism

The term *idealism* is a general label for philosophies that hold that the essence of all reality is Mind, which, in itself, is static. It is monistic, that is, mind inheres in God, nature, and man as a common core. Before anything ever appeared there was Mind and all things shall return to Mind. Mind is the ground of all being.

Unity is found in the coherence of thought or logic. Though the universe seems to be diverse and chaotic, behind the appearance of things, basic laws bind the whole as one. Though life is filled with contradictions and destructiveness, man's mental capacities can probe behind the surface and behold the Absolute Mind, which is One.

The human mind is primary; it is a system builder, and it is self-sufficient.

At the end of the eighteenth century, the German philosopher Immanuel Kant was a system builder who, in his famous work, *The Critique of Pure Reason,* proposed a system that has greatly influenced Western thinking. He speaks of three faculties of the mind; the faculty of sense or phenomena, the faculty of intellect, and the faculty of reason.

The faculty of sense or phenomena seems to give us information about the world outside of us by means of seeing, hearing, smelling, tasting, and touching. The faculty of reason provides three basic ideas: of the self, of the material world, and of God. The faculty of intellect gathers data from both of these two faculties and classifies it according to its twelve forms, which in turn are divided into four groups. The forms of unity, plurality, and totality are grouped under quantity; affirmation, negation, and limitation are aspects of quality; substance-accident, cause-effect, and action-passion are brought together under relation; existence-nonexistence, possibility-impossibility, and necessity-contingency are grouped under modality.

Kant discussed each aspect of this framework in detail and made a lasting impact on Western thinking as a whole, including some Old Testament scholars. As other idealists, Kant held that the objectivity of natural phenomena is an expression of the mind and is transitory. But, being a scientist and a mathematics teacher, Kant regarded the natural world with great respect.

Within a few decades of the early nineteenth century, Kant was overshadowed by another German philosopher, Georg W. F. Hegel, whose system molded the thinking of many scholars for almost a century. Especially his philosophy of history influenced Protestant Old Testament scholars, the most important of whom was Julius Wellhausen.

Hegel accepted the dictum that mind is the essence of reality and tied it to a dynamic growth concept. He adapted Kant's forms of the faculty of intellect to a dialectic of thesis, antithesis, and synthesis, which has been manifested in nature and human history as an ever-evolving clarification of ideas to higher and higher levels of perfection. This pattern has been applied to the Old Testament in a number of ways.

Religiously, the Hebrews started out as primitive animatists who encountered others worshiping nature gods and goddesses. Under Moses a synthesis was made for the Hebrews when they borrowed a god named Yahweh from nomads in the Sinai desert and made him more important than other deities. Moving into Canaan the Hebrews mingled with the sex-centered Canaanites and adopted many of their ways. King David elevated Yahweh into a national god much like the Canaanite Baal, and it was not until the Exile that an unknown prophet exiled in Babylon conceived of an exclusive, universal deity for all mankind.

196

From another vantage point, the followers of Wellhausen have declared that the Hebrews began as hunting, roaming nomads who had a difficult time adjusting to the farmer-based city-states of Canaan. The Hebrews finally settled down on the land and during the kingdom period became more and more international merchants. Caught in the maelstrom of international conflicts, the Hebrews were uprooted from their land and lost their nation, but many became educated career men in the empires of Babylon and Persia. These are only two of many treatments of Hebrew life and thought that have been worked out by those who are debtors to Hegel.

Integral to idealism is the belief that in every person there is a spark of divinity imbedded in his mental capacities. Sometimes, scholars in this tradition have tended to set the mind over against the body as though they were alien to each other. The body and its feelings usually draw a low value rating; the mind and its power to reason is placed at the top of the list.

Because man is a thinking, logical being, he is the means by which the Ultimate Mind achieves itself, and the destiny of man is to be reunited or absorbed back into the Ultimate Mind.

In this system, from whence does the new come? How can improvement be brought about? Fundamentally, all achievement and progress springs from the reflective creativeness of human thought, the Ultimate Mind working through the logic of the mind.

The Liberal Approach

This point of view grew out of the Renaissance and the rise of the various sciences that dominate today's world. It was nurtured in German Protestantism during the nineteenth century and became dominant in Protestantism during the first three decades of the twentieth century. Its mainstream drew heavily on Kantian and Hegelian philosophy for its governing principles.

The liberal view is a basic rebellion against all forms of objective authority, whether the pope or the Bible. The scholars of this persuasion root authority in reason, that is, in a logical philosophical way of thinking. All claims must be tested in the crucible of reason to discover whether they be true or false.

Scholars of a liberal frame of mind claim they take nothing for granted. They have varied from mildly to extremely skeptical of the historicity and truth-value of the Scriptures and of traditional theology. They have been highly selective in retaining any parts of the Bible as of present-day significance.

In the face of problems of the biblical text, scholars of this point of view treat the Bible as they would any other literary production. The text is carefully taken apart and examined. Words, phrases, sentences, syntax, and the construction of paragraphs or stanzas and of larger units are analyzed. If apparent contradictions or illogical arrangements of thought are noted, the text is rearranged into new sentences or sequences of ideas. Portions of the text may be regarded as insertions from a later time and removed to recover the genuine work of the original author.

Generally, liberal scholars have employed a historical-critical method in which facts for their own sakes are of basic concern. The goal is to discover what actually happened. But, since it has been joined to a naturalistic outlook, the activity of a living God has been ruled out. Hence, the testimony of the Bible that God has revealed Himself to man, has acted in nature and in history in a miraculous way, cannot be true. Details of this method will be discussed in the next chapter.

Having ruled out a living God in their world view, liberal scholars have tended to prefer a naturalistic concept in which all events are the expressions of laws of cause and effect mechanically operated; or, a humanistic frame of reference in which man is given a much more creative role in the shaping of history. Revelation is but a human discovery of what had been unknown about life previously. God never has and does not speak to individuals, nor does He interfere with natural law to perform miracles.

These scholars have commonly held that the Old Testament can be best understood in terms of some non-Hebrew culture. At the end of the nineteenth century, the Bedouin Arabs were the favorite model, then the Babylonians or the Egyptians or the Canaanites.

The Wellhausen "School"

Almost a century of intensive study culminated in a way of understanding the Old Testament that was popularized by Julius Wellhausen in the 1880s. The theory he championed has been often labeled the JEDP theory, which has held that the Pentateuch was originally a series of four documents that were composed during the kingdom and exilic periods and were blended into the present five books about 450 B.C. Hegel's understanding of historical dialectic heavily influenced this theory. Details of this influence will be discussed later. This theory dominated Old Testament studies in Germany, England, and America during the last decades of the nineteenth century and the first two or three decades of this century.

The System of Thought Called Positivism

Not all Western philosophers have equated Mind with the essence of the universe or of the human soul. A prominent reaction against the systems of Kant or Hegel has been called *positivism* because it holds that only the knowledge provided by our five senses—hearing, seeing, smelling, tasting, and touching—are of positive value. This view had its roots in ancient

Greek philosophy and gained new prominence through the teachings of such men as Auguste Comte, during the first half of the nineteenth century, and John Stuart Mill, later in the century. Much of the work of scientists to the present day has been guided by this point of view.

A number of Old Testament scholars have been similarly guided in their research in the disciplines such as archaeology, linguistics, and textual criticism, which bear upon the Old Testament. They have little concern for biblical theology.

In regard to reality, positivists have generally held that nature itself is the totality of all things and is ever changing. Nature is pluralistic, that is, it is made up of many separate parts. The laws of nature unite and hold all things together, keeping it working fairly smoothly and reliably.

For the positivist, the mind is a tool, a problem-solver that gathers, classifies, analyzes, and relates data to a functional purpose. The mind is like a bee, which goes out into the world to seek its treasures and then transforms them into materials that meet its needs. The facts of nature provide the raw material for problem-solving, which process becomes the technology of modern industrial society.

Nature possesses an inherent power to develop, to evolve into ever higher forms, and constantly puts that power to work. Most positivists have rejected the dialectics of Hegelian philosophy, preferring rather a steady, emerging development of the universe and of man.

Man himself is but a higher form of animal, a naked ape, the highest form to develop to date. More perfect beings are yet to appear in the evolutionary process. Yet, man is the creature who can unravel objectively the mysteries of nature and bring the unknown into the realm of knowledge and utility.

Though man is not the apex of natural achievement, he is destined to dominate nature, or in a crude, insensitive attitude, ruthlessly exploit nature completely. Even in a spirit of exploitation, man is confident that, given some time to reflect and plan, he can employ his technology to solve satisfactorily any problem that may confront mankind.

As to the source of uniqueness, the positivist believes that natural forces, whether social, economical, political, psychological, or whatever, working through man, produce the new, the unique. One need not look outside of nature for creative power; nature has it and manifests it every time it bursts forth into a new combination of atoms, into a new plant, or into a new creature. If there is a God, his name begins with a capital N; he is Nature.

Gunkel and the Form-Criticism "School"

At the turn of this century, a German scholar, Hermann Gunkel, decided that the JEDP theory did not go far enough into the history of how the Pentateuch was composed. This belief was, in part, the result of archaeological discoveries of ancient Babylonian inscriptions, and the new science of history of religions, which stressed oral tradition. Instead of talking so much about "documents," Gunkel sought to search out ancient literary types and forms in the biblical text. He tried to identify the oldest types and all later variations. He believed that this method would yield a more reliable history of the Hebrew people than either the Bible or the JEDP theory could provide. Gunkel's view did not gain popularity in Germany until after World War I, and in England and America not until after World War II. By and large, this new form-critical method has blended with other newer types of Western philosophy than that of Hegel, preferring positivism over other views.

The System of Thought Called Existentialism

Somewhat as in the case of the Bible, one has to stretch the phrase "system of thought" a bit to apply it to existentialism. Precisely speaking, existentialism is not a philosophy, though it is a way of understanding human life. It, too, has its roots in some aspects of Greek thinking and had an able exponent in the Dane, Soren Kierkegaard, early in the nineteenth century. But it was not until the defeat of Germany at the end of World War I that existentialism began to have appeal among German scholars. Hegel's views were no longer popular, and the agonies of defeat seemed to parallel existentialism's concern to take suffering, alienation, despair, and death seriously. The German author Martin Heidegger gave prestige to the existentialist view of life, and it has profoundly affected Western thinking during the past several decades.

In a true sense, existentialism does not have a world view of reality, though it has been much more friendly with positivism than with idealism. For the existentialist, true reality is found in man's inner consciousness, which is ever changing. Hence, reality is pluralistic, for there are many human beings. The will to choose is an essential aspect of reality.

Personal, individualistic consciousness provides unity for each man. Existentialism has found it difficult to look at the universe or society in terms of unity.

The existentialist regards the mind as the means by which nature is utilized for human benefit. This is much like the positivists' understanding of the mind's function, but there is a difference. The existentialist has limited appreciation for a so-called "objectivity" in nature; he is much more interested in what man understands nature to be. Factuality, then, is man's inner estimate of the world out there, and this estimate may differ from person to person.

200

What is development? It is a movement from unauthentic existence to authentic existence, a decisive turning away from falsity to that which is truly human. Man is caught in a nasty predicament in life; but by choosing to be himself, he can be an absolutely free man. Man is an animal with an awesome power to choose, to make a decision. And man is the creator of his own freedom, his own laws, and his own self-projection. That is what man is supposed to do, and his higher achievement is an authentic existence in total freedom by means of a will to opt for the highest and best. Nothing is superior to a free man.

The matrix of uniqueness is the inner self of intuition, or self-knowledge. Man has within himself the capacity to project himself creatively, to constitute himself as a new, free man.

The Neo-Orthodox Approach

Germany's defeat in World War I was fatal for the credibility of Hegel's philosophy of history in the eyes of German scholars. The demise of Hegel's popularity had far-reaching effects on biblical studies in that country. Because the Wellhausen view was closely allied with the Hegelian dialectic, it became suspect, and German biblical scholars searched for a new base. A new interest in Kant and the rise of Barthian theology and existentialism created a variety of new points of view, which often have been grouped under the catch-all label *neo-orthodox.*

This point of view is more thoroughly a revolt against objective authority than liberalism, for it rejects the pope, the Scriptures, or any system of logic as ultimately authoritative. It tends to center authority in personal encounter with reality and one's response to it.

Since scholars in this viewpoint tend to be individualistic, attitudes range across the spectrum from positive to strongly negative toward the Bible. Neo-orthodox scholars have been selective as to values in the text.

There has been a renewal of interest in some kind of unity in the Scriptures, yet little agreement as to the real nature of that unity. Like the liberals, the neo-orthodox scholars have been more problem-conscious than solution-conscious.

The form-critical method gained wide acceptance among neo-orthodox scholars, though the older JEDP symbols have been retained. The history-of-religions approach has been popular as well as archaeology, though some are more interested in a typological method in biblical theology.

The world view of these scholars tends to be dualistic; that is, they separate the inner realm of thought and experience from the outer world of fact. Almost all are humanistic. Hence, their biblical theology is experience-centered and is not affected seriously by historical study.

Those whose special interest is the Old Testament stress the point that its content is relevant only as it relates to present-day needs. This concern for relevance thus has become the basic key that unlocks the real values of the Old Testament for us today.

The Heilsgeschichte (Salvation History) View

Heilsgeschichte is a term often used by nineteenth-century evangelicals for what we would call God's plan for salvation. After World War I, the term was taken up by German scholars who had become disillusioned with Hegelian dialectics. They joined it with a modified Kantian distinction between *noumena,* the idea realm, and *phenomena,* the factual realm. They applied to noumena the term *Geschichte* (i.e., inner, personal happenings) and to the realm of phenomena they utilized the term *Historie* (which refers to outer, factual data). Therefore, this view has a built-in split between the inner and the outer aspects of man's life.

This view understands that God encounters man in his inner being but does not speak to him intelligibly. God does act in human affairs of epochal dimensions, but man is left to build inferences as to the meaning of these acts. The sum of all human inferences is revelation. The Exodus is the favorite event for study of these scholars, and generations of Hebrew religious communities are the favorite matrix for the inference built up concerning the meaning of the Exodus. Factual data are of interest to scientists, but not to the biblical theologian. A popular slogan is that revelation comes to us in history. As a result, the scholar is faced with two versions of Hebrew history, the one produced by secular historical studies and the one produced by the *Heilsgeschichte* scholars with the help of form-criticism.

Demythologizing the Scripture

Although existentialism has had most of its impact on New Testament studies under the leadership of Rudolf Bultmann, it has influenced Old Testament studies to some extent.

Bultmann wanted to make the Bible relevant to modern thought and in the process relied heavily on Heidegger's thought and on the naturalism of logical positivism. The term *demythologizing* is associated with this view. Bultmann held that the world view of the Bible must be torn away and the basic existential meaning of the Bible be put in modern ways of understanding the nature of man. He stripped away all historicity from the Gospels except that there was a man called Jesus of Nazareth who died on a cross. All else is the result of what the believing community later built up in its thinking about this man Jesus.

Because Bultmann maintained a low view of the Old Testament's value, he has not been popular among Old Testament scholars. An illustration of what Bultmann's theory could do to the Old Testament is

202

seen in an article by E. L. Allen.[1] Using Bultmann's methods, Allen has decided that the following would have to be removed from serious consideration by modern man: (a) the concept of Israel's election by God as a chosen people, for it is too nationalistic, too racist; (b) the concept of a personal, jealous God, for it is inappropriate to employ personal terms for God's attitudes toward us, though we may use personal terms for our attitudes toward Him; (c) the concept that God is active in history is incorrect, for it ties moral retribution with history; (d) the concept of an end to history is misleading, for the Old Testament writers have presented history as though it were prophecy; and (e) the idea of a resurrection of the dead, for it unrealistically regards death as transitory and the continuation of the body as more important, at least as important, as the continuation of the soul.

In a more moderate tone, J. M. Robinson has suggested that Heidegger's way of thinking has much to offer to Old Testament scholars.[2] Particularly stressed is Heidegger's focus on the wonder of being, that things are existent rather than nonexistent. Robinson holds that this awareness is "inherent in the biblical concept of Creation." It is also present in the marvel that Israel is a nation at all; that is, the Hebrews understood their nation to be the result of God's act. Robinson feels this kind of approach moves the Old Testament away from an out-of-date, other-worldly use in devotion and worship to a new appreciation of the down-to-earthness of the Old Testament.

The correlation of these several systems of thought with various theories about how the Old Testament came to be and what it means for us today is not easy. But knowing that these views continue to have impact on the molding of theories about the significance of the Old Testament should aid one to analyze and evaluate what men have said and continue to say about this portion of the Bible.

---

1. E. L. Allen, "On Demythologizing the Old Testament," *Journal of Biblical Literature* 22 (1954): 236-241.
2. J. M. Robinson, "The Historicality of Biblical Language," *The Old Testament and Christian Faith,* ed. B. W. Anderson (New York: Herder & Herder, 1963), pp. 124-156.

Suggested Books for Further Reading

Braaten, C. E. *History and Hermeneutics.* Philadelphia: The Westminster Press, 1966.

Castell, A. *An Introduction to Modern Philosophy.* New York: The Macmillan Co., 1963.

Clements, R. C. *A Century of Old Testament Study.* London: Guildford and London, 1976.

Cohon, S. S. *Judaism: A Way of Life.* New York: Schocken Books, 1948.

Hahn, H. F. *The Old Testament in Modern Research.* Philadelphia: Fortress Press, 1954.

Hegel, G. W. F. *On Art, Religion, Philosophy.* New York: Harper Torchbooks, 1970.

Kauffman, W. *Hegel.* Garden City: Doubleday & Co., 1965.

Kraeling, G. *The Old Testament Since the Reformation.* New York: Lutterworth, 1969.

Langan, T. *The Meaning of Heidegger.* New York: Columbia University Press, 1961.

Moore, G. F. *Judaism.* Cambridge: Harvard University Press, 1930.

Mounier, E. *Existentialist Philosophies*. New York: The Macmillan Co., 1949.

Payne, J. B. *New Perspectives on the Old Testament*. Waco, Texas: Word Books, 1970.

Rad, G. von. *The Theology of Israel's Historical Traditions*. New York: Harper & Row, Publishers, 1942.

Robinson, H. W. *Redemption and Revelation*. New York: Harper & Bros., 1942.

Rowley, H. H. *The Old Testament and Modern Study*. New York: Oxford University Press, 1961.

Royce, J. *Lectures on Modern Idealism*. New Haven: Yale University Press, 1964.

Ruler, A.A. van. *The Christian Church and the Old Testament*. Grand Rapids: William B. Eerdmans Pub. Co., 1971.

Spier, J. M. *Christianity and Existentialism*. Philadelphia: Presbyterian and Reformed Publishing Co., 1953.

Tenney, M. C. *The Bible: The Living Word of Revelation*. Grand Rapids: Zondervan Publishing House, 1968.

Wright, G. E. *God Who Acts*. London: SCM Press, 1952.

The white cupola of the Shrine of the Scrolls in Jerusalem. This museum is the primary repository for the recovered Dead Sea Scrolls.

9

The Manuscripts
and Mosaic Authorship

From a consideration of general background for the Pentateuch in the ancient Near East, we turn now to matters more closely associated with higher criticism. The aims of this chapter are to examine the actual manuscripts that have come to us bearing the books of the Pentateuch and the rest of the Old Testament—to ascertain what Mosaic authorship has meant to the Hebrew people, to Judaism, and to the Christian church through the ages; to trace the history of controversy through the past two centuries that involve a rejection of Mosaic authorship; to examine the methods and results of literary criticism of the biblical text; to do the same with the more recent methods of form-criticism, redaction criticism, and other modifications that bear on Mosaic authorship; to evaluate the views of recent exponents of Mosaic authorship; and to summarize the evidence and arguments that bear upon Mosaic authorship.

Mesopotamia, Egypt, and the upper Levant have documents that go back to the beginning of the third millennium B.C. Anatolia has documents from the second millennium B.C. Palestine has only fragments of short inscriptions from the second millennium and the first part of the first millennium B.C., due to use of papyrus and leather as a common medium for writing. Less than a dozen Hebrew inscriptions of any length come from the Hebrew kingdom period and these are all nonbiblical. Before A.D. 1947, the oldest Hebrew manuscripts of the Old Testament did not date back before the sixth or seventh centuries A.D., with the exception of the fragment called the Nash Papyrus, which is dated about 100 B.C. The oldest Greek translations of the Old Testament did not date before the second century A.D., and the best ones were from the fourth century A.D.

The lateness of these manuscripts and the long span of time during which copies had to be made created questions in the mind of many concerning the actual date that the Pentateuch was written in its present form.

The manuscripts known before A.D. 1947 were of two types: scrolls and codices. Scrolls of parchment, or vellum, were restricted to the books of the Pentateuch and the Megilloth, or Five Scrolls: The Song of Solomon, Ruth, Ecclesiastes, Esther, and Lamentations. These scrolls were used in the worship services of the synagogue and are unpointed, i.e., they do not have special vowel markings. The codex is our book form, which was invented in the first century A.D. and became popular among Christians. Jews also adopted this form, and many of the Old Testament manuscripts of the Middle Ages are codices, which were popular for private study purposes. Most manuscripts of this type are pointed (i.e., have special markings for vowels).

The oldest manuscripts of the Middle Ages were found in the genizah of an old synagogue in Cairo, Egypt in A.D. 1890. A genizah is a storage room related to a synagogue in which worn out, defective, or Apocryphal manuscripts are stored until they are destroyed collectively by burial. The contents of the Cairo genizah had not been buried and the manuscripts in it were found to date to approximately the sixth or seventh centuries A.D. The most important manuscript, however, is not of the Pentateuch, but is Codex Cairensis made up of the Prophets and written in A.D. 895 by Moshe ben Asher. Also in this collection is Codex Petropolitanus of the Prophets, dated A.D. 916. Of about the same date, but not from the Cairo genizah, is a codex of the Pentateuch in the British Museum and labeled Or. 4445. A more important codex of the entire Old Testament, dated in the early tenth century A.D., is the Aleppo Codex. It had been kept in a synagogue in Aleppo, Syria, until 1948 and was presumed lost in the destruction of the synagogue. Fortunately, it had been rescued and smuggled into Israel where it is now in safekeeping. This is considered the best manuscript produced in the Middle Ages.

A Russian Jew, Abraham Firkowitsch, made trips through the Near East and gathered a large number of manuscripts, which he deposited in Leningrad in 1863 and in 1876. The most important of these manuscripts is called Codex Leningradensis, or B19a. It is definitely dated to A.D. 1008 and contains the entire Old Testament. Thus it is the oldest dated Hebrew Bible in existence. The last several editions of the standard printed Hebrew Bible are based on this manuscript; this Bible is called Kittel's *Biblia Hebraica,* and each page has a critical apparatus at the bottom. Actually, the first printed Hebrew manuscript was the Psalter; it came off the press in A.D. 1477. The first printed Pentateuch dates to 1482, and soon afterwards, 1488, the entire Old Testament came off the press.

The Work of the Masoretes at Tiberias

For centuries it was normal for Hebrew manuscripts to be written with consonants only, as was true also of Phoenician and Aramaic inscriptions. The manuscripts and fragments from the Cairo genizah and among the Firkowitsch collection reveal that along with these consonantal texts there arose efforts to indicate vowel sounds as well. This procedure affected private copies, never the synagogue scrolls. The small signs that represented vowels were gradually added to consonantal texts about the sixth or seventh century A.D. Previously, vowel sounds were transmitted by memory from teacher to pupil. This method was not difficult while Hebrew was a spoken language, but variants in traditions of how to pronounce the consonantal text arose as the Jews were scattered far and wide and different native languages became their means of speech. The introduction of vowel and accent markings sought to stabilize pronunciation and became known as the vocalic, or spoken, text.

The manuscripts of the Cairo genizah have witnessed to a Babylonian type of vocalization, or pointing. Fragments from the seventh and eighth centuries A.D. show that six vowel marks were placed above the consonantal line. In the eighth and ninth centuries, a more complicated system of four abbreviated consonants and two other signs were placed above the line of consonants. These manuscripts also had specimens of a Palestinian type, which had eight vowel signs placed above the line and dots employed for showing accents of words. A faction of orthodox Jewish scribes called Qaraites (Karaites) seemed to be largely responsible for this development.

During the eighth and ninth centuries, Jewish scholarship became concentrated at schools in Tiberias, on the west bank of the Sea of Galilee. The scribes at this school became known as Masoretes because they placed marginal notes on the pages of the text. These notes were called *Masora,* hence the title "Masoretes" designates the tendency of these scribes to adhere closely to tradition. The Masoretes felt dedicated to preserve the traditional text with all possible care. They studied many old manuscripts and made an up-to-date recension, which is known as the Masoretic text. This is the text that has been preserved in the West. The Masoretes found the Palestinian method of indicating vowels and accents inadequate, so they devised a carefully fashioned system of dots, dashes, and other markings which are called "points," which appear in printed Hebrew Bibles today. The vowel points are made up of seven signs grouped in combinations and placed either in, under, or above the consonants. There are thirty-two accent marks.

The most prominent scribes of the Masoretic school were of the family of ben Asher, and so important were their contributions that the Masoretic text is sometimes called the ben Asher texts. The Codex Cairensis, the Aleppo Codex, the Codex Leningradensis were all produced by the ben Asher family.

The Samaritan Pentateuch

At the fall of the city of Samaria and thus the end of the northern kingdom of Israel, in 722/21 B.C., the Assyrians deported many Israelites to the Mesopotamian valley and imported other captured people, who were pagan, into the hill country of Samaria to prevent revolts (cf. II Kings 17:24; Ezra 4:2, 9, 10). A hybrid people developed who mixed both Israelite and pagan theology and practice. When Jews returned from Babylon after the Exile, they refused to unite with this mixed Samaritan community. A schism took place between the Jews and the Samaritans during the fifth century B.C.

When the Greeks invaded Palestine in 332 B.C., the Samaritans sought and obtained permission from the Greeks to build a temple on Mount Gerizim. This temple was later destroyed and replaced with a Roman temple, but the Samaritans have observed their sacred festivals, including the Passover, on Mount Gerizim ever since.

A small building of worship exists today at Nablus, and only a few hundred Samaritans still live in Palestine. This community has preserved copies of the Pentateuch in a script only slightly different from the old Hebrew characters. The text is in the Hebrew language, however.

The Samaritans changed the text of the Pentateuch at several points, the most famous of which is Deuteronomy 27:4. Here Mount Ebal is replaced with Mount Gerizim as the place where the law was to be inscribed on a plastered stone and an altar of stones was to be erected. They also inserted a statement after Exodus 20:17 that a sanctuary was to be built on Mount Gerizim. In all, the Samaritan Pentateuch has about six thousand variants, about nineteen hundred of which agree with the LXX (the Septuagint). Extant copies appear to date about A.D. 1100.

At least two copies of the Pentateuch are at the sanctuary at Nablus, but the first Samaritan copy to come to Europe was imported in A.D. 1616 and published in 1632. More copies are now available. Recently the Samaritan community at Nablus has allowed one of its copies to be photographed page by page.

Early Translations of the Hebrew Old Testament

Other old manuscripts of the Old Testament are translations from the Hebrew text. The earliest translation was the Pentateuch into the Greek language about 250 B.C. The remainder of the Old Testament was rendered into Greek during the next century. This translation is known as the *Septuagint,* or by the symbol LXX. Three later translations or revisions of the LXX are known. One was by Aquilla, who produced his work about A.D. 130. Fifty years later, Theodotion came out with his Greek version, and about the same time Symmachus made a free translation of the Hebrew into the Greek. All three of these translations were incorporated by Origen in his *Hexapla,* which was completed about A.D. 245. The Hexapla had six parallel columns: one was the Hebrew text, one a transcription of the Hebrew into Greek letters, and four different versions of the LXX were in the other columns.

Two recensions of the Septuagint were produced. One was by Hesychius in Egypt about A.D. 250 and the other by Lucian in Antioch, Syria, about A.D. 300.

The oldest LXX manuscripts that were available before 1947 are fragments of the John Rylands papyri, mostly of Deuteronomy and dating to the second century A.D.; portions of the Freer Greek Manuscripts at Washington, from the third century A.D.; the Berlin Genesis of the fourth century A.D.; and some of the Chester Beatty papyri from the early second century A.D. The most complete Septuagint manuscript is Codex Vaticanus, which dates to the middle of the fourth century A.D. and is the basic text of the present-day printed Septuagint. Codex Sinaiticus and Codex Alexandrinus also have portions of the Old Testament, and both came from the early part of the fifth century A.D.

The Hebrew text was translated into Aramaic and its official revision, called the *Pentateuch Targum,* was made by Onkelos about A.D. 125. The term *targum* means "translation," and the earliest targums seem to be Jewish in origin. Other targums are the Palestinian Targum, the Targum of Jonathan ben Uzziel, and the Targum Jerusalemi.

Another early translation was into the Syriac and is commonly called the *Peshitta,* meaning "simple." Its oldest extant manuscript is dated at A.D. 442, and is the oldest dated Bible in any language. In the fourth century, the Vatican commissioned Jerome to make an official Latin translation. He based his work on the Hebrew, the LXX, and Old Latin versions. The result was the Vulgate, for centuries the official Bible of the Roman Catholic Church. Jerome's Psalter is still in the Vatican Library.

The foregoing has dealt only with the most important manuscripts of the Hebrew Old Testament, most of which have all or parts of the Pentateuch. There are many other fragments and later specimens. Information about these can be found in encyclopedias, Bible dictionaries, and Old Testament introductions. Also see books listed at the end of the chapter.

The Qumran caves in the Judaean desert near the northwestern shore of the Dead Sea. Cave 4, marked by a circle in the photo, contained what seems to have been the bulk of the library of the Qumran community.

The Rich Treasure in the Dead Sea Scrolls

The Dead Sea Scrolls were discovered in a cave in a cliff high above the northwest corner of the Dead Sea. This event happened in 1947, but the find was not made known to the world until the spring of 1948.

Due to tensions between Arabs and Jews, an agent in Bethlehem found difficulty selling the scrolls but finally found two buyers. Six scrolls (including a portion of Isaiah [IQIsa.b], some Psalms, a tract called "War Between the Children of Light and of Darkness" [a scroll about a holy war], and some Thanksgiving Hymns) were sold to Dr. E. L. Sukenik of the Hebrew University. Other scrolls (including a complete scroll of Isaiah [IQIsa.a], the Manual of Discipline, a commentary on the Book of Habakkuk, and the Genesis Apocryphon) were sold to Saint Mark's Monastery in Jerusalem. All of these are now at the Shrine of the Book near the new Hebrew University of Jerusalem.

The scrolls at Saint Mark's Monastery were taken in February to the American School of Oriental Research in Jerusalem where they were photographed by Dr. John Trever and made known to the world in April 1948.

The cave from which the first scrolls were taken was located and excavated in the winter of 1949. It was situated high on a cliff above the ruins of an ancient village called Khirbet Qumran. Fragments of over seventy

Inside view of the Dome of the Shrine, with the cylinder containing the Book of Isaiah from Qumran, Cave 1. The Shrine of the Scrolls is on the campus of the Hebrew University.

more manuscripts were found in the cave, along with pottery fragments.

In November 1951, Arabs found some more manuscripts in caves at Wadi Murabba'at in the highlands about twelve miles southwest of Qumran. Official excavation of these caves has brought to light the oldest sample of writing on papyrus outside of Egypt; it is in proto-Hebrew, with an earlier erased inscription dating to the eighth century B.C. and the super-inscribed text dating from the sixth century B.C. (nonbiblical), a good manuscript of the Minor Prophets from the second century B.C., and many other manuscripts from the first and second centuries A.D., in Greek, in Aramaic (many dated), in Hebrew, and an Arabic text of the tenth century A.D.

A section of the Isaiah scroll from Qumran.

The Qumran portion of the account of the War of the Sons of Light and the Sons of Darkness.

Intensive excavation of Khirbet Qumran, and a search for more scroll-yielding caves, took place in 1951, 1953, 1954, 1955, 1956, and intermittently since then. The Arab Bedouins were more successful than the archaeologists in finding caves. By February 1956, eleven caves were found close by Qumran. Many manuscript fragments were also excavated in these caves by archaeologists who followed the Arabs. The Arabs were paid $2.80 per square centimeter of inscribed surface for the fragments they turned over to the Jordanian government. To them the caves were virtually gold mines. A great number of these manuscripts and fragments have been published.

Excavation of Khirbet Qumran has revealed that its main occupation was from about 150 B.C. to A.D. 68, with a period of abandonment during the reign of Herod the Great (37–4 B.C.). The village had been destroyed by the Roman army. The inhabitants of the village have often been identi-

Two views of the exhibit of Dead Sea Scrolls housed in the Shrine of the Scrolls.

fied with a people known as the Essenes, an orthodox offshoot of Judaism. They were the ones who had studied, copied, and hidden the scrolls that have been found.

Of the caves that have yielded fragments of manuscripts, caves IV and XI have been the most prolific; about 380 manuscripts were represented in fragments from cave IV alone. One scholar, J.A. Sanders, has said that Genesis was represented by fifteen scrolls, Exodus by fifteen, Leviticus by eight, Numbers by six, and Deuteronomy by twenty-five manuscripts. Other popular books are Isaiah (nineteen manuscripts), Psalms (thirty manuscripts), the Minor Prophets by eight, and Daniel by nine.[1] All other books of the Old Testament are represented by at least one scroll, except Esther, which has not yet been found among the Dead Sea Scrolls. Ten manuscripts are written in proto-Hebrew, five are of the Pentateuch, and four manuscripts are of the Septuagint. The listing, however, was not complete.[2]

Beginning with 1953, manuscripts have been found at Khirbet Mird near Qumran. This was a Christian community, and it yielded manuscripts of papyrus and leather in Greek, Syriac, and Arabic, dating from A.D. 400-800. One manuscript is the Minor Prophets in Greek dating from the first century B.C.; it seems to be the prototype of later LXX recensions and is identical with one recension in Origen's Hexapla.

Arabs found scroll fragments in a cave near En Gedi in 1958, and this sparked a series of searches in the area between En Gedi and Masada during 1960 and 1961. A number of manuscripts written on papyrus, leather, and wood and in the Greek, Hebrew, and Aramaic languages were recovered from caves. They date from A.D. 88-132 and belonged to Jews who died in the Second Revolt against the Romans. In 1964, while excavating Masada, Israeli archaeologists found three papyrus manuscripts that included Psalms 81-85, five chapters from a first century B.C. scroll of Ecclesiasticus, and a scroll called "Songs of Sabbath Sacrifice."

During the spring of 1962, Arab Bedouins found about forty Samaritan manuscripts made of papyrus at a large cave at Daliyah about nine miles north of Jericho. After the Six Day War of 1967, Dr. Y. Yadin of the Hebrew University recovered from a merchant in Bethlehem a leather scroll about twenty-eight feet in length. He has called it "The Temple Scroll."[3]

---

1. J. A. Sanders, "The Dead Sea Scrolls: A Quarter Century of Study," *Biblical Archaeologist* 36 (1973): 110-143.
2. P. W. Skehan, "The Biblical Scrolls from Qumran and the Text of the Old Testament," *Biblical Archaeologist* 28 (1965): 87-100.
3. Y. Yadin, "The Temple Scroll," *Biblical Archaeologist* 30 (1967): 135-139.

This copper scroll, discovered in Cave 3, was sawed into strips at the University of Manchester, England, and published. It contained a puzzling report of hidden treasure, the authenticity of which is doubted by most scholars.

The Significance of the Dead Sea Scrolls

About a quarter of the total manuscripts are of Old Testament books in Hebrew, Greek, and Syriac and are at least one thousand years older than previously known Hebrew texts that can be definitely dated. The texts of the Dead Sea Scrolls indicate that four basic families of Hebrew texts are represented, namely, (a) the standard Masoretic Text, (b) the Septuagint of Alexandria, (c) the Samaritan Pentateuch, and (d) independent Qumran specimens. The discipline of textual criticism must now wrestle with the witness of each of these families to search for an archetype text for the various books of the Pentateuch and the rest of the Old Testament.

The Dead Sea Scrolls throw important new light upon the transmission of the Old Testament books, both before and after the time of Christ. Since the oldest manuscripts of the third and second centuries B.C. indicate text types that lie behind the standard Hebrew Bible called the Masoretic Text, the LXX, and the Samaritan Pentateuch, it seems highly probable now that Ezra of the fifth century B.C. had a great deal to do with a recension of the text. In a general way, this view has been held by traditional scholars for centuries. Ezra has been long regarded as the "father" of the scribes who are mentioned in the New Testament and who were prominent until about A.D. 200.

218

It would seem that sometime during the Exile, the proto-Hebrew letters were exchanged for the more nearly square Aramaic letters, and that Ezra, or someone closely associated with him, popularized in Palestine this new character form. That the older form of writing continued into the third century and became somewhat popular during the Maccabean period seems well supported by the Dead Sea Scrolls. Other manuscripts had been preserved in Egypt and became the basis for the translation into the Septuagint. During this same period, the Samaritans had become isolated and retained their own text type.

Because the Christians made effective use of the LXX in the first century A.D., it would seem that the main core of Judaism in Palestine reacted against the LXX and made a serious effort to establish a semiofficial Hebrew text. The matter cannot be settled for certain, but Rabbi Akiba, who died in A.D. 135, is generally credited with completing this project. The text he had brought through a process of recension, is now held to be basically the Masoretic Text of the Middle Ages.

In summary, schools of thought that either downgraded the Masoretic Text or the LXX of the Samaritan Pentateuch have faded away. There is now a healthy respect for each of these text types, and a new day of serious textual criticism of the Old Testament has dawned.

Writing tables and bench, excavated from the Scriptorium at Qumran.

The Dead Sea Scrolls bear witness to a history of letter forms of Hebrew from B.C. 200 to about A.D. 600 and of Greek from about 100 B.C. to A.D. 800. Many of the scrolls reveal early usage of certain consonants to serve as indicators of long vowels. The LXX scrolls, which transliterate Hebrew names, provide valuable insights as to the pronunciation of Hebrew during this period of time.

The nonbiblical scrolls throw revealing light on Jewish thought immediately before and during the New Testament era. As a result, the date of John's Gospel has been pulled back to the first century A.D., and it is seen as Jewish rather than Greek in thought. Paul's thought is also now regarded as basically Jewish rather than Greek.

The Oldest Specimens of the Biblical Text

During three seasons (1975–1980) of excavating ancient structures, mostly burial caves, a number of artifacts of the final years of the First Temple period were recovered from debris on a site next to the St. Andrew's Church of Scotland, which is located on the west side of the bend of the Hinnom Valley. Several generations of the same family were buried in tombs on this site, all of which but one had been plundered. In the untouched tomb (number 25), an array of items belonging to the dead were found. Among these items were two thin silver plaques that had been rolled up. When they were unrolled, one measured 97 x 27 mm, the other, 39 x 11 mm; each was an inscription in the ancient Hebrew script.

The script was difficult to decipher because the silver is thin, with cracks and missing portions. The letters had not been pressed into the silver with force, so in many instances they are faint or indistinct.

The larger of these two silver sheets has seventeen lines with ninety-three letters, of which seventy-one have been identified. The smaller sheet is incomplete and probably was originally the same as the larger one, but it can be only partially deciphered. The conclusion reached by Israeli scholars is that the biblical text of these plaques is that of Numbers 6:24–26, often called the Priestly Benediction.

The silver sheets and their inscriptions have been dated to approximately 650 B.C., which makes them the oldest portions of Scripture yet discovered.

The Traditional Meaning of Mosaic Authorship

The first five books of the Old Testament have been known as the "Pentateuch" at least since the time of Origen. The title is a compound of two Greek words, *pente,* five, and *teuche,* scroll. In the Old Testament itself, these books were known as "the law of Moses" (cf. I Kings 2:3; II Kings 23:25; Mal. 4:4), "the book of the Law of Moses" (cf. Josh. 8:31; 23:6; II Kings 14:6; Neh. 8:1), "the book of the Law" (cf. Josh. 8:34), or "the book of Moses" (cf. II Chron. 25:4; 35:12). Many have assumed that these terms include all five of the books of the Pentateuch, but this assumption is not necessarily correct. Later, as in the preface to Ecclesiasticus or in Luke 10:26; it is simply called the "Torah" or *nomos,* both meaning law. In Judaism, Torah is a common title for the first five books. In recent years, some Protestant scholars speak of a Hexateuch, i.e., the first six books of the Old Testament, or a Tetrateuch, the first four books.

A limited number of statements attribute some portions of the Pentateuch directly to Moses (see Exod. 17:14; 24:4-8; 34:27; Num. 32:2; Deut. 29:21; 31:9, 22, 24). Constantly in Exodus, Leviticus, and Numbers, however, the text declares that God revealed much of the content directly to Moses, and in a few instances to both Moses and Aaron. The Book of Deuteronomy, except chapter 34, repeatedly is presented as words of Moses to the people of Israel. There is no explicit statement whether Moses himself wrote these oracles and sermons, whether scribes under his direction wrote these portions, or whether this content was transmitted for a period of time orally and then written down at a later date. The text of the Book of Genesis nowhere states that Moses wrote it; the title in many English Bibles, "The First Book of Moses," was first employed by Martin Luther in his German translation. The statement was not Luther's invention, but represented a belief of long standing.

The term "the book of Moses," found in II Chronicles 25:4; 35:12; Ezra 3:2; 6:18; and Nehemiah 8:1; 13:1, surely included the Book of Genesis and also testifies to a belief in Israelite circles in the fifth century B.C. that all five of the books were the work of Moses. Ben Sira (Ecclus. 24:23), Philo, Josephus, and authors of the Gospels held that Moses was intimately related to the Pentateuch. Philo and Josephus even explicitly said that Moses wrote Deuteronomy 34:5-12. Other writers of the New Testament tie the Pentateuch to Moses. The Jewish Talmud asserts that whoever denied Mosaic authorship would be excluded from Paradise. Christians of the early centuries after Christ were not that strong in their statements, but the vast majority of them believed that Moses was the author of the Pentateuch, including Genesis. This view continued in Judaism and in Christianity until the nineteenth century A.D. with few exceptions.

There have been a few scholars in the traditional view of Mosaic authorship who have held that Moses wrote or dictated every word in the Pentateuch. Note Philo's and Josephus's claims that Moses wrote Deuteronomy 34. This view would resist any idea that later additions or interpolations entered the text after the time of Moses. Some scholars have held that Moses did not have sources from which he gained information found

221

in the Book of Genesis; rather, it is held that God revealed the content of Genesis directly to Moses while he was on Mount Sinai.

By far the greater number of recent traditional scholars are not so rigid. References in the Pentateuch that Moses wrote some parts of it are held as valid, and the statements in the Pentateuch that God revealed to Moses the content of large portions of Exodus, Leviticus, and Numbers, and that Moses delivered the orations in Deuteronomy are also accepted. However, allowance is made for Moses to supervise the work of scribes who did the actual recording, accounting for some of the differences of style in the text. Even a period of oral transmission is allowed by some, so long as it is recognized that the content was regarded as sacred and therefore not open to the free additions common to folklore or campfire tales. The oral transmission would, then, not last beyond the beginning of the time of David or Solomon. It is quite common for traditional scholars to recognize that Moses had sources before him as he composed the final form of the Book of Genesis. Nor are later additions to the text ruled out, with the understanding that there must be solid textual evidence for these additions.

The practice of textual criticism in New Testament manuscripts has shown that later additions may happen during the process of copying texts and that these additions do not in themselves determine the authorship of a particular book. Hence, the process could, and probably did, happen during the centuries of transmitting the text of the Pentateuch. The presence of post-Mosaic additions do not in themselves determine the authorship of the five books of the Pentateuch.

Since the Middle Ages, and especially during the first part of the twentieth century A.D., portions of the following verses were the center of argument—whether or not they were late additions and whether or not they denied Mosaic authorship. These verses are: Genesis 12:6b; 13:7b; 13:18; 14:14; 22:14; 23:19b; 36:31; 49:5-7; Exodus 6:26, 27; 16:33-35, 36; Numbers 4:3; 12:3; 13:16; 21:14; 24:7; Deuteronomy 1:1; 2:4-7; 2:26-30; 3:14-17; 10:6, 7; 32:7-12, 13-20; 34. Their relationship to Mosaic authorship has properly faded out of discussion. Other so-called additions have been proposed, but these should be ascertained on the basis of solid principles of textual criticism and not be paramount in evaluating the problem of Mosaic authorship.

Challenges to Mosaic Authorship

This section could take on an appearance somewhat like a telephone directory, with many names and dry statistics. The thrust will rather be in the direction of summarizing the major tenets of views that have denied

Mosaic authorship. The intent of the discussion is to provide a history of thinking that lies behind present-day Old Testament scholarship.

Pre-Nineteenth Century Views

Before the nineteenth century, those challenging the validity of Mosaic authorship were few in number, but some important voices have been involved.

Jerome had a difficult time deciding whether Moses or Ezra had written the Pentateuch; sects like the ancient Nazarenes and the Gnostics denied Mosaic authorship altogether. There was objection to anthropomorphisms and to ethical practices that seemed to be sub-Christian, to stylistic differences, and to apparent contradictions. A few such as Ibn Ezra of the twelfth century, began to see the force of the post-Mosaic additions; and Carlstadt, a rival of Luther, held that since Moses could not have written Deuteronomy 34, therefore Moses was not the author of the rest of the Pentateuch. A few Roman Catholic writers, such as Masius, preferred Ezra as the author instead of Moses.

Two philosophers, Thomas Hobbes and Spinoza, raised doubts about direct Mosaic authorship and opted for later writers, Ezra again being prominent among the possibilities. A daring suggestion for the seventeenth century was advanced by Vitringa, who asserted that Moses had before him ancient scrolls from which he selected materials. A century later, a French physician was to propose the same idea, although neither man had any direct knowledge of ancient Near Eastern literature. This physician, Jean Astruc, firmly believed in Mosaic authorship, but he held that there was evidence for several different sources that were older than Moses. He noted that two different names, *Elohim* (translated into English as "God") and Jehovah, appeared separately in stories in Genesis and only occasionally together. He put all passages with Elohim in a source labeled A, and passages with Jehovah he labeled as B. In addition, he identified ten other fragmentary sources. Astruc thought that Moses had set these sources in four parallel columns, but later editors had combined them into our present Genesis. Astruc published his views in A.D. 1753, but they did not gain acceptance in France itself.

Astruc's two-document theory was snatched up and made popular by a German scholar, Eichhorn, at the University of Jena. He took his symbols for the two documents directly from the divine names and suggested a J document and an E document, plus several smaller sources. Besides using divine names as a guide, Eichhorn added criteria of style and thought content; he differed from Astruc in that he soon gave up Mosaic authorship. Some have acclaimed him as the "Father of Higher Criticism." His views were more successful than Astruc's theory, because he had a pupil and successor, Ilgen, who developed the criteria for recognizing sources further. The E document was seen to be two instead of one, and the J document was suspected of being twins, also.

Nineteenth-Century Theories

Once the method of identifying documents caught fire in the German universities, a great deal of earnest effort was poured into the task of unraveling the puzzle of authorship and date of various sections of the Pentateuch. The nineteenth century was marked by a series of theories before one was settled on as the most reasonable explanation. The following are a few of these views.

The Fragmentation Theory. As noted above, the two-document theory began to break down as more and more criteria were utilized in the search for sources in the Pentateuch. An English Roman Catholic priest, A. Geddes, published a book in 1800 in which he rejected the two-document theory in favor of a group of fragments. Both Eichhorn and Ilgen had found that the law sections were the most difficult to analyze, for they had no ancient Near Eastern law codes or legal tablets to aid them. It was a study of the laws that caused Geddes and a German professor by the name of J. S. Vater to propose independent fragments of material that in the time of Solomon or later, were knit together by a redactor (i.e., editor). The symbols J and E were retained, but not the concept of documents. Vater even found a total of thirty-eight fragments. Geddes popularized the concept of a Hexateuch.

Another German scholar, W. de Wette, was won to this view and is famous for proposing the idea that Deuteronomy was produced in the seventh century and was made the law of the land in Josiah's reform in 621 B.C. (II Kings 22-23). W. de Wette began to have doubts about the cogency of the fragmentary theory, for the procedure was a disintegrating process and contradicted the fairly well-organized character of the books of the Pentateuch. Many others were deeply dissatisfied, for the theory denied the historicity of the Mosaic material and spread it over a span of at least three centuries, during the Hebrew kingdom period.

The Supplemental Theory. Influenced by de Wette's more mature thinking, a young German scholar by the name of H. Ewald declared in 1823 that there was one basic core document in the Pentateuch, the E document. To this basic account, the J items were added, and a redactor/s of the same frame of thought put the Pentateuch into its present form. Others accepted this theory, but twenty years later Ewald abandoned it.

The Crystallization Theory. The criteria of analysis that had been devised during the first half of the century had the prestige of being scientific, but their tendency to divide and classify small units of literature ran counter to concepts of unity of the whole. Ewald was so impressed with the precision of source analysis he gave up his basic E document and proposed another view, which combined elements of the older documentary and the supplementary hypotheses. He wrote a book, *History of Israel,* in the 1840s, in which he suggested that there were two E sources. One was made up of annals and originated during David's reign; the other was more theological and was joined to the first one during the divided kingdom. A third source, J, was concerned with Mosaic history and dated from the eighth century. A fourth narrator was prophetic in attitude; the fifth in the J tradition, was an editor who fused or crystallized all of the strands into one body of literature during the sixth century B.C. Some preferred an exilic date for this crystallization activity.

The Modified Document Theory. The champions of unity were not quieted; somehow the cohesiveness of the present books had to have a better explanation. In the 1850s Hermann Hupfeld promulgated a core J document rather than a fragmented group of J items, and E was two documents rather than one, a view already popular. He also proposed that Deuteronomy was a separate D document, thus making four basic documents: E^1, E^2, J, and D. Above these four, J towered as the dominant document. Hupfeld made much of a fifth factor in Pentateuchal criticism— the redactor or editor. In Genesis, for instance, all items that could not be fitted into E^1 (later known as P), or into E^2, or into J, were ascribed to a redactor who probably lived in the late exilic period. The order of the documents listed above was also the sequence of chronology for them. Thus, E^1 came from David's reign, E^2 and J from the divided kingdom period, and D from Josiah's reform in 621 B.C.

The Developmental or JEDP Theory

In the 1860s, it was rapidly becoming apparent that a basic dilemma was facing the scholars who denied Mosaic authorship of the Pentateuch. If the criteria of analysis were carried to logical conclusions, the Pentateuch fell apart into a mass of fragments with no adequate base for explaining the unity of the present books. If the structural unity of the books was maintained, there seemed to be little possibility of squaring the content of the Pentateuch with increasingly popular theories of growth and change within human history. If structural unity was rejected, there seemed to be no substitute to account for the cohesiveness of the community of Israel through the centuries. If a Torah was not present at the beginning of their nationhood, what had held Israel together?

Spasmodically, a few Old Testament scholars in Germany had suggested a philosophical base for unity in an understanding of Israel's history and literature. C. P. W. Gramberg, Wilhelm Vatke, and J. F. L. George made proposals that fell on deaf ears. Gramberg had stressed a line of development in the religious institutions of the Israelites; Vatke had said that law did not appear as the foundation of a state, but as the product of its long existence, hence, law portions in the Pentateuch, including Deuteronomy, were very late, even exilic. George set up three periods of Israelite history, a view strongly influenced by Hegelian philosophy. George said the Israelites went through preprophetic, prophetic, and hierarchical stages of development and that the content of the Pentateuch should be dated accordingly. As early as 1834, E. Reuss had advocated that E^1 was not the earliest book, but was later than even the J document. It was not until thirty years later that this idea caught on.

K. H. Graf, in 1866, finally gained the attention of his German colleagues and got the points across that law was exilic, if not postexilic in date, and that D was firmly grounded in Josiah's reform. About the same time, other scholars took a new look at E^1 and decided that it was a priestly document, and thereafter the symbol P became popular. An argument developed between German scholars concerning the dating sequence of the documents, so the order of the symbols became important. Should they be listed as PEJD, or JEDP?

Julius Wellhausen is the scholar generally credited with resolving the issue of dating sequence. Drawing heavily upon the implications of Hegel's postulates—thesis, antithesis, and synthesis in the processes of history—Wellhausen opted for the sequence JEDP. In his famous book, *Prolegomena to the History of Ancient Israel,* first published in 1878, Wellhausen argued so persuasively for his position that he won the day.[4] His theory became standard in Old Testament liberal circles for more than half a century and still is a powerful voice.

LITERARY CRITICISM

The procedures of source analysis are often called literary criticism because the raw material of the study is literature itself and its characteristics. The goal of this section is to summarize the methods and results of

---

4. J. Wellhausen, *Prolegomena to the History of Ancient Israel* (New York: Meridian Books, 1957).

literary criticism and the major modifications that have changed the thrust of the method.

Its Criteria and Assumptions

From Astruc on, the criterion of two divine names, Elohim and Jehovah, has been elemental to analysis of the Pentateuch and the basis for three of the four documents. The sources E and P had the name *Elohim,* and J had *Jehovah;* each of these sources or documents had separate histories. The fact that the old West Semitic divine names *il* and *ya(w)* appear interchangeably on the Eblaite tablets practically destroys the significance of this criterion.

Another of the criteria centered on duplications and triplications of incidents. Genesis provides most of the examples. Note how different sources are related to each set listed: (a) Gen. 21:22-34 (E) and 26:26-33 (J) have to do with the naming of Beersheba; (b) Gen. 28:10-22 (J) and 35:13-15 (P) refer to the naming of Bethel; (c) Gen. 32:22-32 (J) and 35:10 (P) explain the change of Jacob's name to Israel; (d) Gen. 12:14-20 (J), 20:1-18 (E) and 26:1-11 (J) are stories of Abraham and Isaac lying about their wives; and (e) Gen. 16:4-14 (J) and 21:9-21 (E) tell us of Hagar's experiences in the desert. The argument is that more credibility is attached to seeing these as separate traditions of one incident in each case, than in understanding them as narrating incidents that were separate but alike.

A third criterion has to do with disagreements within or between narratives and laws. A few examples: (a) two creation stories, Genesis 1 and 2; (b) two accounts, J and P, blended in the story of the flood and evidenced by differences in dates, numbers, and order of animals; (c) contradictions in accounts about the tabernacle and about the spies; (d) disagreements between Exodus laws and Deuteronomic laws.

A fourth criterion is variety of style and vocabulary. Genealogies that belong to J are said to have different terms than those belonging to P. The narratives of J and E are much more lively than are those associated with P, in which prose is said to be dull and repetitious. Stories of J and E have their own distinctive words and phrases.

A fifth criterion has to do with concepts, particularly those that are basically religious and theological.

These criteria are said to be cumulative in force so that totally they demonstrate the correctness of the analysis and present adequate explanations for otherwise disturbing traits of the literature. A basic assumption was that methods of analyzing Western literature could, without modification, be applied to story forms coming from a distant past and from a totally different culture. No literary specimens were needed from that ancient past and from that different culture, other than that which is in the Pentateuch, to check the rightness of the theory.

The Stylistic Traits of the Documents

The fourth and fifth criteria mentioned above need to be expanded, for they tend to gather to themselves the force of other criteria and, in a measure, intersect each other. Early in the task of analyzing the sources of Genesis, it was realized that there is a dry, formal style with repetitious phrasing in Genesis 1, in some of the genealogies, and in the cultic laws of Leviticus. Also, there are many lively stories composed in a simple, direct manner, which denote a superb storyteller. In both, the divine name *Elohim,* or "God" in English, is predominant. Likewise, there are many stories loaded with vivid action that possess the divine name *Yahweh* (Jehovah), or in most English Bibles, LORD, as its usual term. In Deuteronomy there is a rhetorical, hortatory style with a group of repeated phrases.

Some analysts have gone so far they have claimed that these styles may lie in closely associated verses and that there are different expressions that belong to each style. Some verses have even been broken into bits and distributed between sources.

In this procedure, style and theological concept are interrelated. The argument declares that the J document that uses the divine name, which is *Yahweh,* or *Adonai,* and in English is LORD, and prefers the tribe of Judah, has a theology that is naively anthropomorphic. Some would hold that its view of God is basically henotheistic, i.e., *Yahweh* was Israel's national God, but the existence of other gods was not denied. Angels appear now and then in this source, but mostly God talks with man face to face.

The content of the J source, or document, is mostly narrative, with but a few genealogies. The style is simple but brilliantly effective. There is dramatic intensity and down-to-earth vividness; the stories are linked in a cause-and-effect chain. The tone is nationalistic and patriotic, with a pacifist overtone.

This theory, often called the Wellhausen theory, regards the E document as preferring Elohim (God) as the proper divine name and favors the tribe of Ephraim. It begins with Abraham in Genesis 12. The theology of E is said to be less naive than J in its anthropomorphism. Dreams and angels tend to give to divinity an aura of transcendence. This source is fond of blessings and farewells, tends to idealize Abraham and Moses; it prefers the men Reuben and Joshua, and the places Beersheba, Bethel, and Shechem. Like the J document, E knows no need for priests and shares with J a sense of national pride, with security under divine guidance. In some places, such as the account of the ten plagues and the Covenant

Code in Exodus and the Balaam stories of Numbers, J and E are so blended together that they cannot be disentangled. However, the E document lacks the epic scope—the dramatic movement and unity—of J, although E has an inner consistency.

The D document has been limited by the Wellhausen theory to Deuteronomy 5-26 and 28. This document utilizes both of the divine names and often pairs them in the phrase "LORD your God." Many exponents of this theory therefore hold that an advanced form of henotheism, but not true monotheism, is present in this document. The tone of the document is too nationalistic, and it is too closely related to the Jerusalem cult to be monotheistic. The primary interest of the D source is supposed to be the cultic purity of Israel's religion, hence, it stresses two major principles. One principle, or law, has to do with insistence on a single sanctuary and the limitations of the offering of sacrifices to the altar in the temple court of Jerusalem. The other principle has to do with retribution and the dictum that sin is the source of suffering, and loyalty will bring prosperity. This document is said to have a strong humanitarian interest. Its style is sermonic, loaded with exhortations and repetitious phrases.

Style and concept are also declared to be fused in the so-called P document. The letter P stands for the Priestly Code and contains the bulk of the law on sacrifice and the priesthood. It is said to begin with Genesis 1 and constitutes a framework for the entire Pentateuch. R. H. Pfeiffer calls the P document "a historical commentary."

The dull, repetitious style of P is held to be consonant with a most transcendent view of God, a truly monotheistic doctrine. God is presented as the invisible sovereign who appeared in a theophany only at Bethel; the awesomeness, the holiness, and the universality of God are everywhere dominant in the document. This would make P more dogmatic than historical, but it is said to show evidences of great care in research and a systematic organization of materials.

The P document is declared to be interested primarily in setting up an ideal, theocratic state, to promote a pure race, and to build up a group of true believers. The priests and the Levites are prominent in the document, and their care by the rest of society is laid out in detail. The P source knows of no sacrifices before Moses and Aaron and takes for granted the principle that the temple in Jerusalem is the only proper place to worship. The document is said to contain a subsection called the "Holiness Code," which can be found in Leviticus 17-27.

The combination of all criteria under the heading of style and concept has been held to prove the existence of the four basic documents in the Pentateuch. Almost every book that promotes the theory has a listing of chapters and verses originally belonging to the independent documents. All isolated fragments that are left over are attributed, much too easily, to redactors or compilers. It should be understood, however, that there are no literary references, no extant manuscripts of any kind, which mention the J, E, D, or P documents, either singly or as a group. They have been created by separating them, with the aid of the above mentioned criteria, from the extant text of the Pentateuch.

Its Dating Conclusions and Consequences

Old Testament scholars have generally recognized that the Hegelian philosophy of history with its dialectic of thesis, antithesis, and synthesis has served the Wellhausen theory as a frame of reference. It is difficult to resist the conclusion that this dialectic also served as one of the criteria, but it is probably best to understand the dialectic as the "glue" that held the criteria together and determined which concepts belonged to the individual sources.

The dialectic of thesis, antithesis, and synthesis was more closely related to efforts to decide a dating sequence for the four documents. Fundamental to the Wellhausen theory has been a thoroughgoing rejection of a concept of a living God who can speak to individuals and independently act in history. Rather, there has been an acceptance of a naturalistic, or a humanistic, view that holds that all ideas are purely the result of human thinking processes and express themselves in evolving institutions.

Indigenous to the theory has been a confidence that Hegel's dialectic framework provides a means to reconstruct the view of history in the Old Testament into a true Hebrew history that accords with the facts of the case. The four documents were made an integral part of reconstructing "what actually happened" during the kingdom, the exilic, and the post-exilic periods of Israel's existence. The reconstruction was based on these propositions: (a) an early simple culture in Israel moved dialectically toward a complex culture; (b) a primitive, animistic religion evolved into polytheism, then into henotheism, and finally, in the exilic period, into monotheism; (c) an early, concrete, and naive type of thinking slowly became an abstract type of thinking; (d) the prophetic spirit preceded legalistic thinking; therefore, the Pentateuchal law must be later than the Hebrew prophets; (e) poetic literature was produced before drab prose, and (f) oral transmission of stories took place for centuries before they were written down, hence the stories went through many changes during oral transmission. Details of oral transmission, however, are largely ignored.

How then did the Wellhausen theory date the four documents? Since the D document was declared to be written in the seventh century and made public in Josiah's reform of 621 B.C., that document became the keystone for the procedure. It was decided that D knew about the contents of J and E, but not of the contents of P; hence, J and E were written before 621 B.C., and P, at a later date.

Dialectically, the J document, with its naive concepts, could be dated before E, and the early phases of the divided kingdom seemed to provide a good historical setting. It could be argued that J was the kingdom of Judah's reaction against the establishment of the kingdom of north Israel. The purpose of J, then, was to provide Judah with a "historical" document that would justify Judah's and Jerusalem's claim to be the governmental center of all Israel. Likewise, E would be the antithetical production of the kingdom of north Israel, led by the tribe of Ephraim, to show that there were historical antecedents in the Patriarchs and in Joshua for the governmental center to be located in the north.

The theory continued to conclude that after the destruction of the northern kingdom of Israel, in 721 B.C., broadminded men during the reign of Manasseh (first half of seventh century B.C.) felt that the E document was too valuable to lose, so they blended it with the J document. This new JE document became a new thesis and the D document its antithesis. The thinking of the D document is said to have triumphed, substantially, during the Exile in Babylon and colored the composition of the historical books Joshua through II Kings. However, the "Holiness Code," tied with Ezekiel, arose as another antithesis to D; and slowly, for perhaps a century, the priests in exile and then in Jerusalem put together the P document and made it the framework of a grand synthesis, the Pentateuch.

In summary, the J document is dated a bit later than 900 B.C., and the E document somewhat later in the ninth century B.C. The two were put together about 650 B.C., and were written about that same time and made public in 621 B.C. The P document appeared in the fifth century and the Pentateuch composed in approximately its present form about 400 B.C.

The consequences that have followed in the wake of the Wellhausen theory can be listed thus; (a) Mosaic authorship is rejected, with only bits of the Pentateuch attributed to the Mosaic period; (b) for many of the scholars who accept the Wellhausen view, the men and women of the Pentateuch were not actual human beings—at best they were idealized heroes; (c) the Pentateuch does not give us a true history of ancient times, but it reflects instead the history of the divided kingdom through the early part of the postexilic period; (d) none of the people in the Pentateuch were monotheistic, and it was the postexilic priests who made them look like believers in one God; (e) God never spoke to any individuals in ancient times, but again, it was the work of the priests that gives that impression; (f) very few of the laws in the Pentateuch were prekingdom in origin; (g) very few of the cultic practices recorded in the Pentateuch were prekingdom, and many were postexilic; (h) the early Israelites never had a tabernacle such as described in Exodus; (i) all claims in the Pentateuch that God acted redemptively and miraculously in behalf of Israel are erroneous; (j) any concept that the present structural unity of the five books was original with Moses is erroneous, and, finally; (k) the skepticism inherent in the theory creates a credibility gap with the ordinary layman to the extent that the Pentateuch becomes practically useless to him.

The Loss of Hegelian Dialectic and the Rise of Existentialism

Neither in Germany nor in Great Britain nor in America, where the Wellhausen theory quickly became popular, did every nontraditional scholar accept the Hegelian dialectic as the philosophical base for the JEDP theory. There were those who preferred the straight-line development theories of Comte or of Darwin, but basically Hegel's dialectic reigned supreme. The German defeat in World War I destroyed Hegel's credibility, for it had become enmeshed with Germany's nationalistic goals.

Old Testament scholars in Germany, for the most part, turned their back on Hegel and began to question seriously the relevance of his dialectic for reconstructing Israel's religious history. The result was that the Wellhausen theory lost its foundational frame of reference and, in a real sense, the four documents lost their cohesiveness. More and more, scholars began to take the documents apart and to question the correctness of the dates assigned them in the Wellhausen scheme. It was not long before Eissfeldt found an L document and split J into two sources. Hempel found three sources in J, and von Rad found two sources in P; Lohr declared there never was an independent P. Volz and Rudolph denied the existence of an independent E. Kennett said D was postexilic in date and Welch said it was very old. These men had gone back to using only the basic criteria, and unity in the Pentateuch or the documents "went with the wind."

After World War I, a view of life that had agitated in the undercurrents of German thought began to come to the surface and slowly infiltrated biblical studies. This point of view is often called "existentialism." (For key tenets of this view, see chapter 8.) Existentialism was a revolt against abstract thought, neat logical arguments, and claims of some scholars that they were completely objective. The categories of this point of view were different; it was interested in human finitude, in despair, in anxiety, freedom, guilt, and death. Exponents of this way of thinking disliked the rigidity of the dialectics in the Wellhausen theory and grew bold in questioning its methods and its conclusions. The new attitude made it possible for new methods to be tried and accepted and for the new sciences of history of religion, anthropology, sociology, and archaeology to speak to Old Testament problems.

The supreme position of the Wellhausen theory slowly dwindled in Germany, but did not begin to give way in England or the United States until after the Second World War. The symbols J, E, D, and P have remained popular in liberal circles, but their meaning has been modified a great deal.

Modifications of the JEDP Theory

As a tight, well-reasoned explanation of literary and historical matters found in the Pentateuch, the JEDP theory seemed beyond challenge within many circles of Old Testament scholars during the early part of this century. If Pentateuchal studies had been kept in isolation, perhaps it would have continued with little change for a long time. But a mass of new knowledge about the ancient Near East was bursting upon the frontiers of knowledge, and ways of thinking in the West were going through a revolution. It was inevitable that major changes were soon made at basic points in the rationale of the JEDP scheme. This section will endeavor to summarize a few of the major factors that enter into the effecting of these changes.

The Return to Fragmentation

The experiences of the first half of the nineteenth-century search for sources revealed that relentless pursuit for sources, using only the criteria of divine names, duplication and triplication of incidents, disagreements in stories and laws, variety of style and vocabulary, development of concepts, leads to reducing the Pentateuch to fragments. A few instances of this trend were mentioned in the heading preceding this section; many more could be marshaled as examples.

The most radical of the methods that produced a fragmentation of the text was form criticism, which is discussed more fully below.

One result of the new trend was that the symbols JEDP lost more and more of their character as documents. Many scholars preferred to speak of a J tradition, J strands or strata, and so on with each of the other symbols. They thus became less clear cut and much more amorphous.

Form Criticism

Since World War II, a new method of studying the literature of the Scripture has become very popular. In English the method is called "form criticism." This procedure is really not new, for it has antecedents.

Following the lead of Aristotle, Greek scholars observed the difference between tragedies, epics, and other literary forms. They made careful metrical studies of poetry, drawing attention to literary phenomena as figures of speech, alliteration, repetition, word play, and metaphors. Biblical exegetes made good use of these insights as they studied the Scriptures. Prose was not of interest to the Greek scholars, and not much was done to identify prose types until the Romanticists studied novels, legends, and fairy tales.

Late in the eighteenth century, Eichhorn set up literary types for biblical poetry; and Herder, later, searched for folklore in the Old Testament. When source analysis became the prime pursuit of German scholars in the nineteenth century, research in literary types practically ceased, and interest in the poetry of the Bible almost faded away.

Herman Gunkel is the German professor who is credited for bringing the study of literary types in the Bible back to focus, but he met with almost a solid wall of resistance. Gunkel's famous commentary on Genesis was published in 1901; but its most important section, the introduction, was not made available in English until 1964.[5] This serves to illustrate the fact that although Gunkel was able to train a small group of faithful followers he did not become accepted until recently. Presently, his approach has, in effect, swallowed literary criticism, exegesis, biblical history, and biblical theology, making them subordinate parts of the system.

Gunkel labeled his method as *Gattungsforschung,* which may be translated as "research into literary types," or as *Literaturgeschichte,* which may be rendered as "history of literature." In 1916, one of his pupils, D. Dibelius, proposed the term, *Formgeschichte* (i.e., history of forms). This term can apply to a study of linguistic forms and an analysis of the history of these forms. The English phrase *form criticism* has in practice been mostly interested in the history of literary forms, though a study of structure has been part of its task.

Gunkel was essentially convinced of the correctness of the JEDP theory, but he had deep-seated misgivings about certain attitudes of Wellhausen and his followers. He believed Wellhausen was an isolationist in his research in that he paid no attention to oral tradition or to the ancient Near Eastern literature that was rapidly being published. Wellhausen regarded the Hebrews as being totally shut off from the Canaanites and other more advanced neighbors, and, as a result of being so primitive and crude, she could not produce literature such as that in the Pentateuch until a later date. Gunkel believed that the Pentateuch contains evidences of oral materials of earlier date and that research needed to be done concerning the history of oral transmission before 1000 B.C.

Form criticism has reached its present eminence for essentially five reasons: (1) The stagnation of source analysis (when all the verses are divided among the sources, what is left for the Old Testament scholar to

---

5. H. Gunkel, *The Legends of Genesis* (New York: Schocken, 1964).

do?); (2) the recognition that Wellhausen's perception of the history of, and interconnections within, the ancient Near East was all wrong; (3) the discovery that, contra Wellhausen, writing something down in the ancient Near East customarily marked the end of the development of the idea, not the beginning; (4) the replacement of an "inspired" individual with the creative society as the source of developing ideas; and (5) the recognition that the basic unit in oral tradition is not the sentence (much less, the word), but a self-contained "paragraph," and that larger units are built by stringing these "pearls" together on a "cord," or common theme.

Thus it may be seen, given these points, that Wellhausen's idea of Ezra writing by himself the totality of P material about 450 B.C. is almost completely without precedent, and that taking this document apart—into sentences, phrases, and even words—and inserting these at will throughout JED is an absurdity.

The form critic does not deny that there is P (dates, cultic) material within the Pentateuch. He does deny, however, that one man created it at a late date, and, in most cases, that it was ever collected into a self-contained source. In summary, the form critic sees it as his task to go behind our present Bible, which to him at best is a witness to a period no farther back than 1000 B.C. (David). He proceeds to break the artificial strands upon which the pearls had been strung, attempting to find the original strands. Then he attempts to bisect the pearl to find its original grain of sand and to see its later accretions. Thus he claims to understand and reconstruct the actual history of Israel.

Its Criteria and Assumptions

Perhaps the most complete exposition of form criticism has been made by the German scholar, Klaus Koch.[6] Much of the content that follows is based on his book.

There are five aspects to form criticism: (1) a study of literary types; (2) a study of the history of each literary type; (3) a determination of the setting of life for each type; (4) a study of the transmission history of each type through its oral stages; and (5) a study of the redaction history of each type through its written stages. Each of these aspects of study has its own criteria, and a set of assumptions undergirds each study project.

Isolating Literary Types. The first step in separating a literary type (also called a literary genre) from the biblical text is to determine the beginning and ending of a literary unit—the identification of an introduction

---

6. K. Koch, *The Growth of the Biblical Tradition* (New York: Charles Scribner's Sons, 1969).

and a conclusion—both of which are thought to be stereotyped formulae that recurred repeatedly in a specific type. Another criterion is a structure which, in a brief and independent manner, comprises a unity of thought. This criterion, plus choice of words, manner of expression, and sentence structure, make up the next step, namely, the identification of the literary type. The units of a type are sometimes called forms or motifs.

Form critics differ concerning the number of literary types that appear in the Pentateuch, but most agree on such types as the myth, legend, poem, saga, genealogy, promise, blessing, curse, legal saying, and speeches such as monologues and dialogues. In Eissfeldt's *Introduction* there are over a hundred pages devoted to literary types in the Old Testament. He has set up three major categories: prose, sayings, and songs, with many individual types in each category.

The following assumptions, sometimes pure assumptions but sometimes based partially on observation, govern the procedure of isolating literary types: (a) a speaker must use established ways of expressing himself; (b) these ways of expressing oneself are completely independent units of speech; (c) the basic units of communication are types and not sentences; and (d) a literary type governs the contents of the unit and marks its function.

The Setting in Life. The techniques of determining the setting in life of each type is basically interrogative. The exegete must ask questions about the identity of the speaker, the kind of audience he spoke to, the mood of the speaker and audience, the content of the event, and the effect sought by the speaker. Word studies must be made to make clear the nature of the setting in life.

The setting in life may be a nomadic narrator telling his listeners—as they sat about a campfire—the traditions of their forefathers, a peasant village with its concern for crops and running a market place, a council of elders at the city gate, a soldier's camp, a courtroom, a royal court, a home, or a cultic festival.

Underlying the search for a setting in life is the conviction that (a) every literary type arises out of a specific life situation and corresponds with it; (b) the variety of types points to the variety of social settings that existed in the ancient communities; (c) a literary type is a social event in a verbal "nutshell"; (d) a particular setting in life may be so complex that a number of literary types may be associated with it; (e) the settings in life were often closely related, if not identical, with institutions; (4) one must know as fully as possible what ancient Near Eastern institutions and thought patterns were like to delineate the setting in life adequately.

The History of Literary Types. Koch does not like any attempt to limit form criticism to determining literary types and their setting in life; he insists that form criticism must include a search for the details of a type's contents and their origin in the history of Israel. The same procedure must apply to the type itself. Its very earliest configuration must be ascertained, and its changes through the years must be marked out.

The basic criteria for reconstructing the history of a literary type are: (a) the researcher discovers as many forms or motifs, i.e., small units, as possible within the literary type; (b) he does not study the motifs themselves as much as the rise and fall of the type as a whole; (c) duplications of stories, poems, sayings, or laws, that can be found in the Pentateuch or can be paired with similar material in ancient Near Eastern literature are brought together for comparison; (d) from the parallel literature, simple sentences and a simple structure that embodies a homogeneous flow of thought are isolated as the earliest specimen of the type. This earliest specimen is the tradition that had been part of the heritage of Israel. The procedure of applying these criteria is pointed to the past prior to 1000 B.C. and pierces the memory of Israel to its beginnings.

Certain assumptions guide the researcher as he unravels the history of each type: It is essential that the history of each type be made clear. The farther back the history can be traced, the better we understand the present passage in the Scripture. The history of a type was from a simple structure and content to ever more complex structures and sentences. The combined histories of a number of literary types provide invaluable insights into the actual history of Israel before the kingdom period, and even during that period.

The Oral Transmission of the Type. The criteria for tracing the history of the transmission of a type from generation to generation are much the same as for determining the history of a type. The basic difference is in the direction of movement. The study of the history of a type unravels two or more parallel portions of literature until the earliest and simplest content is exposed. The study of the transmission of the type moves forward from this early simplicity to the very last stages of oral transmission, i.e., just before the literary type was written down. Since interrogation of the texts being studied has already isolated items that were later than the original literary form of the type, the task now is to "peg" these items to settings in life in different periods of Israel's history. One criterion has to do with changes in pronouns, verbs, and nouns; and this must be paired with another criterion, namely the relationship of the people to each other in the literary type. A third clue is the presence or absence of motive clauses or of explanatory glosses and their relationships to a changed setting in life for the type. A fourth clue is the presence of a negative or a positive emphasis; a fifth is the presence of interpretative clauses, and finally evidences of merging of a type with other types. All of these criteria must be related as closely as possible to dated events; if these are lacking, uncertainty persists. The goal is to follow the changes through which a tradition passed to bring out the background of biblical text.

Guidelines that supposedly aid the researcher to produce a history of oral transmission are (a) the recitation of stories, laws, and poems over a period of time caused changes in the literature itself; (b) the changes that are observable in the text can be arranged in a sequence that leads to ever greater complexity, (c) the changes in the text are tied to specific periods in Israel's early history, kingdom period history, or exilic history, thus providing a better understanding of the Old Testament; (d) the process will reveal tendencies of growth in Israel's belief, thought, and teachings; (e) the reconstruction of Israel's past will not so much bring to light facts as it will clarify her traditions; (f) almost all of the stories, most of the legal sayings, and some of the cultic rules had a long history of oral transmission, (g) the larger the piece of literature, the more profitable its study, for it can give a historical outline for interpreting Israel's early history; and (h) this procedure can ferret out information for periods in Israel's history for which no contemporary documents are available.

The History of Redaction of Written Documents. Gunkel and a few of his followers did some work in redaction history, but the method as it is practiced now, developed since World War II.

Redactors were popular with many of the literary critics who understood them to be faceless individuals, whose function was to edit the four great documents. Most did a clumsy job of it. The form critics regard the redactors as compilers who gave order to the already formed literary types. Redactors collected the literary units, organized them, and wrote them down.

Redaction history is much like textual criticism in that both are primarily interested in written documents, but they move in opposite directions. Textual critics start with late manuscripts, work their way back to families of texts, and seek to bring to light the archetype or ancestor of the several families of texts. Redaction history endeavors to begin at the moment oral tradition was written down and work forward to the presently existing manuscripts.

In redaction history, clues are of a different kind than those used in transmission history. The researcher first looks at the introductions and the conclusions of present books of the Pentateuch as evidences of the redactor at work. He then looks for transition passages between literary types or sections of the books. He looks for an overall framework, a unifying theme, or underlying principles that give the book a structure. He selects sentences that link people to each other, or people to places. He would pick out late words, phrases, or thoughts that seem out of place in an old literary type. He would take note of interpretive passages or explanatory details bearing on chronology or geography. He would have interest in clues that indicate that the redactor had inserted some of his own opinions in the speeches of his ancient heroes.

Form critics, for the most part, have assumed that (a) no book of the Pentateuch, and no other book in the Old Testament, still retains the form it had when it first was written down; (b) the written text must be interpreted against its background of literary type, its setting in life, and its oral transmission—hence, redaction history must rest on them; (c) the redactors put oral material into written form and thus slowed down change, to some extent freezing the material in a manuscript; (d) many form critics regard the first redactors to be those such as the Yahwist and the Elohist, using the symbols of the JEDP theory as their clues; (e) there were also generations of redactors, through whom the texts were rewritten, modified, and enriched with new doctrines; (f) because most redactors had great reverence for the text, additions were not many; (g) since the period of transmitting the text was lengthy, redaction history is vitally important to show that the setting of life was changed for the literary types and to provide evidences of how this new setting crept into the text.

If all original manuscripts and their revisions have been preserved, a researcher can easily examine them and determine what changes were made at various stages of composition and often determine why the changes were made. In such a situation there is no great problem with redaction criticism, for the evidence is available.

The problem of applying redaction criticism to a study of biblical texts is that the original compositions of the books of the Bible no longer exist. This kind of criticism of biblical books cannot be truly objective because the oldest manuscripts available are many years, even centuries, removed from the moment of their original composition. As with source critics, form critics have no recordings of oral storytelling or singing to verify their theories, which have varied from scholar to scholar.

The German scholar, Gerhardt von Rad, seems to have been the first to look at additions and arrangements made by redactors and suggest theological motivations for what they did. He felt these people made changes intentionally in order to remove an older polytheistic theology and replace it with a theology that was currently in favor with religious leaders. Therefore, von Rad's interest moved away from what many scholars called older sources to an effort to determine what redactors wanted readers to understand with the aid of their revisions. A new aspect of research soon became popular, that of analyzing editorial changes in order to ascertain the intention of each redactor. Reaching a consensus on what these intentions were has proved difficult; dead redactors could not be questioned, so no scholar's opinion could be proved right or wrong.

The Stylistic Traits of Literary Types

Only a few of the most important literary types that are said to appear often in the Pentateuch are described here. The names of the literary types are obviously Western and not Semitic, mainly because the Pentateuch does not provide names for its literary types. Form critics tend to look for traits in the biblical units that correspond to those found in similar Western types. Burke O. Long lists an array of literary types.[7]

Myths. Myths are held to have words and phrases that are the same as, or like, those found in pagan mythology. The interest of the myth is supposed to be in the long ago, such as in the creation, the fall of man, and the flood. The myth is said to have a lofty and arrogant style and to be loaded with awe and terror. God is always victorious and His opponents are very sinful. The myth is held to be connected with a priestly setting in life.

Legends. This type is said to be interested in the origin and history of cultic centers and to major in details about the cultus. It is also interested in human personality, but in terms of its religious significance. Stress is placed on the divine power, which is dominant in an individual's life.

Sagas. This material typically begins with "It came to pass. . . ." It gives little or no information about people or time but is quite definite about places. Sagas are marked by long lists, bits of humor, long speeches, and frequently includes word plays of sounds and meanings.

Legal Sayings. The legal material has an objective, conditional style in prose. It is marked by either strong prohibitions, positive commands, or "If —then" constructions.

Cultic Regulations. These units are mostly in the form of lists and reports, rarely in direct address. They are basically directed toward priestly circles.

Its Dating Conclusions and Consequences

Since form criticism, as a total discipline, is concerned about the historical milieu of each literary type, it must endeavor to correlate the types

---

7. Burke O. Long. *I Kings,* vol. 9 of *Forms of the Old Testament Literature* (Grand Rapids: William B. Eerdmans Pub. Co., 1984).

with events in history. The last three aspects of form criticism—history of literary types, history of oral transmission, and history of redaction of manuscripts—are intimately involved in dating processes of one type or another.

Basic to the procedures of many form critics is the conviction that literary types developed according to the rigid laws of growth said to inhere in human societies, the evolution of life, individual mental growth, and government. Hence, when parallel types or specimens of a type are dissected, it follows as a matter of course that the simplest, most unencumbered expression of the type is the earliest. It also follows that each type progressively became more complex until it was written down. This kind of change continued at a much slower pace during the transmission of the written text. The art of analysis produces a mass of small items that can be strung out like the "teeth" of one side of a zipper. The other side of the zipper is made up of the series of settings in life that existed during the sequence of experience in the Israelite community.

When a setting in life or events in that setting can be dated by other means, i.e., nonbiblical inscriptions or by artifacts recovered by archaeologists, they are paired with a matching stage in the history of the literary type. So far this has not happened often for material in the Pentateuch. The next best procedure is to match stages in the history of a literary type with settings in life through probable correlation. Success is realized when the "teeth" on each side of the zipper are paired; the researcher then has a history of Israel.

In many respects, the dating conclusions of most form critics have been at variance with both Wellhausen's reconstruction of Israel's history and the sequence presented in the Pentateuch and the early historical books like Joshua, Judges, and I Samuel. A number of items that Wellhausen dated late are dated early by the form critics, and many items that the Pentateuch presents as patriarchal or Mosaic are dated late.

Most form critics hold that some motifs or simple literary types in the Pentateuch were associated, in their earliest setting in life, with Canaanite cultic centers such as Shechem, Bethel, Mamre, and Beersheba. Other motifs and simple literary types are related to nomadic pre-Israelite tribes who wandered in the deserts south and east of Palestine and occasionally went to Egypt. Certain tribes gravitated toward certain cultic centers, and similar literary types in each group tended to blend together. In the process of time the separate tribes built up a confederation, a setting in life that caused further changes in the types. Then a kingdom was set up, an event that radically complicated many literary types.

For the kingdom, exilic, and postexilic periods, most form critics have accepted, with modifications, the JEDP theory. The writer of the J document, the Jahwist, is supposed to be the first to break the oral transmission chain and freeze the literary types on papyrus or leather. Next was the Elohist and then the Deuteronomist (they find it difficult to speak of the priestly author of the Priestly Code as a Priestess). The dates that the Wellhausen theory had given to these documents are accepted by many form critics.

Very few of the form critics have attempted to explain the dating sequence of the method in the terms of Hegelian dialectics. The kind of development popular among the logical positivists—an emergent, almost organic, growth influenced by Darwinian thinking—has guided the theories of most form critics to date. Those who have been enamored with existentialism, particularly Heidegger's brand, have interpreted ancient settings in life in existentialist categories.

There is much in the procedures of form criticism that is commendable. All of the aspects of form criticism, as Koch defines them, are legitimate concerns for the Old Testament scholar. The study of literary types has been a most neglected phase of biblical studies, though the raw material for such a study has been present as long as manuscripts have been written. It is a pity that those responsible in the Middle Ages for our present format of chapters and verses were not aware of the basic literary types and their confines. The Bible would be easier to read and to study if they had possessed this awareness and divided the text into chapters and verses accordingly.

A study of literary types is the most objective of the several phases of form criticism. Its material is the text itself and the conclusions of a researcher can be checked directly against the witness of that text. There is one major failing in form criticism at this point. Many form critics have castigated other scholars for looking at and interpreting the Old Testament from the standpoint of Western thought patterns and customs. Yet the names given to Pentateuchal literary types and the criteria for isolating and labeling these types are Western to the core. The observation that names for types do not occur often in the Pentateuch does not justify this procedure. Efforts must be made to devise labels that accord with and arise out of the biblical materials themselves (see pages 241-258).

A study of the setting in life for each literary type is a legitimate task. A tendency to ignore the historical rootage of the biblical text has been a malady in both traditionalism, which has stressed doctrine or piety, and liberalism, which has emphasized universal, abstract ideas or truths. The Pentateuch has its "feet" solidly planted in the rugged, realistic affairs of this world; therefore, to fully understand the Pentateuch one must understand the settings in life of its literary units.

The manner in which many form critics have reconstructed settings in life for many Pentateuch literary types has some serious shortcomings. No one can object when clear-cut biblical data is employed to clarify a setting in life; but some attempts, of which there are several examples in Koch's book, range far and wide to gather isolated bits of information, and in the procedure tend to proof-text a setting in life for a particular type, or the history of a type. Nor can one seriously object when pertinent data is drawn from other ancient Near Eastern religions, if that data is used judiciously; but any assumption or assertion that the Hebrews were pagan in their thinking during the Middle Bronze and Late Bronze ages can only prejudice a setting in life that is reconstructed for a type. It is remarkable that many form critics have only selectively drawn data from the discipline of archaeology for their studies.

Research in both the oral and the written transmission of the biblical text is a proper occupation. We need to know much more than we do at present about how the Pentateuch was passed from generation to generation until we reach the manuscripts in the Dead Sea Scrolls. An informed understanding of this history of transmission can only enhance and clarify our understanding of how the Pentateuch was preserved for us. Participants in the traditional stream of scholarship need to do their share in this discipline.

It is in the area of the oral transmission history and of redaction history that form critics, such as Koch, are too cocksure. They could even be charged, with some reason, with an attitude of imperialism toward other disciplines. Koch frankly claims that form criticism is the master discipline, and that literary criticism, archaeology, sociology, psychology, theology, anthropology, history of religions, and textual criticism must all be subsumed under form criticism.

In the studies of transmission history and redaction history, there is presently too much room for subjectivism, too much opportunity for the researcher to mold Israel's past into a contrived, even a pseudo, history. If one marks provisional or tentative phrases, such as "it is likely," "we may suppose," and "likely to have been," in discussions of the above "histories" with a highlighter pen, one soon has pages that appear to have a bad case of scarlet fever. Dependable histories should have a firmer base that that.

Another disturbing element is the average form critic's resistance to an association of the element of sacredness of divine authority with literary types at an early date. His concept of growth demands that oral transmission be kept open-ended and fluid for long periods of time. He understands the origins of early or intrusive motifs in a type as coming out of the creative matrix of the community. All things come from the community; as a whole, nothing comes from the creative individual or from a speaking God. This is the reason the reduction of much of the Pentateuch to writing is placed well into the kingdom period and later. Both sacredness and writing tend to fix or, at least, seriously slow down changes within a type.

A traditional scholar can accept a period of oral transmission, say of the literary units of Genesis, if it is understood that the Patriarchs and their descendants accorded the contents of these units divine authority and told them to their children with a deep sense of reverence. Neither does a traditional scholar regard the event of putting these stories into written form a near catastrophe. Manuscripts also marked as sacred merely aid and abet oral transmission; there is no reason why they could not have functioned side by side from early times.

An Alternative Treatment of Literary Types

This discussion will center upon the first aspect of form criticism. This limitation should not be interpreted as an intentional snubbing or downgrading of the other aspects of the method. It is understood that traditional scholars are faced with a legitimate challenge to engage in research in these areas, from a stance that is free to criticize the philosophical and theological frame of reference of many form critics.

This analysis rejects Western labels and criteria for the literary types that are considered. Since this treatment is only an example of what might be done, only narrative prose is brought under scrutiny. That decision still leaves much untouched in the Pentateuch.

It should be axiomatic by now that the predominant, if not the overarching, framework of Israelite thought and practice was the covenant relationship between God and man. An impact of this covenant framework should be apparent in the literary types that became current in Israel. Since the Abrahamic covenant is the starting point of Israel's existence (at least the Scripture gives that strong impression), the study will begin with the stories of the Patriarchs.

The first story in the Abraham series is in Genesis 12:1-9. The basic components of the narrative are: (a) a divine communication, 1-3; (b) a positive response, 4-6; and (c) a theophany, 7-9.

This story could be called a *Positive Response* type. There are other narratives of this construction in the Pentateuch.

Units	Genesis 22:1-19	Exodus 24:12-18	Exodus 34:1-9	Exodus 40:1-38
(a) Divine Communication	1-2	12	1-3	1-15
(b) Positive Response	3-10	13-15a	4	16-33
(c) Theophany	11-19	15b-18	5-9	34-38

In each of these stories, God gives specific instructions that the addressee must carry out. There are no negative reactions by the person addressed; without a question he does as directed. His obedience is blessed with another appearance of the Lord, who speaks again directly, except in Exodus 40:36-37, which indicates that the cloud and fire symbolically gave directions. The cloud is prominent in the Exodus stories but is not present in the Genesis accounts.

The second story in the Abraham series is Genesis 12:10–13:1, which has an organization made up of: (a) orientation of people, place and/or time, 12:10; (b) an act of disobedience, 12:11-12; (c) a discussion of the disobedience, 18-19a; and (d) the aftermath of the affair, 12:19b– 13:1. The label *Moral Violation* might be applied to this type, and there are other specimens to be found in Genesis and in two other books of the Pentateuch. The following chart indicates the structure of the several patriarchal stories.

Units	Genesis 20:1-18	Genesis 26:34–28:9	Genesis 37:1-36	Genesis 38:1-30
(a) Orientation of People, Place and/or Time	1	26:34–27:4	1-11	1
(b) Act of Disobedience	2	27:5-29	12-28	2-19
(c) Discussion of the Disobedience	3-16	27:30-40	29-33	20-26a
(d) Aftermath	17-18	27:31–28:9	34-36	26b-30

Several narratives of this type appear in the account of Joseph's life:

Units	Genesis 39:1-23	Genesis 44:1–45:28
(a) Orientation of People, Place and/or Time	1-6a	44:1-5
(b) Act of Disobedience	6b-15	44:6-13
(c) Discussion of the Disobedience	16-18	44:14-34
(d) Aftermath	19-23	45:1-28

Having established the basic structure of this story form we may look backward and see that it appears in Genesis 1-11; the most striking difference is that God is more directly involved in the discussion of the violation, that is, in activity contrary to the will of God.

Units	Genesis 6:1-8	Genesis 11:1-9
(a) Orientation of People, Place and/or Time	1	1-2
(b) Act of Disobedience	2	3-4
(c) Discussion of the Disobedience	3-6	5-7
(d) Aftermath	7-8	8-9

Two examples of this sequence of components are to be found in Exodus:

Units	Exodus 1:15-22	Exodus 2:11-15
(a) Orientation of People, Place and/or Time	15-16	11
(b) Act of Disobedience	17	12
(c) Discussion of the Disobedience	18-19	13-14a
(d) Aftermath	20-22	14b-15

In the first of these stories, the disobedience is toward a command of the pharaoh, but is actually also an act of obedience to Yahweh's wishes. Moses' crime is also an act of disobedience against the pharaoh's law and order system, but there is no mention of Yahweh's attitude toward the act.

In the Book of Numbers, there are two specimens of this kind of story composition:

Units	Numbers 22:22-35	Numbers 22:36-40
(a) Orientation of People, Place and/or Time	22a	36
(b) Act of Disobedience	22b	37a
(c) Discussion of the Disobedience	22c-35a	37b-38
(d) Aftermath	35b	39-40

One of the parallel passages to Genesis 20:1-18 is 26:1-25. It is similar in structure but has an added component, a divine word. The sequence of the story is (a) orientation, v. 1; (b) divine word, 2-5; (c) act of disobedience, 6-7; (d) discussion of the disobedience, 8-10; (e) the aftermath, which includes God speaking to those involved, 11-25. There are examples of this structure in Genesis 1-11.

Units	Genesis 2:4–3:24	Genesis 4:1-16
(a) Orientation	4-15	1-5
(b) Divine Word	16-17 plus creation act 18-25	6-7
(c) Act of Disobedience	3:1-7	8
(d) Discussion of the Disobedience	8-12	9
(e) Aftermath	13-24	10-16

The third story in sequence in the Abrahamic block of narrative is Genesis 13:2-18, which may be designated as a *Moment of Decision* type. Again, examples of this form appear throughout the Pentateuch. An important characteristic of this type is that the decision can be made either positively or negatively in relation to the divine will or an established custom of society, and the aftermath will reflect the nature of the decision.

The structure of this kind of story is (a) orientation, 13:2-4; (b) the problem, 5-7; (c) the alternatives, 8-9; (d) the decision, 10-11a; (e) the aftermath, 11b-18. Observe this same sequence in the following examples:

Units	Genesis 19:1-29	Genesis 43:1-15	Exodus 2:5-10	Exodus 18:13-27	Numbers 14:39-45
(a) Orientation	1-3	1-2a	5	13	39
(b) The Problem	4-11	2b-3	6	14-16	40
(c) The Alternatives	12-17	4-10	7	17-23	41-43
(d) The Decision	18-23	11-14	8-9a	24-25	44
(c) Aftermath	24-29	15	9b-10	26-27	45

In several of the stories, the alternatives are quite clearly stated, and, in several, only partially so. In Genesis 19:12-17, the angels urge Lot and his family to "arise . . . escape for your life" and stated the consequences if they did not do so, "lest you be consumed. . . . "

The cruel choices set forth in Genesis 43:4-10 were stated by Judah: "If you send our brother with us, we will go down and buy you food; but if you will not send him, we will not go down." The implied result would be starvation. Primarily, Jacob had to make a choice and his heartrending statement in 43:14 reveals his pain: "And God Almighty give you mercy before the man, that he may release your other brother and Benjamin. If I am bereaved of my children I am bereaved." In this same story, Judah was also faced with alternatives that entailed a decision. He could stay in the background and let some other brother help solve the dilemma; or he could take responsibility for Benjamin and bear all blame for failure to return him to Jacob. He chose to risk all.

In Exodus 2:7, the baby's sister voiced one side of the possibilities: "Shall I go and call you a nurse from the Hebrew women, that she may nurse the child for you?" The other possibility is in the context: obey the pharaoh's edict and give up the boy to be destroyed.

Moses' father-in-law forthrightly presents the choices the overworked leader had. Moses could keep on doing all the judging and wear himself out; or, he could appoint a number of judges to help bear the burden (Exod. 18:17-23).

After the report of the Hebrew spies had been heard, some of the men reversed themselves and suddenly decided to make an unauthorized invasion into Canaan. Moses laid the outcome of this act before them; they could go up to Canaan but they would be defeated (Num. 14:41-43). The implied alternative was that they could change their plan and live peaceably among their fellowmen.

The next narrative in the Abrahamic series is 14:1-16, which is much like those cited above, except the alternatives are implied rather than expressed. The organization of 14:1-16 is (a) orientation, 1-9; (b) the problem, 10-13; (c) decision and act, 14-15; and (d) the aftermath, 16. The implied alternatives enshroud stories like this one with a certain mystery and suspense, which captivates the reader. Several examples elsewhere in Genesis are these:

Units	Genesis 16:1-15	Genesis 19:30-38	Genesis 21:1-21	Genesis 32:1–33:4
(a) Orientation	1-3	30	1-8	1-5
(b) Problem	4-6a	31	9-11	6-7a
(c) Decision and Act	6b	32-35	12-14a	7b-29
(d) Aftermath	6c-16	36-38	14b-21	32:30–33:4

Notice these five specimens among the Joseph narrative group:

Units	Genesis 41:1-57	Genesis 42:1-38	Genesis 43:16-25	Genesis 43:26-34	Genesis 46:28–47:12
(a) Orientation	1-7	1-6	16-17	26-29	28-30
(b) Problem	8-24	7-8	18	30	31-33
(c) Decision and Act	25-36	9-25	19-22	31	34
(d) Aftermath	37-57	26-38	23-25	32-34	47:1-12

The force of these hidden alternatives becomes clear when they are drawn into actual expression in sentences. In Genesis 14, Abram could ignore Lot's plight and regard it as his just punishment, thus playing it safe; or, he could go to Lot's rescue and risk possible heavy losses of valuable servants. Abram chose the later course of action.

In Genesis 16, both Abram and Sarai faced alternatives. Abram could retain Hagar and endure the family squabble; or he could side-step the problem and force Sarai to make the decision. Sarai could retain Hagar and endure her attitude; or she could make Hagar's life miserable, hoping she would run away. Hagar ran.

Again a choice had to be made in regard to Hagar and her child (Gen. 21). Abraham could refuse to expel Hagar and endure family tensions; or, to please Sarah, he could expel Hagar, thus ignoring his responsibilities as the father of Ishmael. Only after God gave instructions did Abraham send Hagar and the boy away.

Facing the arrival of Esau and his four hundred men, Jacob was in a dilemma. He could sacrifice some of his family and cattle to Esau's supposed wrath and thus save his life, plus some of the family and goods, by escaping; or, he could confess his sins, yield to God, and present himself to Esau. God led him through the latter course of decision and action with marvelous results.

One of the intriguing aspects of the Joseph narratives is the series of decision-making incidents that Joseph himself faced and that he forced his brothers to face and inevitably forced his father to suffer through. Consider this sequence of painful choices that had to be made.

There is a hint in Genesis 41:16 that Joseph knew he had to make a decision as he stood before the pharaoh for the first time. Joseph voiced his rejection of the one possibility, to attempt to interpret the pharaoh's dream by means of the arts of divination that would emphasize his own superior skill of interpretation. The other possibility was to depend on God to give him wisdom to understand the dream and then tell the monarch its true meaning. God did not fail him, and Joseph won great fame and power.

When Joseph's brothers appeared in Egypt to buy grain, he faced a painful decision. Joseph could have immediately revealed his true identity and punished his brothers for their past crimes against him. Joseph took the other, surprising, course of action. He remained unrecognized by his brothers and proceeded to test them. Part of the aftermath of Joseph's actions was the dilemma that now faced the brothers. If they regarded the money as theirs on the basis of the "finders, keepers" principle, they could be charged as thieves and punished should they enter Egypt again to buy grain. Even if they returned the money and claimed to be innocent, they could still be punished as thieves should the Egyptian ruler choose to be cruel. He had already kept Simeon as hostage.

When the brothers returned to Egypt (Gen. 43:16-25), Joseph had to make the same decision again. He could now reveal his identity, since Benjamin was among his brothers; or, he could be patient and test the older brothers further. He chose to do the latter and the brothers found themselves in another, similar, dilemma. Though the brothers returned double the money found earlier in the grain bags, they discovered that the incident created no serious repercussions; instead, they were invited to a banquet.

The situation changed when they started home with the new supply of grain; they soon found a silver cup in Benjamin's bag of grain (Gen. 44), and the mystery was not resolved until Joseph let his true identity be known (45:1-3).

When Jacob's clan arrived at the borders of Egypt (Gen. 46:28-34), a new set of alternatives faced Jacob and Joseph. Implicitly, they could conspire to slip the clan into Egypt, but they would risk being discovered and expelled. On the other hand, they could be honest and straightforward by approaching the pharaoh and depend on his good graces for land and provisions. Under Joseph's guidance they chose to approach the pharaoh and negotiate for an agreement.

There are two stories in Exodus and one in Numbers in which alternatives are implied and a decision had to be made:

Units	Exodus 2:15-22	Exodus 17:8-16	Numbers 25:6-9
(a) Orientation	15b-16	8a	6a
(b) Problem	17a	8b	6b
(c) Alternatives	17b	9-12	7-8a
(d) Aftermath	18-22	13-16	8b-9

The story in Exodus 2:15-22 has Moses sitting by a well in Midian watching the flocks come to drink. Observing the shepherds discriminate against the shepherdesses, Moses could have ignored the injustice and perhaps won favor with the shepherds; instead, he chose the other alternative and drove the shepherds off, helping the girls water their flocks. At the moment it must have seemed to be risky business, but the results were favorable.

The appearance of the warlike Amalekites presented the Israelites with alternatives that are not stated but lie behind Moses' decision. As the leader he could decide that wisdom dictated surrender to the Amalekites with great cost to his own people; or he could (as he did) prepare for battle and pray that God would give them victory, which God did (see Exod. 17:8-16 for details).

The story in Numbers 25:6-9 is brief and serves as an introduction to what follows but in itself has the structure of a *Moment of Decision* type. When Phinehas of the priestly tribe saw an Israelite bring a pagan woman into the camp, he could have done one of two things. He could have pretended he did not see the pair and let someone else act; or, he could punish them himself, though he had no authority from Moses to do so. He killed both the man and the woman.

The fifth story in the Abrahamic series, Genesis 14:17-24, has a structure of three main parts: (a) orientation, 14:17-20; (b) bargaining, 14:21-23; and (c) outcome of bargaining, 14:24. The narrative is concerned with relationships between ethnic groups, which may be made harmonious if a covenant can be made between them. The alternatives facing the groups involved are dealt with in the bargaining dialogue but are not separately stated. Abram had a problem because he had regained the property of several other ethnic groups when he had rescued Lot. Those groups were interested in getting their property back. Abram could have refused to give the loot back and earned the hostility of his dispossessed neighbors; instead, he worked out an agreement with them that seemed satisfactory to all. The label, *Covenant Negotiation,* could be given this story.

There are other stories in Genesis that portray incidents of negotiation between ethnic groups, or intertribal groups.

Units	Genesis 21:22-34	Genesis 23:1-20	Genesis 24:1-67	Genesis 26:26-33	Genesis 29:1-30
(a) Orientation	22	1-2	1-32	26	1-14
(b) Bargaining	23-30	3-15	33-60	27-29	15-27
(c) Outcome	31-34	16-20	61-67	30-33	28-30

Units	Genesis 29:31–30:43	Genesis 31:1-55	Genesis 33:5-17	Genesis 33:18–34:31
(a) Orientation	29:41–30:24	1-24	5-6	33:18–34:3
(b) Bargaining	30:25-34	25-44	7-15	34:4-24
(c) Outcome	30:35-43	45-55	16-17	34:25-31

Consider also these specimens among the Joseph narratives:

Units	Genesis 47:1-12	Genesis 47:13-17	Genesis 47:18-20	Genesis 47:21-26	Genesis 47:27-31
(a) Orientation	1-2	13-14	18a	21-22	27-29a
(b) Bargaining	3-6	15-16	18b-19	23-25	29b-31a
(c) Outcome	7-12	17	20	26	31b

Units	Genesis 48:1-22	Genesis 50:4-14	Genesis 50:15-21	Genesis 50:22-26
(a) Orientation	1	4a	15	22-23
(b) Bargaining	2-20	4b-6	16-21a	24-25
(c) Outcome	21-22	7-14	21b	26

There are four records of negotiation in Exodus:

Units	Exodus 8:25-32	Exodus 9:27-35	Exodus 10:7-11b	Exodus 10:24-29
(a) Orientation	25a	27a	7-8a	24a
(b) Bargaining	25b-29	27b-30	8b-11a	24b-26
(c) Outcome	30-32	31-35	11b	27-29

Three specimens may be found in Numbers:

Units	Numbers 10:29-32	Numbers 20:14-21	Numbers 21:21-35
(a) Orientation	29	14a	21
(b) Bargaining	30-31	14b-19	22-23a
(c) Outcome	32	20-21	23b-35

Although narratives of this variety deal with family, clan, tribal, and national problems, the presence of the living God overshadows each transaction. Especially the negotiations in Exodus and Numbers have unsatisfactory outcomes.

Genesis 15 is a record of a divine-human covenant-making event. Its first component is a mixture of divine word and Abram's responses in a dialogue format (1-9). The second portion is Abram's obedience in preparing for the covenant event itself (10-11). The last section is a ratification, or sealing, of the covenant by the symbolic presence of the divine sandwiched between two divine words of promise (12-21).

The next covenant event (17:1-27) has the same basic components:

divine word, positive response of the man, and the sealing of the covenant by act, in this case by circumcision. In this account, there are a series of divine words (1-22) and an intermixture of positive response and sealing act (23-27).

The record of the covenant-making event between God and Jacob has first a short orientation, or setting (28:10-11), then the divine word (12-15), followed by Jacob's positive response by verbal commitment and ratification by anointing a standing stone (16-22). The covenant renewal incident in Genesis 35:9-15 has a brief statement of orientation (9), a divine word (10-13), and Jacob's positive response, which again involved the anointment of a standing stone (14-15).

The story in Genesis 18:1-15 is related to the covenant promises but has more of a messenger/message context. It does not have the same basic components of the covenant-making/renewal accounts, nor does it have the formulas of the standard message delivery situation. More about that later.

The account in Genesis 18:16-33 is a description of an intercessor praying to the Lord in behalf of others. It begins with an orientation, or setting, involving both a divine soliloquy and a divine word to Abraham (16-22), but it alerts the reader to the crisis facing Lot and his family in Sodom. A hallmark of intercession is the sequence of the dialogue; in this instance man speaks first and then God responds by word and/or act. Actually, Genesis 18:23-32 is a series of intercessions. Verse 33 is a concluding observation. There are no other descriptions of an intercession situation in Genesis, though references are made to men worshiping God.

Five records of intercession events can be found in Exodus:

Units	Exodus 5:19–6:1	Exodus 17:1-7	Exodus 31:18–32:16	Exodus 32:30-35	Exodus 33:7-23
(a) Crisis	19-21	1-3	31:18–32:10	30	7-11
(b) Intercession dialogue	5:22–6:1	4-6a	32:11-14	31-34	12-23
(c) Aftermath		6b-7	15-16	35	

Two such stories are in Numbers:

Units	Numbers 11:4-25	Numbers 12:10b-16
(a) Crisis	4-10	10b-12
(b) Intercession dialogue	11-23	13-14
(c) Aftermath	24-25	15-16

Examples of a similar composition can be detected, but one which is lacking the dialogue format because the intercessory request is referred to rather than verbalized.

Rebekah went to "inquire of the Lord" (Gen. 25:22b) because of a crisis in her life (22a), and she received a divine word (23). The result is reported in verses 24-26. Both Exodus and Numbers have this kind of narrative. Note these in Exodus:

Units	Exodus 8:8-15	Exodus 10:16-20	Exodus 14:9-25	Exodus 15:22-27
(a) Crisis	8	16-17	9-14	22-24
(b) Reference to prayer	12	18	15a	25a
(c) Divine Response	13	19	15b-25a	25b-26
(d) Aftermath	14-15	20	25b	27

Three more such accounts can be observed in Numbers:

Units	Numbers 9:6-23	Numbers 11:1-3	Numbers 21:4-9
(a) Crisis	6-7	1	4-7a
(b) Reference to prayer	8	2a	7b
(c) Divine Response	9-16	2b	8
(d) Aftermath	17-23	3	9

Note that in Exodus 14:19-25, a theophany of the divine presence by angel and by cloud accompanied the divine word. Compare with Numbers 9:15-16 in which both cloud and fire appeared with the giving of the divine word.

In recent years, the research of Claus Westermann has clarified the structure of the messenger speeches uttered by the great prophets, such as Amos, Isaiah, Jeremiah, and preserved in their writings.[8] He points out that the sending of communications via messengers either orally or by written document was a common practice in the ancient Near East, especially in the Mesopotamian valley, from whence many letters in cuneiform script have come to light. These letters reveal that certain standard statements,

---

8. C. Westermann, *Basic Forms of Prophetic Speech* (Philadelphia: Westminster Press, 1969).

or formulae, were basic components of communication and that contents of the message were put in fixed formats. He points out messenger situations described in the Old Testament that help us to understand how messages were sent and received. These biblical descriptions are in conformity with the customs of ancient times.

Though a part of a larger narrative, there is a limited description of a messenger-sending situation in Genesis 32:3-6. Verse 4 makes it clear that Jacob intended the message to bear his personal authority. He also used one variation of a commissioning formula, "Speak thus to my lord Esau" and a standard messenger formula, "Thus your servant Jacob says." The message has two parts: a resumé of Jacob's condition and a request. It is not clear whether the messengers actually delivered the message.

Joseph commissioned his brothers to be messengers to his father, Jacob (Gen. 45:9-13, 24-28). Joseph commissioned his brothers with the words, " . . . say . . . " and employed the messenger formula, "Thus says your son Joseph." The message relates how God had helped Joseph and makes a request and a promise. He reinforces the authority of the message by declaring, " . . . it is my mouth that speaks to" and their responsibility, " . . . you shall tell my father of all . . . " (vv. 12–13).

The brothers delivered the message, but Jacob found the message unbelievable. When he saw the Egyptian wagons that Joseph had sent, hope kindled in his heart; but it was not until God confirmed the truth of the message that Jacob accepted it.

The contacts between Balak and Balaam (Numbers 22) were initially by means of messengers. There are no formulae, but the crucial verb of commissioning "sent" is present (v. 5a), and mode of transmission is indicated by the word "saying" (v. 5b). The message deals with the situation in Moab and bears a request, a task, a goal, and flattery. The messengers verbally delivered their message and waited the reaction of the addressee, Balaam. Balaam desired a message from a higher authority, and he received one from God that night. The messengers returned Balaam's refusal to their master, Balak.

Another set of messengers were sent to Balaam, and this time the message they delivered is recorded (16-17). The message is prefixed with a messenger formula, "Thus says Balak the son of Zippor . . . " The message has a request, a promise, and a task. Balaam again desired word from a higher authority and God gave it to him that night. This time Balaam could go, conditionally; Balaam must speak only God's word.

Compare the above with the various situations in Judges 11:12-28; I Kings 2:29-30; I Kings 20:1-12; II Kings 1:1-16; II Kings 18:28-37; II Kings 19:1-7, 9-34 (cf. Isaiah 36 and 37. Do not overlook Isaiah 38:1-8).

Westermann pursues his analysis of the Old Testament prophets by noting in their speeches such components as announcements of judgment with their accusations, pronouncements of divine intervention, reasons for judgment, and effects of judgment.[9]

K. Koch also speaks of announcements of salvation comprised of an appeal for attention, a resumé of the present situation, an exhortation, a divine intervention to save, and reasons for the salvation.[10]

Neither Westermann nor Koch applies his examination of messenger speeches to Exodus or Numbers, though even a casual reading will show that Moses was involved in many messenger tasks. It would appear, then, that an analysis of some narratives as descriptions of several aspects of the messenger relationship to a higher authority and to an audience is in order.

The primary event for a messenger is his commissioning to carry a message, and it has been traditional to refer to the initial commissioning as a call. Moses' call to be a messenger for God is recorded in Exodus 2:23–4:17. The setting for the event (2:23–3:1) places Moses in the desert tending his sheep. God makes His approach via a burning bush and quickly gains Moses' attention (3:2-4a). The remainder is a dialogue in which the divine word alternates with Moses' responses.

Scattered through the dialogue are several components belonging to a messenger situation.

God's selection of His messenger and His contacts with him are represented by such statements as "God called him . . . said . . . " (3:4); "and He said" (seven times); and "[X] said to [X]" also seven times. The commissioning formulae prefer the verbs send, go, say or their synonyms in the proper tense (see Exod. 3:10b, 15b, 16a, 18b; 4:12a, 15a). The last reference, 4:15a, also involves Moses' commissioning of Aaron to be his spokesman to the people. The same verse has an equivalent to the formula, namely, "put the words in his mouth. . . . " Moses was not merely to speak a message; the other part of his task was "that you may bring forth My people, the children of Israel, out of Egypt" (3:10b).

Some of Moses' responses were focused on how he could demonstrate the authority of his message source and on the authenticity of the commission. God answered by giving him authenticity formulae as part of the message to be delivered and also physical tokens. The completion of the Exodus from Egypt would be one of these tokens (Exod. 3:12b), but Moses wanted more immediate signs; they were given (4:5, 8). In terms of authority, Moses was told to say, "I AM has sent me to you" (3:14), and "The Lord God

---

9. Ibid.
10. Koch, *The Growth of the Biblical Tradition,* pp. 183–220.

[etc.] has sent me to you . . . " (3:15), or "appeared to me" (3:16). A variant is found in the message to be delivered to Pharaoh, "The Lord God of the Hebrews has met with us" (3:18b).

The core of the message is an announcement of salvation, that God was intervening in human affairs in behalf of His people. Note this emphasis in Exodus 3:8, 17, 20-22. The reason for God's action is given in 3:7, 9. There are also two promises to Moses (3:12, 18).

Part of the dynamics of the dialogue is a basic dilemma that God's visit brought into Moses' life. The dilemma is not explicitly stated, but it lurked behind all of Moses' objections and came the nearest to surfacing in Exodus 4:14. If Moses should positively respond to God's task for him, a difficult future lay ahead of him. He knew that the Egyptians probably would not forget his crime of killing an Egyptian years before, and he was by now a forgotten person in the Hebrew community. Surely, he had no military power to bring his enslaved people out of Egypt. On the other hand, not to respond positively meant that he would always hereafter be under the wrath of God. Divine mercy alone delivered him from wrath when Moses said he wanted to turn down the task (4:13-14). The stories that follow in the Pentateuch demonstrate that Moses got the message.

Two accounts of messenger commissioning are found in Exodus, chapter 6. In the first one (6:10-13), the commissioning to speak is in verses 10 and 11a, with the brief message in the last part of verse 11. The messenger reacts to the commissioning (v. 12) and God gives an answer (v. 13). The second story (6:28–7:7) has the same components but in a different order, with a verse (6:28) serving as an orientation. The components are the commissioning (6:29), messenger's reaction (6:30), the message content (7:1-5), and a closing statement that the message was delivered (7:6-7).

Observe these more regular examples in Exodus:

Units	Exodus 7:14-18	Exodus 7:25–8:4	Exodus 9:13-21	Exodus 14:1-8	Exodus 25:1–30:10
Orientation	——	7:25	——	——	——
Messenger Commission	14-16a	8:1a	13a	1	25:1-2a
Message Content	16b-18	1b-14	13b-21	2b-4a	25:3–30:10
Obedience				4b	

There are nine examples in Numbers; in many cases the message content deals with legal and cultic matters.

Units	Numbers 5:5-10	Numbers 5:11-31	Numbers 6:1-21	Numbers 6:22-27	Numbers 15:1-16
Messenger Commission	5	11-12a	1-2a	22-23a	1-2a
Message Content	6-10	12b-28	2b-20	23b-27	2b-16
Notation		29-31	21		

Units	Numbers 16:36-40	Numbers 18:25-32	Numbers 35:1-8	Numbers 35:9-34
Messenger Commission	36-37a	25-26a	1-2a	9-10a
Message Content	37b-38	26b-32	2b-8	10b-34
Reaction of Addressee	39-40			

The rules and regulations in Leviticus that deal with everyday moral problems and religious observances are largely couched in a messenger-commissioning framework. Rarely is there reference to the delivery of the messages. The beginning of each section has two standard statements with few variations: "The Lord said to Moses . . ." (and/or Aaron) and the commissioning formula "Speak to . . ." (individuals named or "the children of Israel"). After these statements is a divine word of varying length. These are the sections which come under this format: Leviticus 1:1–3:17; 4:1–6:7; 6:8-23; 6:24–7:21; 7:22-27; 7:28-38; 11:1-47; 12:1-8; 15:1-33; chapters 16; 17; 18; 19; 20; 21; 22:1-16; 22:17-33; 23:1-8; 23:9-22; 23:23-32; 23:33-44; 25:1–26:46; 27:1-34.

In Exodus, chapter 4, one finds accounts that present a broader view of the total messenger situation; they are 4:18-23 and 4:27-31. But these stories do not fully parallel and each lacks certain basic components.

In Exodus 4:18-23, a brief verse of orientation (v. 18) leads to the commissioning of the messenger (v. 19) and then a journey to meet the addressee (v. 20). A messenger commissioning occurs again (v. 21-22a) and then a message of judgment is given (vv. 22b-23).

The messenger situation described in Exodus 4:27-31 begins with a commissioning (v. 27a) and a statement that Aaron went to meet Moses (v. 27b). Moses delivered God's message to Aaron (v. 28), and together they went on to meet an assembly of Israelites (v. 29) to whom they delivered God's message (v. 30). In response, the people believed and worshiped God (v. 31).

Also consider these rather complete descriptions of the messenger situation in the Book of Exodus.

Units	Exodus 6:2-9	Exodus 10:1-6	Exodus 12:1-42	Exodus 19:1-8a	Exodus 20:18–24:3
Orientation				1-2	20:18-21
Messenger Commission	2-6a	1-2	1-3a	3	20:22a
Message Content	6b-8		3b-20	4-6	20:22b–24:2
Going and Speaking to Addressee/s	9a	3a	21a	7	24:3a
Message Delivery		3a-6a	21b-27		
Reaction of Addressee/s	9b		28	8a	24:3b
Aftermath		6b	29-39		

Examples may be found in Numbers with slight variations:

Units	Numbers 17:1-19	Numbers 22:41–23:12	Numbers 23:13-26	Numbers 34:1-15
Orientation		22:41–23:4	13-15	
Messenger Commission	1-2	23:5	16	1
Message Content	3-5			2-12
Going and Speaking to Addressee/s	6a-7	23:6	17a	
Message Delivery		7-10	17b-24	13-15
Divine Act	8			
Reaction of Addressee/s	9	11-12	25-26	

Three stories in Exodus have a slightly different format.

Units	Exodus 8:20-24	Exodus 9:1-7	Exodus 11:1-3
Messenger Commission	20a	1a	1-2a
Message Content	20b-23	1b-5	2b
Divine Action	24a	6a	3a
Aftermath	24b	6b-7a	3b
Reaction of Addressee/s		7b	

Another set of reports is found in Exodus; only one is in Numbers. Observe the plot of these reports; they basically cover only the delivery of the message. The chart has the Exodus narrations.

Units	Exodus 5:1-14	Exodus 11:4-10	Exodus 32:25-29	Exodus 35:1-3	Exodus 35:4-29	Exodus 35:30–39:43
Orientation			25-26			
Going and Speaking to Addressee/s	1a	4a	27a	1a	4a	30a
Message Delivery	1b-3b	4b-7	27b	1b-3	4b-19	30b-35
Reaction of Addressee/s	4-9		28a		20-29	36:1–38:20
Aftermath	10-14	8a-10	28b-29			38:21-43

The narrative in Numbers 30:1-16 has three units: the oral transmission of the message to the assembly (30:1); the delivery of the message itself (2-15); and a brief account of the aftermath of the meeting (v. 16).

In Exodus there are narratives that assume a messenger situation but have a different format and a different function.

The following charts present plots of these reports, which may be called *Miracle Authorization* types.

Units	Exodus 7:8-13	Exodus 7:19-24	Exodus 8:5-7	Exodus 8:16-19
Miracle Authorization	8-9	19	5	16
Obedience	10	20-21	6	17
Reaction of Adversary	11-12	22-23	7	18-19
Aftermath	13	24		

Units	Exodus 9:8-12	Exodus 9:22-26	Exodus 10:12-15	Exodus 10:21-23	Exodus 14:26-31
Miracle Authorization	8-9	22	12	21	26
Obedience	10-11	23a	13a	22a	27a

Divine Action	12a	23b	13b	22b-23	27b
Reaction of Adversary	12b				
Aftermath		24-26	13c-15		28-29

One more major structural type is to be found among the narratives of Exodus and Numbers. Since each story begins by a report of opposition to Moses' administration over the tribes of Israel, the type may be called a *Leadership Challenge* format. Another important feature is a dramatic theophany in which God suddenly appears in a cloud and/or in glory.

Units	Exodus	Numbers				
	16:1-36	12:1-10a	14:1-45	16:1-35	16:41-50	20:1-13
The Challenge	1-3	1-2	1-10a	1-19a	41	1-6a
Divine Word	4-5	3-4	10b-12			
Message Delivery	6-10a					
Theophany	10b-14	5	14a, 21	19b	42	6b
Interchange: God's Word, Messenger Speeches, Reaction of Addressee/s	15-35	5-8	20-35	20-30	43-47	7-12
Notation or Aftermath	36	9-10a	36-38	31-35	48-50	13

The foregoing analysis of narrative structure in the first four books of the Pentateuch is not exhaustive; it does suggest that this aspect of literary research may not yet be complete. A minute examination and correlation of the details, on which much has been done, has not been attempted here but needs to be done.

Several observations may be in order. The close parallelism of structure within each of the narrative types points to more homogeneity within the story classifications than most literary critics have been willing to allow for.

And this homogeneity appears to be rather closely tied to the life situation with which each literary type deals.

A check of these story classifications with the so-called sources, J, E, P, reveals that in almost every classification of narrative forms at least two, and often all three, are found. Often the so-called J and P sources are found in the same story grouping, even both of them in the same story. The conventional date given the J source is ca. 900 B.C., and that of P, 500 B.C., about four hundred years apart. Would the same basic story structure be retained for this period of time in two different social classes? Surely doubt could be raised at this point. Such doubts would not have to be brought forth if all these stories are regarded as Mosaic.

The Swedish School of Tradition History

In the 1930s, rumblings of discontent and attitudes of outright rejection of major aspects of the Wellhausen theory began to come out of Sweden. Since most of the opinion of the Swedish scholars was written in Swedish, scholars in other countries, especially in America, were slow in learning of the views of these men. These views had been influenced by Gunkel and ancient Near Eastern literature, and they explored the relationship between oral and written material. The University of Uppsala has been the center for this brand of thinking that has been called *Tradition History,* or the traditio-historical method.

H. S. Nyberg was the first to spark the interest of Scandinavian scholars in this method and to publish the results of their research.[11] He rejected the evolutionary scheme of the Wellhausen school and an association of the symbols JEDP with documents. He held that the symbols represented segments of oral tradition. Nyberg rejected the traditional methods of textual criticism. He believed that this method was unnecessary, because the Masoretic Text was very reliable, and because before the writing of the Masoretic Text, the oral tradition that preserved the Scripture was reliable. He claimed that a study of ancient Near Eastern literature shows that oral materials suffered fewer changes than written texts. He posited "bearers of tradition" for Israel; these groups would pass knowledge from generation to generation with great care.

In the same decade, H. Birkeland also declared that oral tradition had fixed forms and the act of writing them down did not effect significant changes.[12] He employed Islamic Arabs as models of how memorization of great amounts of tradition was common in the Semitic cultures. Birkeland claimed that oral tradition acted as a check on written texts in late Judaism.

---

11. H. S. Nyberg's books have not been translated into English.
12. H. Birkeland's books also remain untranslated.

After World War II, I. Engnell became a prolific writer in several languages and thus could disseminate the new views more widely.[13] He followed Nyberg's and Birkeland's views quite closely but kept himself more solidly grounded in ancient Near Eastern literature. He believed in both oral and written fixity of the biblical text and in schools of tradition in Israel's history. The symbol P represented such a "school" in Judah, and it faithfully preserved priestly material until it was written in the time of Ezra. The symbol D represented a "school" in northern Israel of long standing, and it became associated with Judah only at a late date. Engnell saw no need for unknown redactors or any point in the criteria of divine names. He was a strong believer in the reliability of the Masoretic Text. The close tie of oral and written material with liturgy was the prime reason for minimal changes.

In summary, tradition history rejected normal textual criticism, the literary criticism of the Wellhausen theory, and the idea of a transmission history of literary units. Some shortcomings might be pointed out. Like many new theories it tended to go to extremes. It had no real basis for schools of tradition in Israel, and its exaltation of oral reliability above textual reliability seems overstressed. On the other hand, it does not give adequate attention to the importance of the written document in Semitic circles in the ancient Near East. The spoken word was valued on a short-term basis, but for long-term preservation, valued data was written down. There is reason to believe that oral transmission and written transmission coexisted throughout the Pentateuchal and other Old Testament periods, and that this phenomena contributed to the reliability of both. As the use of the term "schools" implies, there is a strong stress upon the "creative community" as the source of the Scriptures. In addition, in denying Wellhausen's concept of an isolated Israel, most of the Swedish scholars have gone to the opposite extreme, making Israel part and parcel of the religious milieu of the ancient Near East.

Biblical Theology

Suffice it to say that the exponents of the Wellhausen theory could write many books on the religion of Israel but almost none on the theology of the Old Testament. The method of literary criticism and evolutionary dialectics could find many theologies, as many as fourteen, but no basic theological theme.

Two factors, the loss of confidence in Hegelian dialectics and the redis-covery of the covenant as the ancient framework of Hebrew' religious

---

13. I. Engnell, *A Rigid Scrutiny: Critical Essays on the Old Testament* (Nashville: Vanderbilt University Press, 1969).

thought, changed scholarly attitudes toward biblical theology. W. Eichrodt[14] broke new ground and sparked a new interest. It was firmly based on the covenant concept. In the past forty years many books on the theology of the Old Testament or on the unifying themes of the Scripture have come off the press. Most of the new books push monotheism and other themes back to Moses, and some, to Abraham. The study of biblical theology is sharpening the contrast between pagan polytheism and the true Hebrew faith as presented in the Scripture.

Biblical theology has not been able to maintain its momentum, in spite of its contributions to one's grasp of major themes that span the books of the Old Testament. Hindsight seems to show that B. S. Childs's book, *Biblical Theology in Crisis* (1970) has been a turning point in attitudes toward the books that proposed an overall theology in the Old Testament. Childs faults the biblical theologians for basing their efforts on the methods of source, form, and redaction criticism and then joining theological truths that are relevant to "modern man" with the non-theological conclusions of the critics. The chasm between the two has proved to be too great. Biblical theology as presented in recent books has not proved equal to the task. If the beliefs and practices of the ancient Hebrew were essentially of low quality and encased in a hard shell of primitive polytheism, how could they possibly have value for present-day Christians? If the redactors freely changed and reshaped their traditions and literature according to their personal prejudices, how could the final result of their labors possess integrity and credibility? Would serious Christians feel comfortable resting their spiritual and moral values on such foundations, to say nothing of a viable hope for the future?

Canonical Criticism

B. S. Childs has proposed an alternative approach to the Old Testament which has become known as "canonical criticism," though he prefers the terms *analysis* or *method* for his approach. In contrast to source, form, and redaction critics who have claimed liberation from the contraints of the authority of a canon of Scripture, Childs freely accepts the context of every book and every passage within each book as being Scripture. Childs has thus placed high value on what words, phrases, and passages mean in the biblical manuscripts presently available to us. Whereas the critics mentioned above tended to view their work as essentially irrelevant to modern Christians (though recent biblical theologians have tried to make it relevant), Childs has deliberately focused his attention on the canon in order to reveal theological truths to the Christian reader. In effect he has sought to join the insights of the

---

14. W. Eichrodt, *Theology of the Old Testament* (Philadelphia: The Westminster Press, 1961).

source, form, and redaction critics with the teachings of the books of the Hebrew Old Testament in their present form. These critics have been very unhappy about this attempted wedding.

In Childs's view, when a Christian reads the Bible, he or she does so as a believer and holds the Bible to be authoritative. The believer understands the Old Testament as an account of how God established and maintained a dynamic relationship with Israel and how this relationship has been extended to all the peoples of the world through Jesus Christ.

True, some believers have been vulnerable to interpreting the text improperly; but, this need not be the case. Childs relies on both the work of his fellow critics and on the theological competence of the believer as safeguards in maintaining the integrity of the Bible.

Structural Analysis

In the late seventies, books and articles in English alerted scholars to a new type of approach to Scripture developed in France. Biblical scholars in that land, dissatisfied with the inability of critics to bridge the gap between ancient Israel and the modern Christian, turned to a secular form of literary criticism called structural analysis. These scholars felt they found in this theory and its procedures a way to bridge the gap between the then and the now. With help from the assumptions and methods of this analytical method, biblical scholars sought to understand the Bible in a new way.

From the vantage point of this new perspective, Old Testament literature was viewed as imaginative and metaphorical. No longer need the student bother with geography, historical accuracy, or authorship; he could gain new and startling insights by accepting biblical literature as the presentation of an imaginative world governed by established conventions. As in many types of literature, fairy tales commonly have an opening statement, "Once upon a time," or something comparable. Fairy tales are marked by elfish creatures and talking animals. Myths have the convention of gods and goddesses talking to men, and so on. Since the Bible is a part of world literature, one should expect such conventions in many of its stories. Fairy tales, epics, myths, etc., are a *genre,* a category of literary compositions distinguished by a definite style. Each genre has its set of conventions; hence, recognizing a biblical genre as the same as that found in other literature, one can use its universal conventions to interpret the biblical example.

Biblical scholars who apply structuralism to the Old Testament do not bother asking whether statements made about human affairs were true; they would rather ask if every part of the biblical story or poem fits the conventions (the standard elements) of that kind of story or poem. If so, all the elements are appropriate and beautiful. The ultimate concern of structuralists is beauty, not truth.

Because structuralism cares little about the past history of a literary unit in the Bible, the proponents of this procedure concentrate their efforts on the way a present-day reader should read that text. They insist on reading a literary work as a whole unit within the context of all literature of the same genre, and accepting it as consistent within itself. To do this kind of reading, one must learn the mechanism used in constructing the unit being read and appreciate the beauty of that mechanism (the conventions that belong to the genre).

The New Criticism

Among American literary critics of the forties and fifties there was a strong negative reaction to the prevailing interest in the historical details lying behind a literary work, and in the familial, social, and emotional aspects of the author's life. The new critics pushed all this aside and focused their attention on the literary work itself. They did not care whether the work possessed information about the past or about the author. These critics were fascinated by the finished text and its beauty, by which the reader would be enriched if the text were perused from this perspective.

Some biblical scholars have studied the Bible in the same manner. The reader is the one who matters, not the historical background or the intentions of an author. What the text means to the reader is most important, since a normative, timeless meaning or truth is not an element of the biblical text. If the reader is religious, what "God says" to that reader through that text is its valid meaning. No outside system of truths or doctrines have the right to declare that meaning incorrect, though that meaning may be evaluated within the context of the entire canon of the Bible.

An Inductive or Discovery Method

A method of bible study that has become popular among scholars who are conservative in their point of view is known among them as the inductive method. Proponents of this approach do not deny that a number of aspects of method in the other kinds of study described in the previous pages are inductive. Indeed, inductive procedures have been employed, that is, observable data have been gathered and analyzed, and hypotheses based on that data have been constructed by scholars who study the Bible according to the theories and techniques of each type of criticism described above.

The inductive method has several characteristics that are similar to the methods described earlier, but also several that differ from these methods. A brief sketch of the historical background of this method may clarify why this is so.

The roots of this discovery method go back to William R. Harper, professor of Semitics at Yale (1881–1891) and president of the University of Chicago (1891–1906). His dissatisfaction with the prevailing way of teaching biblical languages was expressed in two books, *Elements of Hebrew Syntax by an*

Inductive Method (1888) and *The Inductive Greek Method* (1888). Harper began his courses by requiring the students to deal directly with the Hebrew or Greek texts and to draw principles of syntax from the text as it was read.

One of his assistants at Yale, a doctoral student named Wilbert W. White, saw possibilities of adapting this method to studying the biblical text in the vernacular and then leading the students to the original languages. Thus, in America, the method is sometimes called "English Bible." In 1900 White founded a school called the Biblical Seminary of New York. Through its Bible-centered curriculum he sought to train educators and pastors to engage in a balanced program of research. He urged pastors to lace their sermons with valid biblical insights and to show believers how to study the Bible properly — on their own in their mother tongue.

The student who uses the inductive method of Bible study should read the biblical text itself as objectively as possible. It is to be understood as a number of canonical books, and its voice should have the right to speak for itself. Meanings should not be assigned to the text but discovered in it. At the outset the biblical text should be read and studied as whole units, whole books, and groups of books as a whole. Their inner consistency may be grasped by outlines of the contents or by visualizing their overall structure by constructing charts.

The first step of the inductive method is observation, the ability to see important data in the text itself. Particular characteristics of the text must be noted exactly and examined carefully. These particulars may include 1) terms of various sorts in their context; 2) elements of internal structure such as introduction, comparison, contrast, repetition, continuity, continuation, climax, cruciality or turning point, interchange, general statements and clusters of particular items, cause and effect, instrumentation, substantiation, explanation, analysis, interrogation, harmony, and summary — singly or variously combined; 3) general literary forms; and 4) the atmosphere or moods evident in the passage.

The next step in the method is interpretation, the first phase of which is interrogation. Portions of the observed data, whether in passages or the book as a whole, are probed by questions in a certain sequence: (1) questions of the who, what and where type that seek basic information and meaning; (2) those of the why and how type which ferret out motives, reasons, and functions; and (3) those which try to bring to the surface implications embedded in the data. Block after block of data are thus analyzed; no source of information is ignored while seeking for possible answers which may correctly interpret the data.

The second phase of interpretation is a process of walking around the data and looking at it from various vantage points, from the perspectives of disciplines of study and opinions of scholars. Undergirding this examination is the conviction that the meaning of Scripture must coincide with what one finds in all of Scripture. External concepts or systems of thought are not to be imposed on the Scripture; rather, they are also probed with questions in order to gain insights which will aid in understanding the Bible as we have it.

The third step is that of evaluation, to determine whether what is found in Scripture is worthwhile, relevant, and useful for whomever, whenever, and where ever. The student seeks to determine which passages are local, that is, of primary significance to people of ancient times and in specific circumstances. The student also needs to identify those teachings which are timeless and thus are relevant at any time and anywhere. At this level of reflection the student must resist making snap judgments or injecting subjective reactions ("I don't like it, therefore I won't consider it").

The student should also realize that a timeless principle may not fit every circumstance that may arise; hence, an effort must be made to identify which present situation matches a timeless teaching of Scripture and then propose an application of the teaching to it. This application may be personal, and thus significant for spiritual transformation and growth; or it may be social, and thus significant for social reform and welfare. The movement here is from literature to life.

The final step is that of correlation, a process of synthesizing all insights gained from the previous steps. The goal is to construct a viable biblical theology and a dynamic Christian understanding, with practice in life, so as to recreate within and without, with the aid of the Holy Spirit, conformity to Jesus Christ.

Correlation on the cognitive level should always be tentative and growing; it is always possible to gain more information and understanding. On this level, correlation should be as broad as possible, looking beyond passages to the entire book, to the entire canon, to all of literature. Often charts and diagrams are utilized to show visually the relationships of themes and principles to the totality of a book.

SUMMARY OF EVIDENCE AND ARGUMENT FOR MOSAIC AUTHORSHIP

The goal of this section is to bring together and to summarize items that bear directly upon Mosaic authorship. Rather generalized statements will be presented on theological aspects of the question.

Internal and External Correlation

A fundamental aim of this study has been to see the Pentateuch in relationship to its cultural environment. Much new knowledge gathered by scholars of a number of disciplines has broadened the horizon so that correlations can now be made more effectively than ever before. But there are still huge gaps in our knowledge of the ancient Near East, which can only mean that correlation is still limited in its scope.

268

Our knowledge of ethnic groups other than the Hebrews has greatly expanded during the past several decades. Many of these groups the Pentateuch does not mention, or does so obscurely. The great civilizations of Mesopotamia and of the Nile are much better understood; and, in the process, the Pentateuch has become a new literature, for it can now be seen in its ancient milieu. Many problems still remain in chronological correlation of the Pentateuch to the dynasties of Egypt, of Mesopotamia, and of the Levant, but there is good basis for hope that more information will further enhance our appreciation of the Pentateuch.

The artifacts recovered by archaeologists have brought together the Patriarchs and the cultural life of the Middle Bronze Age in a remarkable manner. Much more data is needed to place them precisely in that age, but a hazy picture is increasingly becoming clearer. The ages before Abraham and the Late Bronze Age afterward still relate poorly with the Pentateuch, but several factors give hope for improvement. Knowledge about the early history of the alphabet is not nearly as vague as it was forty-five years ago; indeed it is quite certain that an alphabetic script was available for the people in Palestine several centuries prior to Moses' time. Ignorance of writing techniques can no longer be claimed for the Israelite leaders.

Literary forms of expression were available for the Hebrew people. The Ras Shamrah tablets demonstrate that the structure of the poetry in the Pentateuch is in line with the poetry produced by the Canaanite people. Though the Pentateuch has some prose types not found elsewhere, if creativity is granted to talented individuals, that problem is not insurmountable. Presently, many form critics refuse to allow this kind of creativity, but they are surely wrong. The covenant structure was well known in the Middle and Late Bronze ages and thus available for the applications of the covenant to the faith and practice that the Pentateuch portrays.

One of the most significant correlations to come to light is in the realm of law. The law codes and legal documents of the Mesopotamian area show that Mosaic laws were premonarchial and fit the time of Moses well.

Another helpful correlation is in the area of language. The Hebrew language was not a strange or unique tongue, but one closely tied to other widely used languages, such as Akkadian, Canaanite, and Aramaic. Many in the Pentateuch long defied translation because their meaning was not known. In many instances this is no longer the case. Recent commentaries and scholarly articles are filled with bits of linguistic gold; they provide the meaning that these words and phrases had long since lost. Our understanding of the content of the Pentateuch is therefore richer.

All in all, the evidence for a close relationship between Moses and the Pentateuch has been strengthened by the vast amount of research that has been done during the century. This evidence has not solved all problems nor answered all questions that surround a claim of Mosaic authorship, but headway in that direction has been made. At the same time it should not be forgotten that a number of prominent Old Testament scholars, most notably the late Martin Noth, have been persistent in denying that there ever was a Moses who took an important leadership role among the Hebrew people.

The Concept of Revelation

An important cog in the argument in favor of Mosaic authorship is the validity of the concept of revelation. Even if Moses may not be regarded as the actual penman of every word of the Pentateuch, it still remains that in Exodus, Leviticus, and Numbers, God repeatedly spoke to Moses. This claim of the text immediately ties the material to Moses.

In contrast to the mind-set of many Western scholars who understand revelation to be basically the result of man's reflective or reasoning processes, the Pentateuch presents a different picture of God's communicative encounter with Moses. Commonly, Old Testament scholars have depicted the religious outlook of the Pentateuch to be the dogmas of a late period superimposed on early traditions.

How are the God-Moses encounters depicted? Time and again God is presented as the first speaker; He initiated the meeting. This is true of the burning bush incident, of the plague series, of the Passover meal, and the several Mount Sinai encounters. In other instances, the encounter began with a prayer request or a question, as in Exodus 5:22 ff; 14:15 ff; and Numbers, chapter 21. In both kinds of encounters, the divine decision to communicate to Moses was crucial; Moses could not force God to speak.

Characteristic of the God-Moses meetings is the "I-Thou" relationship, but even this is not fully accurate, for the third party, Israel, is constantly in the context. It was God's concern for the welfare and destiny of Israel, which overshadowed each of these meetings. The revelatory experiences were not just for Moses' sake; they were for the sake of Israel. But Moses was important. The Pentateuch does not present God as generalizing His revelations in natural phenomena and historical events, leaving the meaning of these occurrences for future thinkers to ferret out. The Pentateuch presents God as giving to Moses information about His estimate of the situation and His intentions to do something about it prior to the occurrence, and oftentimes while the occurrence was taking place and after it had happened.

Glancing back to Genesis, one notes that this same pattern of God-man encounter is present from Adam and Eve to the last of the Patriarchs. Turning one's scrutiny to the remainder of the Old Testament, one finds this pattern wherever a God-man encounter is described, especially among the prophets.

The Concept of Inspiration and Authenticity

A complement of revelation is inspiration. In discussing inspiration one can emphasize the source of inspiration, namely, the Spirit of God, who moves in the inner consciousness of an individual; or one may stress the experience of the individual, whether it be one or that of several varieties; or one may highlight, even limit the discussion to, the proclamation of the individual. Some would focus their attention on only the written form of the proclamation.

All three aspects are in the Pentateuch: God who is the source of inspiration, the experiences of the individual who meets God, and the message that is proclaimed. Crucial to an argument in favor of Mosaic authorship is the authenticity, the genuineness, of this inspiration. The Pentateuch presents the religious experiences that it describes as genuine, real-life experiences. Integral to each are rugged, nasty life problems. Imaginative literature does not produce or reproduce concrete experiences such as these *ex nihilo,* nor does reflective literature linger long with the concreteness of everyday life; its natural environment is abstraction and speculation.

The very fact that the common man can read the stories preserved in the Pentateuch and can see meaningful correlations with his own life situations (for centuries Jews and Christians have experienced this fact) speaks volumes in favor of its authenticity.

Several characteristics of inspiration in the Pentateuch can be noted. First, individual after individual discovered that the living God is not easily accessible to man; there is a power, a mystery, and a glory about the presence of God that frightened every one of them. Israel learned that Mount Sinai could not be ascended unless God gave an invitation; they could not approach the tabernacle without an atoning sacrifice. The hinderpart of God's glory was almost more than Moses could endure. God's presence was a threat to life. Yet God did move into the experiences of individuals and of the nation to give a saving word to them.

Divine inspiration did not degrade, demolish, or annul the self-consciousness of any of the people with whom God communicated. Each was vividly aware of personal sins and weaknesses and of the seriousness of the dangers that threatened others in the world. What they experienced was not to be simply a private, priceless possession; the experience was to fit them for the task to which God called them. There was variety in the human experiences, but an induced "trip," or a severance of inner and outer consciousness, was not among them.

Thirdly, the stress in the inspired encounters was not on the condition of the experience; the emphasis was on the content of the communication.

Many scholars cannot endure the concept of a speaking God, but He is everywhere present in the Pentateuch. The claim is that God had promises, prohibitions, commands, instructions, exhortations, challenges, and judgments for men and women of ancient times, and He delivered them personally. Consequently, the message was important whether in oral or in written form. This fact gave to the message of God an aura of sacredness that would contribute to fixity in oral transmission or to the written transmission of God's Word through the centuries.

The Concept of Infallibility and Inerrancy

Neither infallibility nor inerrancy are biblical terms; they are both from the Latin language and have been utilized to convey convictions that the Scripture is supremely important to the believer in the one true God and that it provides for him reliable information for faith and practice. The term *infallible* has been popular among traditional scholars in Great Britain; whereas in America the term *inerrancy* has been more favored among Calvinists and *infallibility* has the lead among traditional scholars who are non-Calvinists.

Both terms, *infallibility* and *inerrancy,* carry with them connotations that have caused their exponents to spend inordinate amounts of time clarifying what they mean when they use the terms. The goals of the exponents of these terms have been to stress the divine source of the message of the Bible; to uphold the validity of the concept of revelation portrayed and stated in the Scripture; to stress the genuineness of the religious experience of the men and women prominent in the Bible; to defend the trustworthiness and dependability of the content of the Scripture; to support the belief that the intentions of the authors of Scripture were unsullied by guile, deliberate falsification of the past, efforts to brainwash the public, or by deceit; and to challenge theories that were undergirded by naturalistic or humanistic philosophies that insisted on reconstructing Israel's history or radically reinterpreting doctrines in the Bible.

Several syllogisms have been joined with infallibility and inerrancy, and these have tended to confuse the matter rather than to clarify it. In a simplified form one syllogism declares, "God is perfect, the Bible is the Word of God, therefore the Bible is without error." Or another one, which is more of a dictum states, "False in one instance; false in all instances." In both cases, time and space must be spent explaining that there are many human elements in the Bible and many difficulties in all extant manuscripts, so only the autographs are intended. But the autographs are not available.

And what is meant by error? Again time and space are expended to admit that no one denies the existence of errors made by copyists of manuscripts or by translators of the Hebrew into other languages. Nor are errors of good style or of good grammar included. Opponents have made long lists of so-called errors, and defendants have written many pages in rebuttal. And few seem to agree whether certain features in the text are contradictions, anomalies, paradoxes, or parts of a greater unifying whole. Nor can agreement be reached whether certain words, phrases, or sentences are to be understood literally, figuratively, or whatever. And what of the intention of the original author in some passages? Would that he were here to explain what he really meant!

The word *infallible* has become obscured by Islam's attitude toward the Koran—that the Koran must not be translated from the Arabic; as soon as it is translated it loses its infallibility. The Koran cannot be joined with commentary without the same loss occurring. Any admission that the text has changed since it left the pen of the prophet is unthinkable. There has been some of this attitude in some sectors of Judaism and Christianity; but basically, translations have been freely made, spellings of words have been updated, late words have been substituted for old words, synonyms have been interchanged, and explanations have been added. All this was done consistently but enough to show, in the minds of most believers, that these matters had not annulled the Scriptures as the Word of God.

By no means do all traditional scholars agree that the terms *infallibility* and *inerrancy* are the best instruments of defense to set out on the front lines. There are some solid believers in the Scripture who hesitate to use either term. Properly understood, both terms can fulfill an important function in higher criticism, but in the controversy that surrounds their presence in the arsenal of polemic, the main front lines ought not be neglected.

It is a conviction of this writer that many of the items that have been discussed have contributions to make in consideration of the genuineness, integrity, reliability, trustworthiness, and truth of the Pentateuch. Perhaps these can be summarized in a series of contrasting propositions as follows.

The biblical doctrine of one true personal God, who is uniquely other than nature or man, is in contrast to the pagan tendency to identify deity with the totality of nature, with human reason, or with a generalized human consciousness.

The scriptural portrayal of the living God is a true picture of how God relates to man in personal experience, through direct communication, through wondrous signs in nature, and through events in history, in contrast to any view that holds the concept of God to be the growing construct of man's reflective and/or intuitive powers.

The creation of material things and the creation of man were acts of

God that "actually happened," and is in contrast to any view that holds that all things emerged out of eternal, physical matter.

There are demonic powers that are neither eternal, nor equal with God, nor have the status of divinity, a view that is in contrast to views that hold the demonic powers are eternal, are equal with God, or that there are really no demonic powers.

The claim is correct that God did reveal to selected men information about Himself, the intentions that prompted the revelation of the meaning of His acts, the plans He had for the future, in contrast to any view that all verbalizations, which traditionally has been called revelation, is in fact the result of rational processes, references, myth-building, or the demythologizing of pagan stories about the activities of gods and goddesses.

The biblical understanding that God is the Lord of nature and of history and can, at any time of His own choosing, use or change natural processes (miracles) and/or intervene in the affairs of mankind (history) to save or to judge either individuals or groups, is true. This understanding is quite different from a view that holds that any or some of the miracles were acts of magic, or that God does not interfere with the laws of nature, hence all miracles can be rationally explained as interpretations of the community.

The concept that God prompted men to speak and/or write the content of the Scripture without negating the humanness of the people involved, without destroying the authenticity of the Word spoken or written, without polluting the purity of motive of the men involved, is valid. Such a concept would be far superior to claims that God did not speak directly to any man, that humanity is of necessity given to falsehood, the distortion of truth, or that historical facts have been twisted by religious or other inferior motives.

The position is correct which holds that the authority of Scripture is intrinsic because it is rooted in the authority of the speaking, acting God, in contrast to a view that regards the authority of Scripture to have been conferred on selected books by human acts of assembly or by a personal response to parts or the whole of the Scripture.

The affirmation is sound that understands that God deals with man, even in revelatory moments, within the dynamics of healthy, interpersonal relationships. This kind of God-man encounter would maintain the unity of his personality, involve the totality of his being, regenerate and cleanse him from sin, and prompt his growth toward maturity. Unsound would be the view that significant religious experiences (including revelatory moments) are marked by a split between man's spiritual "self" and his physical "self" and by pathological traits. Equally unsound would be the view that the great experiences of God's men were much like a "trip" or were basically limited to the mental and emotional life.

The understanding of the covenant as a framework of interpersonal relationships that is tri-dimensional—including God, the individual, and the community—is valid. To be more explicit, God is the Sovereign who creates, commands, invites, calls, saves, and judges the individual who must choose to obey or disobey Him, and the community who must choose to obey or disobey God's Word, whether spoken or written. Not valid would be understandings of the covenant relationship as strictly legal regulations, or a private affair with no social concerns.

The propositions set forth as valid in the above discussion should undergird and be compatible with interrelating activities of biblical studies:

> All serious activity in the discipline of textual criticism that seeks to ascertain the original reading of any passage of Scripture.
>
> All serious activity that seeks to attain to a correct understanding of any aspect of the grammar of Hebrew, Aramaic, or Greek texts to possess the true meaning of the written material and to grasp the intention of the writers.
>
> All serious activity that seeks to analyze the structure, types, and functions of literary units in the Scripture to understand the intentions of the writers.
>
> All serious activity that seeks to discover the environment, way of life, and mode of thinking of the writers and of their contemporaries within and without the believing community.
>
> All serious activity that seeks to ascertain the chronological sequence and correlation of events mentioned both in the Scripture and in nonbiblical inscriptions, and the correct dates for those events so far as it is humanly possible.
>
> All serious activity that seeks to identify and to understand all linguistic devices, such as similes, metaphors, and idioms, that the Scripture writers employed to convey their thoughts.
>
> All serious, positive evaluation of any and all interpretations of Scripture, by individual scholars and by the believing community, to test their accordance with the total message of Scripture. The evaluation should weigh in the balance of truth the fairness of an interpretation to the biblical witness and whether or not improbable or false relationships have been established between passages of Scripture or between Scripture and nonbiblical writings.

All of the points mentioned bear upon Pentateuchal studies, and they should furnish guidelines for a fruitful pursuit of truth in the Word of God.

Suggested Books for Further Study

Archer, G. L. *A Survey of Old Testament Introduction.* Chicago: Moody Press, 1964. See, especially, pages 31-350.

Bruce, F. F. *The Books and the Parchments.* Old Tappan, N. J.: Fleming H. Revell Co., 1963.

Childs, B. S. *Memory and Tradition in Israel.* Naperville, Ill.: A. R. Allenson, 1962.

Cross, F. M. *The Ancient Library of Qumran.* Garden City, N. Y.: Doubleday Anchor Books, 1961.

Flack, E. E. *The Text, Canon and Principal Versions of the Bible.* Grand Rapids: Baker Book House, 1956.

Gaster, T. H. *The Dead Sea Scriptures.* Garden City, N. Y.: Doubleday Anchor Books, 1964.

Gerhardsson, B. *Memory and Manuscript.* Lund, Sweden: C. W. K. Gleerup, 1961.

Harrison, R. K. *Introduction to the Old Testament.* Grand Rapids: Wm. B. Eerdmans Publishing Co., 1969. See, especially, pages 1-82, 495-662.

Kapelrud, A. S. *Israel.* Oxford: Blackwell, 1966.

La Sor, W. S. *The Dead Sea Scrolls and the Christian Faith.* Chicago: Moody Press, 1962.

Mansoor, M. *The Dead Sea Scrolls.* Grand Rapids: Wm. B. Eerdmans Publishing Co., 1964.

Nielson, E. *Oral Tradition.* Chicago: A. R. Allenson, 1954.

Roberts, B. J. *The Old Testament Text and Versions.* Cardiff: University of Wales, 1951.

Trever, J. *The Untold Story of Qumran.* Old Tappan, N. J.: Fleming H. Revell Co., 1965.

Tucker, G. M. *Form Criticism of the Old Testament.* Philadelphia: Fortress Press, 1971.

Vermes, G. *The Dead Sea Scrolls in English.* Baltimore: Penguin Books, 1962.

Wurthwein, E. *The Text of the Old Testament.* New York: Macmillan Co., 1957.

Young, E. J. *An Introduction to the Old Testament.* Grand Rapids: Wm. B. Eerdmans Publishing Co., 1964. See, especially, pages 15-154.

Tiberias, by the Sea of Galilee, became a primary center of Talmudic Judaism after the fall of Jerusalem in A.D. 70. The Tiberian school of the Masoretes established the Palestinian canon, the order of the books in the Hebrew Old Testament.

10

The Pentateuch
and Canonization

The question of why certain books were selected and why other Hebrew writings were rejected in the process of putting together the Old Testament has long been of interest to students of the Bible. Most discussions of this process, called "canonization," have regarded the Pentateuch as foundational to the entire Old Testament canon.

The aims of this chapter are to define what is meant by the term *canon,* to become acquainted with the organization of the several orders of the Old Testament books that have been preserved in Judaism and in Christianity, to examine possible factors said to have determined the make-up of the canon, to analyze the Wellhausen concept of canonization, and to analyze the traditional understanding of why the present books are in the Old Testament canon.

The term *canon* is a transliteration of the Greek, *kanon,* which appears twice in the New Testament (II Cor. 10:12 and Gal. 6:16) in which the meaning is "measure," or "rule." There is rootage for the word in classical Greek in which the word refers to a straight rod, or bar, especially made to keep a thing straight. Some Greek authors were regarded as canon or models for literary excellence. The word with much the same meaning, i.e., a measuring device, can be traced back into ancient Near Eastern languages. Worthy of note are the words *gi-na* in Sumerian, *qanu* in Assyrian, *qn* in Ugaritic, and *qaneh* in Hebrew.

Athanasius (about A.D. 350) seems to have been the first to apply the word *canon* to the Scriptures, especially the Old Testament. The connection was not ill-advised because an essential idea, related to the use of a measure or a ruler, is control over other objects: it is a standard of authority. Jesus and the apostles regarded the Old Testament as authoritative, and the Jewish Talmud regards the Old Testament, especially the Pentateuch, as authoritative. In the Talmud, the idea of authority is present in the ritualistic formula "defiling the hands," which refers to the practice of washing the hands after the scribes have handled sacred things or the sacred books (compare with a similar thought in Leviticus 16:24).

The idea of authority was present in the Old Testament. Deuteronomy 31:10-13 exhorts the priests to read the law to Israel, ". . . that they may hear and that they may learn to fear the Lord your God, and carefully observe all the words of this law . . . " (v. 12b, RSV; cf. Deut. 17:18–20; Josh. 8:30–35). In I Samuel 15:19-23, the same emphasis is on "obeying the voice of the Lord," which in context seems to refer to the previous oral messages of Samuel. The same stress upon the authority of the words of "My servants and prophets" is found in II Kings 17:7-23. In II Chronicles 14:4, King Asa is commended because he "commanded Judah to seek the Lord, God of their fathers, and to observe the law and the commandment" (RSV). The verbs "command" and "observe" have the ring of authority. In the postexilic period, the leaders in Jerusalem were guided in their religious actions by a standard. Note the phrases, "as it is written in the Law of Moses the man of God" (Ezra 3:2). The authority of "the Book of the Law of Moses which the Lord had given to Israel" is obvious in Nehemiah, chapters 8 through 10.

The *Century Dictionary* defines the word *canon* well. The canon is "the books of the Holy Scripture accepted by the Christian churches as containing an authoritative rule of religious faith and practice."

The Hebrew, Alexandrian, and Protestant Canons

The order of the books in the Hebrew Old Testament is often called the Palestinian canon and is associated with the Tiberian school of the Masoretes. Before the adoption of the codex (the book form) by the Jews, the Hebrew Old Testament was written on many scrolls, and because each scroll was independent of the others there was no order *per se*. When the codex became popular, it was possible to place the books in a sequence, and the order of books in the early codices probably had a tradition behind it. One indication of this tradition is a reference to the books of the Old Testament made by Josephus of the first century A.D. He held that there were twenty-two books.

The earliest codices of the Middle Ages (Codex Leningradensis is the oldest complete Old Testament and is dated A.D. 1008) have twenty-four books. The order of contents is: The Torah made up of Genesis, Exodus, Leviticus, Numbers, and Deuteronomy; The Prophets (Nebiim), which is divided in two sections — the Former Prophets comprised of Joshua, Judges, Samuel, and Kings, and the Latter Prophets made up of Isaiah, Jeremiah, Ezekiel, and the Twelve; The Writings (Kethebim); this section has three subdivisions, which are the poetical — Psalms, Proverbs, and Job; the five scrolls or Megilloth — Song of Solomon, Ruth, Lamentations, Ecclesiastes, and Esther; and the historical — Daniel, Ezra-Nehemiah, and Chronicles. Jewish scholars frequently refer to the Old Testament as the Tanak. The term is an acronym of the initial letters of the Hebrew titles of the three divisions of the Old Testament. The "T" is taken from Torah, the "N" from Nebiim, and the "K" from Kethebim. An "a" vowel is added twice to make the acronym pronouncable.

Some scholars think that Josephus had combined Ruth with Judges and Lamentations with Jeremiah to obtain his count of twenty-two books. As can be seen in the list of books in the early codices, the number is twenty-four. Later in the Middle Ages, Jews began to divide Samuel, Kings, and Chronicles into two books each, and as such they are printed in the Hebrew Old Testament.

Some observations may clarify some features in the Hebrew canon. The Torah is the Jewish name for the first five books of the Old Testament and thus equivalent to our title, the Pentateuch. Its meaning, however, is law or instruction, and Jews sometimes refer to the entire Old Testament as Torah, which can be a bit confusing. The Twelve are the books of the Minor Prophets. The five scrolls are separately read at important Jewish feasts. The Song of Solomon is read at the Passover; Ruth, at the Feast of Pentecost; Ecclesiastes, at the Feast of Tabernacles; Esther, at the Feast of Purim; and Lamentations, at the anniversary of the Fall of Jerusalem.

The Alexandrian canon has been best preserved in the Septuagint manuscript, Codex B or Vaticanus, dated to the middle of the fourth century A.D. This Codex came from Christian circles, and its table of contents are: The Pentateuch—Genesis, Exodus, Leviticus, Numbers, and Deuteronomy; the Historical Books—Joshua, Judges, Ruth, I, II, III, and IV Kings, I and II Chronicles, I Esdras (Greek Esdras), and II Esdras (Ezra-Nehemiah); the Didactic and Poetical Books—Psalms, Proverbs, Ecclesiastes, Canticles, Job, Wisdom of Solomon, and Ecclesiasticus of Ben Sira; the Story Books— Esther with additions, Judith, and Tobit; the Prophetical Books—the Twelve, Isaiah, Jeremiah, Baruch, Lamentations, Epistle of Jeremiah, Ezekiel, Daniel with additions, and I and II Maccabees. Some other contemporary manuscripts have III and IV Maccabees.

Some information about the order of the Old Testament books, as understood in the early Christian church, comes from the writings of the early Church Fathers. These writings have been gathered in a series of volumes and edited by J. P. Migne.

Belonging to the Eastern branch of the early church, there are twelve lists dating from the third century A.D. In all of the lists the Pentateuch comes first, and the order of the five books is constant. The sequence of the books in the remainder of the Old Testament varies from the Pentateuch on. Several features are interesting. Esther is missing in four of the twelve lists, and seven lists have from one to four Apocryphal books. In eight of the lists, Psalms, Proverbs, Ecclesiastes, and Song of Solomon appear as a block but in different places in the sequence.

Ten lists come from the Western branch of the church and date from the late fourth to the fifth centuries A.D. The Pentateuch is constant in order and place, and Esther shows up on all lists. The block including Psalms, Proverbs, Ecclesiastes, and the Song of Solomon is present in seven lists but in differing places in the order. Apocryphal books, from four to six, are in seven lists.

Many of the canons from the Western church are related to the Vulgate. Jerome, the translator of the Vulgate, was a strong opponent to the presence of the Apocryphal books in the canon. On the other hand, Augustine accepted some of the books as authoritative and so did several assemblies of the early church. The Synod of Hippo (A.D. 393) and the Synod of Carthage (A.D. 397) accepted the Apocryphal books as part of the canon. The Eastern Orthodox Council of Trullo (A.D. 692) also recognized the Apocryphal books as authoritative. The Roman Catholic church in Europe did not take official action in regard to the Apocryphal books until the Council of Trent. In A.D. 1546 that council declared that eleven of the Apocryphal books belonged to the canon; this decision remains unchanged.

The Protestant canon comes out of the Alexandrian tradition and was forged in the controversies between Protestants and Roman Catholics during the sixteenth century A.D. The traditions of the Hebrew Bible and the views of Jerome led Protestants, particularly Bodenstein of Carlstadt, to redefine the extent of the canon. Some of the basic proof texts of the Roman Catholics for the doctrine of purgatory come from the Apocryphal books. This factor entered into the decision among Protestants to separate the Apocrypha from the other books of the Old Testament and insert them as a corpus between the two testaments. Later, the common practice was to leave the Apocrypha completely out of the Bible, though the pulpit Bible of many Protestant churches contains the Apocryphal books scattered throughout the Old Testament. Quite consistently, Protestants refuse to accord canonicity to the Apocryphal books. A glance at the table of contents of any printed Old Testament commonly distributed by Protestants will provide a comparison with both the Hebrew order of the canon and the Alexandrian order.

Arguments About the Extent of the Canon

How the Lord Jesus Christ and the apostles understood the extent of the Old Testament is unclear. Jesus spoke of the Law and the Prophets

(Matt. 5:17; Luke 16:16) as though there were only two sections of the Old Testament. On the other hand, He spoke of the Law and the Prophets and the Psalms in Luke 24:24, and this may indicate three sections. In Matthew 23:35 and Luke 11:51, Jesus mentions the death of Abel and Zechariah, which suggests that He understood Chronicles to be the last book of the Old Testament; this would suggest the three divisions of the later Hebrew manuscripts. The apostles quoted from all sections of the Old Testament; but other noncanonical literature is never cited by name, though there are statements in the New Testament that point to that body of writings.

As noted above, Josephus's enumeration of the books of the Old Testament indicates that he understood the limits of the Old Testament in much the same way as later Jewish scribes. Among the Dead Sea Scrolls, all the books of the Old Testament are represented by at least fragments of manuscripts, except Esther. There are manuscripts or fragments of a number of noncanonical writings in the corpus of Dead Sea Scrolls materials, but scholars are generally agreed that these writings were not regarded by the community at Qumran as canonical.

Farther back in history, the most definite statements are in the prologue to the book of Ecclesiasticus of Ben Sira. There are three statements that mention the first two sections of the later Hebrew codices, namely the Law and the Prophets, but the last phrase in each statement is enigmatic. Some consider "the others who follow after them," "other books of our fathers," "the rest of the books," to be either open-ended—thus the extent of the canon not yet determined—or variant designations of the last section of the Old Testament that the Jews called The Writings.

Two main factors have kept active the controversy about the extent of the canon of the Old Testament. First, the Talmud contains scattered references to a rabbinical school at Jamnia (Jabneh), south of Joppa, during the late first century and the early second century A.D. There was discussion in this school whether several books in the Old Testament ought not be taken out and several Apocryphal books inserted in their places. The books most seriously questioned were Ecclesiastes, Song of Solomon, and Esther; the books favored to replace them were Ecclesiasticus of Ben Sira above all, and next in line, I Maccabees. But the books already in the canon won the day.

The second factor is the presence in Greek and Latin translations, in codex form, of Apocryphal books. As previously mentioned, the Dead Sea Scrolls have yielded manuscripts of noncanonical writings, many of which had not been known by recent scholars before their discovery. Obviously, they were valued by the community at Qumran. For reasons not yet clear, the Christian communities in Egypt, and a few elsewhere, had begun to include a few of these writings in their lists of the Old Testament canon.

Of prime interest to questions about the extent of the canon is the group of books called the Apocrypha. This title comes from the Greek and means "hidden" or "concealed," and seems to have its source in the Apocalypse of Ezra (also known as II Esdras, IV Esdras, or Ezra) 12:37 ff.; 14:45 ff. This book was possibly written in Aramaic during the latter part of the first century A.D. in Jerusalem. Whether it was written by Jews or by Jewish-Christians is not known. Jewish rabbis referred to extracanonical books as "outside books." Jerome used the term Apocrypha in this sense and so did the Reformers Luther, Karlstadt, and Coverdale. Some Jews think the term comes from the practice of keeping these books stored in the genizah, attached to each synagogue, away from public access. Roman Catholics call these books the Deutero-Canon.

The Apocrypha is listed as containing these writings in five main divisions, as follows: (1) Didactic or Wisdom books—Wisdom of Solomon, dated about 125 B.C. and Ecclesiasticus of Ben Sira, dated about 180 B.C.; (2) Historical Books—I Esdras* dated about 135 B.C., I Maccabees, and II Maccabees; (3) Romantic Stories—Tobit and Judith; (4) Prophetic Literature—Baruch, the Epistle of Jeremiah and the Apocalypse of Esdras; (5) Legendary Additions—Prayer of Manasseh, additions to Esther, The Prayer of Azariah, the Hymn of the Three Men, Susanna, and Bel and the Dragon. The last three were added to Daniel.

Since the Pseudepigraphal literature has been referred to, the writings that make up this corpus are listed as follows: (1) Primitive history—Jubilees, dated about 50 B.C.; (2) Apocalyptic writings—I Enoch, dated about 95 B.C., Apocalypse of Baruch, Assumption of Moses, Apocalypse of Esdras, dated about A.D. 69, Martyrdom of Isaiah, Lives of the Prophets, and Sibylline Oracles, dated about A.D. 138; (3) Legendary books—Letter of Aristeas, the Book of Adam and Eve, The Testament of the Twelve Patriarchs, and the Testament of Job; (4) Poetical—Psalms of Solomon; (5) Didactic discourses—Magical books of Moses, Story of Achiarcharus, and Pirke Aboth; (6) Unclassified—III Maccabees and IV Maccabees.

Factors Determining the Canon

Much effort has been expended to discover what it was that led to the establishment of an Old Testament canon. The fact that the Old Testament does not speak of acts of canonization or of motives for canonization has encouraged some to make the quest. The answers scholars have come up

*Caution: the title *Esdras* has different meanings in the several translations. In the LXX Lucianic recension, II Esdras is Ezra-Nehemiah; in the Vulgate, I Esdras is Ezra, II Esdras is Nehemiah, III Esdras is the Apocryphal listed above, and IV Esdras is the Apocalypse of Esdras in the Pseudepigrapha.

with have been varied and have not satisfied everyone. Mostly the search has been made by those who have rejected the biblical concept of revelation.

Late in the eighteenth century, Eichhorn had suggested that the age of the material was the determining factor. He did not have available the information that the people of the ancient Near East were producing written documents as early as 3000 B.C. Lack of information about ancient languages led another scholar, Hitzig, to claim that Hebrew was the mark of canonical literature. He had assumed a limited ability in olden times to produce Hebrew literature.

A more popular view has been that the law was the model by which the Israelites decided what was canonical. Josiah's reverence for the book of the law and Ezra's similar high regard for the law are held up as examples of this testing procedure in action. Others have pointed back to the claim in the Code of Hammurabi to divine sanction for the law given to the king and then passed on to the people. Others were not impressed by this view, for the Pentateuch is by no means all law; there are many narratives in its content. The historical books have little law, and the same could be said for the prophets and for the wisdom literature.

Others have held that a book or some kind of written tradition was a model for determining canon. Again, Josiah's reform and Ezra's act of reading the law to the people have been appealed to as evidence. The rebuttal is that oral tradition can just as well have canonical dignity, especially if it is recited in a religious service or festival.

A popular view has been that the presence of inspiration, or a belief that inspiration was involved, was the standard that determined which books were worthy of canonization. This may be paired with a belief that authority accompanies inspiration.

Two recent introductions popular among nontraditionalists may be cited as examples. R. H. Pfeiffer holds that the idea of canonicity arose out of a common belief in the inspired word of a spoken prophecy, especially if the message was accompanied by an ecstatic experience.[1] In a similar way, the results of casting the lots by the priest was regarded as inspired, although ecstasy might have been absent in that case. Eissfeldt speaks of the belief in the inspired nature of the instructions of the priests, the oracles of the prophets, the songs of the singer and the proverbs of the wise men.[2] This argument may be carried further by saying that a declaration by a prophet that a writing was canonical would be determinative. Reference is then

---

1. R. H. Pfeiffer, *Introduction to the Old Testament.* (New York: Harper & Bros., Publishers, 1941), pp. 50-51.
2. Otto Eissfeldt, *The Old Testament, An Introduction.* (New York: Harper & Row Publishers, 1965), pp. 9–11.

made to the role of Huldah, the prophetess in Josiah's reform (II Kings 22:14-20).

R. H. Pfeiffer coupled the idea of inspiration with several other factors, namely, the mere survival of the writing, anonymous authorship, an early belief that a book had to be written before the time of Ezra because prophetic inspiration ceased then. Josephus is cited as evidence. But there was an alternative: a late anonymous book such as Daniel could be attributed to an ancient prophet as long as its contents looked as if it happened before the time of Ezra!

G. Ostborn has maintained that all of the above-mentioned factors are secondary, and many are the result of a more basic primary cause for canonicity.[3] He finds the real standard for canonicity in the contents of the biblical materials; and the contents were rooted in the cult, for it was recited at its feasts and in its services, whether temple or synagogue. He claims that the underlying cause is a belief in Yahweh's activity in history in relation to central individuals and the nation of Israel. The motif is struggle or distress and God's victory that brings a new order of peace and goodness. This motif started as a cultic story and expanded to include narrative, hymns, laws, and words of wisdom. Since all these materials were recited in the cult services, they had holiness and authority. All historical, prophetical, and wisdom literature that was appended to the core must meet the standard of portraying divine activity, i.e., victory over chaos. Where did this motif come from originally? Ostborn has declared the motif comes from the Canaanite cult, and previous to that from Mesopotamia. These cults were sources that fed to Israel its basic motifs over many centuries, so that the canon was open-ended until the Council of Jamnia (Jabneh).

The Wellhausen View on the Steps of Canonization

The Wellhausen concept of canonization has changed little in basic outline during the past century. Exponents of "Salvation History" and form criticism have accepted this point of view as completely as did the literary critics.

There were antecedents to the Wellhausen theory of canonization, but the fundamental framework has been the four-document J, E, D, and P scheme of composition for the Pentateuch. There have been those who have traced the beginnings of the idea of canon into J and E and even back into oral tradition, but the crux of the theory begins with the D document and continues with close ties with the three-divisional make-up of the Hebrew Old Testament. These three divisions are the Torah, the Prophets, and the Writings.

---

3. G. Ostborn, *Cult and Canon* (Uppsala: Lundequistsaka bokhandlen, 1950).

The D document has been important to the Wellhausen point of view because it is regarded as a written document made up of Deuteronomy, chapters 5-26, plus chapter 28, and because the scroll found during Josiah's reign is held to be that document (II Kings 22-23). This correlation of the D document with the Josiah reform also provides a key date, 621 B.C. The passage in question refers to the scroll as either the "book of the law" (II Kings 22:8, 11) or as the "book of the covenant" (II Kings 23:2-3).

Wellhausen regarded Deuteronomy as the first book that was written with the intent that it be a written law, the public authority of the land. The project succeeded marvelously but was far from being a blessing to Israel, for the written law, now declared to be canon by act of assembly, destroyed the old freedom in worship and killed the prophetic spirit.

In Wellhausen's argument, one sees a dictum that has undergirded the theory through the years, namely, that canonization is an act of assembly that confers authority upon a writing or a group of writings. Also in the theory is the operation of the Hegelian dialectic, for Deuteronomy was the antithesis to the prevailing religious thought and practice in Israel.

The grand synthesis of Israel's thought came during the Exile and the early postexilic period. The priests slowly brought together the contents of the Priestly Code and utilized it as the framework for the corpus called the Torah or Pentateuch. Ezra is said to have brought the process to a climax at the assembly where the Torah was read to the people, who thus made it the authority that henceforth would govern their lives (Ezra 7:14; Neh. 8-10; esp. 9:38; 10:28-29).

There are no literary references to other assemblies that in like manner had the books of the Former or Latter Prophets or any of the books in the Writings read to them prior to the translation of the Old Testament into Greek (250-100 B.C.). For the Prophets, understood as a division of the Hebrew Old Testament, there is a terminal point. The prologue to Ecclesiasticus of Ben Sira (180 B.C.) mentions the Prophets as a unit, thus the Wellhausen theorists must posit some type of assembly or series of assemblies before that date for its canonization. There are no references that speak of such assemblies, and this is a problem for the theory.

The Writings are normally understood by the exponents of the Wellhausen theory as being open-ended as late as the second century B.C., and then canonized separately. According to this theme, the Psalter would be closed about 150 B.C., Proverbs and Job about 132 B.C., and Daniel just before 100 B.C. The other books of the Writings would be closed and canonized at the turn of, or early in, the first century B.C. Again, there are no records of any assemblies that accorded these books the status of canon.

The Wellhausen school almost invariably focused on a so-called

Council of Jamnia (Jabneh), dated about 90 A.D., as a final canonizing body that closed the Old Testament for Judaism and conferred authority on all its books. The Jewish Talmud mentions discussions about books of the Old Testament, but an explicit statement of canonization it does not have.

The Traditional View of Canonization

Scholars in the traditional stream of opinion have never understood that acts of assembly in Old Testament times, during the intertestamental period, or at Jamnia conferred authority on the books of the Old Testament. In Roman Catholicism and in Eastern Orthodoxy, the idea that assemblies of the church had the power to determine the extent of the canon became a practice by the late fourth century A.D. Roman Catholicism, at least, has not found it difficult to accept the Wellhausen theory of canonization. Their common definition of canon could be "an authoritative list of books." Protestant exponents of the Wellhausen theory, however, have been freer to hold that what man had once declared to be authoritative can be later declared not authoritative.

The heart of the traditional scholar's rejection of the Wellhausen view of canonization has to do with the source of authority; it is rooted in the reality of God's speaking in revelatory event and acting redemptively. The biblical claim that God selected men to proclaim the divine message and that they faithfully obeyed, not as robots, but as free men, is taken as valid. In this view, intrinsic authority in oral message or written message is a casual factor of ratification, not a result of ratification.

Ostborn's contention is valid that the content of the books is the place to find information about what "canon" meant to the Hebrew people. He is right in seeing Jahweh's activity in the lives of central figures and in the affairs of the nation as the crucial theme of the Old Testament, especially the Pentateuch. But he is surely wrong when he claims that the rootage of this theme was in Canaanite cultic mythology. He saw that the word *covenant* was important to the theme of Yahweh's victorious defeat of evil, but he failed to see it as vital.

M. G. Kline has recently contended that a second look needs to be taken at the beginning and growth of the Old Testament canon.[4] His position is based on recent research in the ancient covenant forms and attitudes of Amorites and Hitties toward these forms. For the ancient people in the upper Levant and in the Hittite empire, the suzerainty treaty was the canon in political affairs.

---

4. M. G. Kline, "Canon and Covenant," *Westminster Theological Journal* 32 (1969): 49–67 and (1970): 179–200.

A sovereign king set up regulations for his vassals, and these were written down. Copies of the written covenant were made for each party and placed in the proper temples. The covenant was read publicly at stated times during the year. An inscriptional curse was a key part of the treaty, giving it canonical sanction. Somewhat similar were professional inscriptions such as incantations, cultic formula, edicts, law codes, and royal land grants with their *kudurru* stones. These authoritative written documents were the common media of administration in the ancient Near East.

The political treaty of the suzerainty type was the model taken over. Genesis depicts God as performing this adaptation, which became the framework of the faith revealed to His people. In the covenant with the Patriarchs and the Sinaitic covenant with Israel, there was no human source of authority; God alone is the suzerain. The narratives of Genesis and Exodus up to chapter 19 may be regarded as the historical prologue to the stipulations, which are the Ten Commandments and the book of the covenant that follows them. The cultic regulations were closely tied to the festivals, hence Ostborn is right when he states that the canon has a cultic setting.

Ostborn should have turned from a thematic background in mythology to a thematic rootage in the covenant literary forms. He would have found there a better understanding of Jahweh's activity and His struggles that brought forth a new order.

The law was conventional law, and the historical narratives were also conventional in interest and in their setting in life. Stipulations are closely blended with the history in the Pentateuch. The Book of Deuteronomy is structured as a covenant and also interweaves the historical elements with stipulations.

As a corpus, the Pentateuch is the core of the covenantal canon; the narratives of Joshua through II Kings have covenant themes. Scholars are right in seeing these books as an expansion of Pentateuchal themes, a theological treatment of Israel's history. These books see Jahweh as Israel's covenant Lord and Israel as the errant, rebellious covenant breakers who must be brought under covenant sanctions repeatedly. Chronicles, Ezra, and Nehemiah would be an expansion with a priestly viewpoint. The basic difference of opinion would be the date of origin for the Book of Deuteronomy. Traditional scholars see it as Mosaic, and those who follow Wellhausen see it as a seventh-century work.

The content of the prophets' messages was rooted in the covenant themes. Recent research has repeatedly brought covenant concerns, such as historical background, violations of law, and the lawsuit and covenant ideas such as justice, loyalty, righteousness, transgression, and rebellion to light. The prophetic literature is loaded with these matters. A prophet was a treaty emissary, a prosecutor of lawbreakers, an evangelist calling the people back to the covenant relationship. They did not hesitate to use the curse.

What of the Psalter? It is covenantal in its themes, in its words, and its concerns. Kline calls the Psalter "an extension of a vassal's ratification response." The purpose was to maintain the proper covenant relationship with Jahweh.

The Wisdom Literature had its function too; it applied the covenant stipulations to life situations. Stipulations became maxims and instructions. The sanctions of the covenant were traced out in life in the home, in the market place, and on the job.

In short, the books of the Old Testament are canon because the covenant God is everywhere present in them and the covenant themes are faithfully expounded in them.

An aspect of canonization was the acceptance by the people; this was ratification of the covenant but not a human conferral of authority upon the books. Authority was already intrinsic to them. The content of the books correlates with genuine religious experience, but human experience itself did not and does not stamp canonicity upon the books. Overshadowing human experience is the presence and guidance of the Holy Spirit.

In a serious discussion of canonicity, an effort must be made to keep in their proper places such matters as ultimate authority, the process of collection of biblical writings (for scrolls were used in ancient times, not books), authentication of scrolls as covenant scrolls, especially during and after the Exile, and the activity of transmitting the biblical materials. Each of these areas of scholarly interest is important and must be carefully studied, but each area must be treated for what it is. Not many of them directly relate to the matter of canonicity itself.

Suggested Books for Further Reading

Blenkinsopp, J. *Prophecy and Canon*. Notre Dame: University of Notre Dame, 1977.

Campenhausen, von, H. *The Formation of the Christian Bible*. Philadelphia: Fortress Press, 1972.

Charles, R. H. *The Apocrypha and Pseudepigrapha of the Old Testament*. Oxford: Clarendon Press, 1913.

Childs, B. S. "The Exegetical Significance of Canon for the Study of the Old Testament." CONGRESS VOLUME. Gottingen (1977): 66–80.

Clements, R. E. "Covenant and Canon in the Old Testament." *Creation, Christ and Culture*. Edinburgh: Clark (1976): 1–12.

Coats, G. W. & Long, B. O. *Canon and Authority: Essays in Old Testament Religion and Theology*. Philadelphia: Fortress Press, 1977.

Guthrie, H. H. *Wisdom and Canon*. Evanston, Ill.: Seabury-Western Theological Seminary, 1966.

Harris, R. L. *Inspiration and Canonicity of the Bible*. Grand Rapids: Zondervan Publishing House, 1957.

Harrison, R. K. *Introduction to the Old Testament*. Grand Rapids: Wm. B. Eerdmans Publishing Co., pp. 199–287, 1969.

Katz, P. "The Old Testament Canon in Palestine and Alexandria." ZNW 47 (1956): 191–217.

Kline, M. G. *The Structure of Biblical Authority*. Grand Rapids: Wm. B. Eerdmans Publishing Co., 1972.

_____. "The Correlation of the Concepts of Canon and Covenant." *New Perspectives on the Old Testament*. Waco, TX: Word Books, Pub., 1970.

Leiman, S. Z. *The Canon and Masorah of the Hebrew Bible*. New York: Ktav Pub, 1974.

Newman, R. C. "The Council of Jamnia and the Old Testament Canon." *Westminster Theological Journal* 38 (1975–6); 319–349.

Ostborn, G. *Cult and Canon*. Uppsala: Lundequistska bokhandlen, 1950.

Sanders, J. A. *Torah and Canon*. Philadelphia: Fortress Press, 1972.

Sundberg, A. *The Old Testament of the Early Church*. Cambridge: Harvard University Press, 1964.

Torrey, C. C. *The Apocryphal Literature*. New Haven: Yale University Press, 1945.

Appendix

The Archives
of the Ancient Near East

Over a period of a century and a half, by archaeological skill or by accident, an amazing number of inscriptions have been exhumed from ancient ruins. Some of these inscribed objects were found by chance by natives and sold to antiquity dealers, who rarely knew precisely where the objects had been found.

This appendix will seek to tell briefly the stories of the discovery and excavation of major archaeological archives, describe the nature and content of each, and summarize the significance of each for Old Testament studies.

Ebla

In 1964 a young Italian archaeologist, Paolo Matthiae, examined ancient Syrian mounds, seeking one that offered the greatest challenge and, hopefully, the most information. He chose a large one called Tell Mardikh, covering about 140 acres located in the northwestern corner of Syria, not far from the Turkish border. Its location made the site a control center of trade moving between the Mesopotamian Valley and the Mediterranean Sea, as well as that moving from the north to the south.

The first indication of the ancient name of the site was provided by a damaged statue found in 1968, bearing an inscription containing the name *Ebla*. Before that discovery, clay tablets associated with Naram-Sin, monarch of the Old Akkadian empire, claimed that he had captured and burned a great city named Ebla (2250 B.C.). No one knew where it was located until the partial statue was uncovered by Matthiae.

The first group of inscribed clay tablets from Ebla, 42 in number, were found in 1974 in a small room connected to a large audience hall. The following year much larger collections of clay tablets were found in two small rooms. One room, probably a scriptorium, yielded about 1,000 tablets, some nearly complete, others as fragments. The other room had an archive of about 15,000 tablets, again some nearly complete, but others as fragments, but all filed in proper order on wooden shelves. The fire that destroyed the building also baked the tablets, contributing to their excellent preservation through the centuries. In 1976 about 1,600 more tablets and fragments were found in nearby rooms. All of these tablets are dated by archaeologists as having been inscribed between 2400 and 2250 B.C., that is, in the Early Bronze Age. Reports indicate that more than 7,000 tablets are complete or nearly complete and in excellent condition.

Probings down to undisturbed soil (through debris as much as fifty feet thick in places) reveal that the site was first settled late in the fourth millennium B.C. The village grew to be a mighty city, reaching its peak of power during the time period in which the tablets were produced, but gradually declining in influence until its final destruction around 1600 B.C. Tablets containing summaries of the population of various areas in and around Ebla indicate a total of about 260,000 people.

Ebla was basically a trading center, with routes reaching across the upper Mesopotamian Valley, north into the area now known as Turkey, and south to the borders of Egypt. Such a powerful and sophisticated trading empire was unknown before the discovery of these clay tablets. Prior to their discovery, the only known civilizations in the ancient Near East were located in the lower Mesopotamian Valley and in Egypt. During the time of the Patriarchs (Abraham, Isaac, and Jacob) the rebuilt and weaker city of Ebla was located just west of the Haran area, where their relatives lived.

Up to early 1984 the inscriptions on some 1,650 tablets had been published by scholars associated with universities in Rome and Naples. G. Pettinato of the University of Rome, the first scholar to study the clay tablets, has published a list of about 6,500 tablets, giving basic data about them in the Italian language.

The writing system used on the tablets is composed of the cuneiform symbols developed by Sumerians of the lower Mesopotamian Valley. It appears that scribes from that civilization had a school at Ebla at which students were trained to use the system. Overall, though many Sumerian script symbols were used, there are indications the words were pronounced in the local language, an early form of later Semitic languages.

The contents of these tablets are classified as follows: 1) economic and administrative records of invoices, taxes, deliveries of agricultural products, offerings, and lists of officials (approximately 3,500); 2) dictionaries (250, of which 32 are bilingual, having Sumerian words with translations into the language spoken by the Eblaites) and Sumerian grammars written in the Eblaite language; 3) treaties, letters of state officials, ordinances, edicts, marriage certificates, and lists of subjugated cities (approximately 100); and 5) tablets of a religious nature (approximately 150): hymns, incantations, proverbs, and myths (including a flood story said to be much like the "Epic of Gilgamesh"). References to creation are said also to be included in the religious materials. The Ebla tablets have the oldest occurrence of *nabi,* the word for prophet in the Old Testament.

Approximately five hundred deities are named in the Ebla tablets concerned with religion. Many are well known from other clay tablets that have been found in the lower Mesopotamian Valley; others were previously known from tablets found at Ugarit and dated one thousand years later (see the description of the archives of Ugarit elsewhere in this appendix); some are found in the Old Testament. The main god in Ebla was Dagan (grain), spelled *Dagon* in the Old Testament. *Resheph* (pestilence) appears as the name of a gate at Ebla, but in the Old Testament it appears as the name of a man (I Chron. 7:25), or it is translated as "pestilence" (Deut. 32:24), "arrows" (Ps. 76:3), "lightning" (Ps. 78:48), or as "flame" (Song of Sol. 8:6). The Canaanite gods Baal and Haddad, variant names of the storm, were worshiped at Ebla, as were Ishtar (spelled *Asherah*), Kamish, Malik, Kemosh, and Molek, all mentioned in the Old Testament. Some personal names end with *il,* which in the Old Testament equals *el* (god). In some instances *il* is displaced by *ia,* which Pettinato equates with *Yah* (the first part of *Yahweh*), an equation denied by others.

The commercial records of Ebla reveal the names of a number of cities in the trade network of the day. Of special interest are names of areas to the south. The earliest reference to Damascus is found on these tablets, as well as the names of Palestinian cities such as Hazor, Beth-Shan, Schechem, Dor, Joppa, Ashkelon, Salim, and Jerusalem. Pettinato's claim that Sodom and Gomorrah appear on several tablets is a matter of controversy.

Over ten thousand personal names are said to be recorded on the Ebla tablets, of which several thousand have been published. Names that are equivalent to those of some persons mentioned in the Old Testament are Adam, Eve, Jubal, Noah, Abram, Ishmael, Hagar, Keturah, Bilhah, Israel, Micah, Michael, Saul, and David. Pettinato has claimed that one name reads "iaramu," the equivalent of Jehorum (Yah is exalted; see references to kings of this name in I & II Kings and II Chronicles). On the other hand, I. J. Gelb has insisted this name should be read "iluni-ramu" (our god is exalted).

Overall, the archive found at Ebla provides us with written material that unveils the presence of a powerful merchant empire in the third millennium B.C., hitherto unknown. We now know that the inhabitants of Ebla spoke a Semitic language that has some kind of ancestral relationship to later Semitic languages spoken in lands east of the Mediterranean Sea.

In regard to the Bible, the archive provides information about the political, economic, social, and religious practices just before the time of the Patriarchs and features of the area in which they lived and moved. In regard to the personal names on the tablets, none specifically designates a biblical person, though they do show that Old Testament names were used in ancient times.

The Ebla tablets need to be published in various modern languages, including English, so a wider range of scholars can read and evaluate the full contributions of these tablets to our knowledge of the ancient Near East and the Bible.

Mari

Another of the important archives of the ancient Near East was found at the city of Mari. The ruins of this powerful trade center are located on the south bank of the Euphrates River, about fifteen and one-half miles north of the Syrian-Iraqi border. The cities of Ebla and Mari were bitter rivals during both the Early Bronze and Middle Bronze ages, with Mari probably the stronger during the latter period. Like Ebla, the first settlement at Mari dates back to the last half of the fourth millennium B.C. The modern Arabic name for the site of about 280 acres is Tell Hariri.

Local officials of the French Mandate were first alerted to the possible importance of the site by the chance discovery of a headless statue by a Bedouin quarrying for stone. The statue bore an inscription, which, when translated, led French authorities in Paris to send archaeologists to Mari. The discovery was made in August 1933, and by December excavation began, headed by a young archaeologist, Andre Parrot. By the end of one month of digging, the team had found a small inscribed statue dedicated to the goddess Istar by one of the kings of Mari. This was the first clear evidence that the site was indeed Mari.

Though not many in number, enough inscriptions were exhumed from the third millennium B.C. stratum to hint at the presence of an old Semitic civilization in the upper Euphrates Valley. However, the hint was not taken seriously until the discovery of Ebla tablets almost forty years later.

The Golden Age of Mari lasted from 1860 to 1760 B.C. Buildings and artifacts from this century portray Mari as one of the wealthiest and most culturally advanced city-states in the Mesopotamian Valley during that time.

The most significant building found at Mari was the palace of King Zimri-Lim of the Middle Bronze Age. This brick palace is one of the largest that existed in the ancient Near East during that era. The building covered nine acres and had some three hundred rooms. A remarkable feature was the function of some rooms as bathrooms, having hard clay bathtubs, lavatories, and a plumbing system. Other rooms served as scriptoria, where scribes wrote or copied inscriptions in cuneiform on clay tablets; yet others were libraries where the tablets were stored.

The Mari inscriptions show that Zimri-Lim's eighteen-year reign was troubled by wars. He gained control of the area between the upper Euphrates and Tigris rivers, and for a time he gathered in his palace an enormous store of wealth. But his power soon waned, and the palace was destroyed by the aggressive Hammurabi.

The Mari archive rooms yielded about 25,000 tablets that cover a wide range of subjects: commercial transactions, farm products and sales, correspondence between rulers and officials, international treaties, diplomatic letters, irrigation practices, laws and court actions, cargo of caravans, the products of many kinds of crafts, and religion. Chronological statements on some tablets aid in relating various kings of the regions of the Mesopotamian Valley, so that writing a cogent history of that time became possible.

These tablets have brought to light the power of the Amorite people, whose name reflects the fact that they lived west of the city-states in the lower Mesopotamian Valley. These people were Semitic, speaking and writing a language much like later Semitic languages used in areas to the west and south. Some tablets bear inscriptions in the Hurrian language, the oldest yet available in that tongue.

Students of the Old Testament gain considerable knowledge from these inscriptions, since they provide a fund of information about the world in which the Patriarchs lived and traveled. Their way of life as migrants and nomads is well documented by the Mari inscriptions and fits well with the biblical portrayal of the patriarchal lifestyle. Even the meaning of the word *Hebrew* is clarified by the Amorite verb *habuaru,* to "emigrate," to "seek refuge." Adoption and inheritance documents found at Mari detail practices similar to those of the Old Testament. Inscriptions on the Mari tablets also describe the practice of slaughtering animals in connection with making covenants. Some of the judges mentioned on the clay tablets were not court officials but governed regional or tribal units, as was the case in the Old Testament.

The most important god of Mari was Dagan. Other deities, known as Canaanite from the Old Testament, are also mentioned: Baal, Ishtar (Asherah), El, and Adad (Hadad). Both temples and names are associated with these and many other deities.

Unique to the Mari tablets is the existence of about thirty tablets, some quite damaged, that include reports of messages received from certain deities by various people. These people, of both sexes and of various ages and occupations, appeared unbidden before the governor of their city or region. They claimed they had received messages from the idols in the temples where they had been worshiping. These messages supposedly came while the recipients were in various mental states: dreams, visions, trances, etc. These people requested of the governor that their messages be delivered in written form to Zimri-Lim, king of Mari, which he did. The most frequently named idol-gods named as the source of the messages were Dagan and Adad.

The content of these messages varies but normally has some combination of accusation (even of some of the king's actions), warning, exhortation, and promises of victory if certain demands were met. The accusations varied from the royal court's neglect to provide adequate offerings to neglect of maintenance of the temple. Some messages claim the king had been unjust in his administration. Some of these people sent with their report a piece of the hem of their garment or a lock of hair, sometimes both. These were to be tested by some technique of divination, perhaps for their authenticity.

In all the non-Hebrew literature so far recovered, there is no other collection of tablets that contains reports of messages received from deities, or in any way provides information about the act of receiving and delivering a prophecy. The Mari tablets show this practice has ancient rootage in Semitic societies. In spite of some similarities, such as the claim of receiving a message marked by accusations and promises, there are marked differences between the Mari messages and those of the old Testament prophets. These differences are pointed out in the discussion of prophecy on pages 164–171.

Mari references to cities in Palestine seem to be limited to Hazor and Laish, the latter being the ancient name of Dan (Judg. 18). Personal names that correspond with biblical names are also few in number. Only Noah, Abram, Laban, and Jacob are clearly alike; controversy exists concerning the inclusion of the names of Benjamin and David in the Mari texts.

In summary, the Mari tablets provide general background concerning politics, the social structure, the legal system, and religious beliefs and practices in Patriarchal times. Hopefully other discoveries will clarify the relationships of the Patriarchs to the people among whom they lived.

Nippur

Late in the nineteenth century scholars were alerted to the possibility of a Sumerian culture in the lower Mesopotamian Valley by the recovery of a few bricks, cylinders, and tablets. However, these archaeological objects were placed in the British Museum, with but little information gained from them.

In 1887 Professor John P. Peters of the University of Pennsylvania left with a team of archaeologists to explore Nippur, the largest of the mounds in what now is known as Iraq. Known in modern times as Naffar, this site is located approximately one hundred miles south of Baghdad, lying between the Euphrates and Tigris rivers. Teams from the University of Pennsylvania led by different archaeologists dug there during the years 1889–91 and 1893–1900. After 1948, joint teams from the University Museum of Pennsylvania and the Oriental Institute of Chicago carried on work at the site every other year until 1958.

Early in the excavations a map of the city was found inscribed on a clay tablet, indicating a number of buildings, including a temple. Subsequently large temples were brought to light and over 30,000 clay tablets and fragments were unearthed.

The history of the ancient city goes back to a settlement of people called Ubaid sometime during the fourth millennium B.C. The village grew to become the chief religious center of the Sumerian civilization during the third millennium B.C., but was destroyed by Hammurabi during the eighteenth century B.C. Subsequently Babylon became the chief city of the region.

The archives of Nippur contain a variety of documents: 1) texts of an economic nature: bills of sale, contracts, loans, receipts, and records of financial accounts; 2) laws, court decisions, and various governmental records; 3) letters of various officials to each other and several cities; 4) inscriptions of historical value; 5) Sumerian dictionaries and grammars; and 6) religious myths, hymns, proverbs, and epics, dated about 1750 B.C. These cuneiform inscriptions are mostly in the Akkadian language.

The Nippur archives are an impressive collection of over two thousand tablets in the Sumerian language, deposited in several museums. About half of them are now found at the University Museum of Pennsylvania, one hundred at the University of Jena in Germany, and about eight hundred at the Museum of the Ancient Orient in Istanbul. One clay tablet is the oldest catalog of religious literature known and dates from about 2000 B.C. Assumed is the fact that the sixty-two compositions listed were already old when the scribe compiled the catalog.

Another important inscription is called the Sumerian King List, which first enumerates a number of kings, whose reigns number in thousands of years, then gives a short account of a flood, followed by another enumeration of kings with much shorter reigns. This list of kings is important because it provides the first chronological framework for the history of the Sumerians.

A large number of names for gods and goddesses appear on the clay tablets; but, though they were well known by the Babylonians and Assyrians by other names, they were ignored by the biblical writers. Most of the inscriptions provide general information about conditions in the lower Mesopotamian Valley about the time tradition has Abraham and his family migrating westward.

Nuzi

One would not expect the ruins of a small city, located far from international ports and major rivers carrying trade cargo, to produce a large cache of clay tablets. But such did happen at the little known mound of Yorghan Tepe, situated in the highlands that rise east of the Tigris Valley toward modern Iran. The mound is about two hundred miles north of Baghdad and twelve miles from Kirkuk in modern Iraq.

Because inscribed clay tablets were appearing in antiquity shops, mostly in Akkadian cuneiform, but having words from an unknown language, scholars began searching for the source of the tablets. The quest led to Yorghan Tepe, so in 1925 Edward Chiera of the American Institute of Oriental Research in Baghdad began excavation there. Almost immediately a family home belonging to Tehiptilla, a wealthy businessman, yielded tablets bearing the legal documents of four, perhaps five, generations. Clay tablets were also discovered in other houses, and eventually a total of over four thousand were accumulated. These tablets, dated from about 1400–1200 B.C., told the excavators that the site was ancient Nuzi. The unknown language was identified as Hurrian (see page 57). Excavation of the site was completed in 1931.

The history of the site goes back to the late fourth millennium B.C. Later it became important in the Semitic empire of Sargon I (c. 2250 B.C.). At that time the city was called Gasur and had a mixed population of Semitic and Hurrian stock. The Hurrians became dominant about 1700 B.C. and renamed the city "Nuzi." It is interesting though that the normal spelling of the name on the tablets is the genitive *Nuzu*.

The tablets of this archive, for the most part, are dated several hundred years later than the archives of Mari, but many of the same kinds of customs were practiced in both places. A striking difference is that whereas most of the Mari records reflect the activities of the royal court and the merchant elite, the records of Nuzi provide a vivid picture of the daily life and practices of individuals belonging to a much lower level of society. The documents are records of deeds, marriages, adoptions, court decisions, wills, and other records important in family affairs. No other site in the Mesopotamian area has yielded so much information of this kind from the early periods of its history. These tablets show that families lower than the elite level placed great value on written documents and preserved their important records carefully.

Scholars were quick to note that these documents helped greatly in understanding unusual customs mentioned in the stories of the Patriarchs in the Book of Genesis. Many of these patriarchal practices were unknown in Israel; at least they are not mentioned in the books of Judges, I & II Samuel, and I & II Kings.

The phenomena of Abraham telling Pharaoh in Egypt and Abimelech in Gerar (Isaac, too) that his wife was a sister may be explained by Nuzi documents that show that a wife could be legally raised to a superior sister level. Perhaps the Patriarchs thought they could better protect their wives by presenting them in this way. If so, the situation was a transcultural misunderstanding rather than a deception.

Marriage contracts at Nuzi contain provisions for the bride to provide a substitute wife for her husband to bear a son, in case she were unable to do so. There are instructions that make clear the wife's authority over the concubine and the primacy of her own son, should she bear one at a later time. A similar situation existed in the marriages of Abraham and Jacob.

Adoption contracts at Nuzi make provision for childless couples to adopt someone to take over inheritance rights and care for them in old age (cf. Gen. 15:2). Inheritance rights were also tied to possession of household gods; whoever had them could claim the properties of a deceased father. Perhaps one should read the story of Jacob and Laban (Gen. 31:17–5) in the light of this stipulation. Inheritance rights could also be transferred to a brother for a price (cf. Gen. 25:29–34). In Nuzi, inheritance was not passed on automatically to the oldest son; if the father had a good reason, he could deprive that son of his rights, much as Jacob did to Reuben (Gen. 49:3).

The arguments between Jacob and Laban over loss of sheep and goats in the flocks under Jacob's control (Gen. 31:38–42) are well illustrated by regulations of such matters in court decisions and contracts found at Nuzi.

The gift of women servants to a daughter at the time of marriage (cf. Gen. 29:24, 29) is attested in Nuzi marriage contracts.

The archives of Nuzi have provided the basic documentation for family practices among average citizens living in the ancient Near East. True, Nuzi was located several hundred miles east of the region of Haran, and the tablets are dated several hundred years later than the Patriarchs. Nevertheless these witnesses to similar practices are ancient and belong to Semitic people influenced by Hurrians much like the relatives of the Patriarchs. Further, family practices of common people tend to remain fairly stable, unless there is a catastrophic invasion or other event that thoroughly disrupts a society. This rather generalized background of family life thus provides windows through which we can view the narratives in Genesis from an ancient perspective rather than from a modern point of view.

Hattusas

The Hittites are mentioned a limited number of times in the Old Testament, but without any indication of their origin or what their native language or racial stock may have been. Assyrian records of about 1100 B.C. refer to the land of Hatti, but seem to tie the word to Syria. On the other hand, Egyptian records of the eighteenth dynasty mention conflicts with the armies of Kheta at Kedesh on the Orontes River in the northwestern part of modern Syria. Some strange carvings on rocks in this area and in central Turkey puzzled scholars during the nineteenth century. A key Hittite site in Turkey was Boghazkoy, where clay tablets inscribed with cuneiform were picked up.

The German scholar Hugo Winkler first dug at Boghazkoy in 1906. Funds came from the Deutsche Orient-Gesellschaft of Germany, but the excavation was under the supervision of the Ottoman Museum at Istanbul, Turkey. Work continued in the following year and then in 1911, 1912, and from 1931 to 1938. After World II excavation was resumed, and shortly thereafter Winkler recovered about 10,000 tablets and fragments which were quickly identified as the royal archives of a powerful empire dating from before 1400 to about 1200 B.C.

Boghazkoy is located about a hundred miles east of Ankara on a bend of the Halys River. The ruins of ancient Hattusas are on the heights where the river makes a sharp bend. They are protected on three sides by the river gorge. The remains of the city are scattered over about four hundred acres.

The earliest settlers of central Turkey are known as Hattians and their coming to the area is dated about 2300 B.C. Their language appears on a few inscriptions and is regarded as non-Indo-European. True Indo-Europeans began to move in about 2000 B.C. and became powerful enough to dominate the Hattians by 1750 B.C., and elevate Hattusas as their capital city in the next century. After the time of the Old Hittite Empire (1800–1600 B.C.), the Hurrians from the East impacted strongly upon the Hittite people (1500–1450 B.C.). then there arose a strong line of native rulers who developed the New Hittite Empire. The city of Hattusas was utterly destroyed about 1200 B.C.

A total of 14,000 tablets, fragments, rock carvings, and inscriptions represent five different local languages and two international languages, Sumerian and Akkadian. Among the local languages, Hittite (sometimes called Nesite) is the most common and the oldest Indo-European language found on ancient inscriptions. Besides the cuneiform script, there are examples of old Hittite hieroglyphic symbols.

The inscriptions can be classified as: 1) legal records and laws, 2) trade records of various kinds, 3) religious myths, hymns, and rituals, and 4) political documents, especially treaties with a number of vassal city-states and kingdoms.

G. Mendenhall's 1954 report on the Hittite treaties and their close similarity to biblical covenants generated much interest. Soon there appeared many books and articles scrutinizing every aspect of this possible relationship. See pages 153–162 for a discussion of how extensive and how helpful study of these Hittite treaties can be.

Another interesting similarity between Hittite and Israelite literature is the existence of narratives that present human activities in a chronological sequence, with some attention to causes and effects. In Hittite inscriptions material of this sort is brief and is found within longer treaties, but the fact remains that no other ancient Near Eastern inscriptions include anything comparable to this Hittite material.

A technological spillover into the life of the Hebrews may be related to the skill of Hittite craftsmen in producing and working tempered iron into agricultural and military implements. There is some evidence that the wave of Philistines into southwestern Palestine included some who came through Hittite territory, perhaps helping to destroy the empire, but learning the art of blacksmithing while doing so. During Samuel's time the Philistines had a monopoly on this craft (I Sam. 13:19–21).

Ugarit

Important archaeological discoveries have come about in unusual ways. One of the most unusual concerns the treasures of ancient Ugarit, whose modern name is Ras Shamra, a site near the small harbor of Minet el Beida, in the northeastern corner of the Mediterranean Sea, in Syrian territory.

In the spring of 1928 a farmer was plowing a field near his home when his plowshare suddenly hit a large stone. Removal of the stone revealed the entrance to a tomb. Entering the tomb, the farmer found a number of objects, some of which he removed and sold to a dealer of antiquities in town. News of the archaeological find soon leaked to French authorities in nearby Latakia, and it wasn't long before archaeologists from Paris came to investigate.

Exploration of the tomb found by the farmer led to the discovery of other tombs, all of which were part of a cemetery that is close to the sea. Its presence indicated that a sizeable settlement must have existed nearby, the ruins of which probably could be found in the large mound approximately one mile from the tombs, covering about fifty acres. Two small streams run past it, then join and flow toward the sea. The deduction proved correct when further exploration revealed the city of Ugarit, or Ras Shamra.

Ugarit was the terminus of a major trade route coming out of the Mesopotamian Valley and lay beside the main trade route coming from the north and going on through Palestine to Egypt. Its harbor became a hub of a busy shipping business with Cyprus and ports along the south shoreline of Turkey and along the eastern Mediterranean coast. The plain around Ugarit produced excellent crops and lumber was plentiful on the slopes of Mt. Bargylus to the east.

The tablets of Ebla, concerned with the period before 2250 B.C., refer to Ugarit as an important port for international trade. By 2000 B.C. links with Egypt had been firmly established. During the next one thousand years the city was at different times subservient to the Hurrians, the Hittites, and the Egyptians. The city was destroyed about 1200 B.C. and apparently never rebuilt.

After being alerted to the archaeological potential of Ugarit, the French government sent Claude F. A. Schaeffer in 1929 to begin digging at the site. In the northeast corner of the tell, Schaeffer noticed stones that probably were part of a wall. Further digging revealed a large building containing many valuable artifacts. Discovered nearby was another large building, housing many clay tablets inscribed with cuneiform symbols.

The work at Ugarit was interrupted in 1939 by World War II, but was resumed in 1948 and continues to the present time.

So far about 1,400 Ugaritic tablets and fragments have been found, all dating from 1400–1200 B.C. The remarkable feature of many of these tablets was the fact that these symbols did not represent syllables as elsewhere in the Mesopotamian Valley. Each symbol represented a letter in a fully functional alphabet (see pages 73–74). Careful study revealed an unknown language (now called Ugaritic), an early form of Canaanite (see pages 59–60). Such an alphabetic script was also used on some Hurrian and Akkadian tablets.

Other tablets from Ugarit have the regular syllabic cuneiform symbols in four different languages: Sumerian, Akkadian, Hurrian, and Hittite. Inscriptions in Egyptian hieroglyphics, in Hittite hieroglyphics, and in a strange script called Cypro-Minoan were also recovered.

Much like the other archives, those at Ugarit had: 1) records of trade activity; 2) governmental documents such as letters of state, reports, and agreements; 3) school boy exercises in the art of writing; and 4) religious hymns, incantations, rituals and myths found in priestly libraries, and divination techniques used in a "magician's" house. Two private libraries had scientific notes and a dictionary in four languages, as well as a flood story. The religious texts are mostly in poetic form.

The inscriptions from the archives of Ugarit have enlarged our knowledge of Canaanite culture significantly. In addition to information about the nature of Ugarit's trade and diplomatic activities, we now have a better picture of the nature of Canaanite religious beliefs and practices. Before this discovery, most of our information about these people came from the Old Testament. The caution one must observe is that the Ugaritic civilization was centered several hundred miles north of Palestine and ended several hundred years before Israel became firmly settled in their promised land. Obviously, differences should be expected.

As at Ebla and Mari, the chief deities were El, Dagan, Baal, Athtart (Ishtar, Asherah) — gods mentioned in the Old Testament. Other deities were Mot (death), Yamm (sea), and Khasis (blacksmith). Other nature gods of lesser importance were also worshiped.

Places in Palestine that are mentioned in the Ugaritic tablets are those along the coast, including Tyre, Acco, Ashdod, and Ashkelon. A personal name of interest to Old Testament readers is that of Danel, a variant of Daniel.

Overall, the tablets of Ugarit have provided us with a much needed background concerning the Semitic world at the time of the Exodus and Conquest. More specifically, the inscriptions contribute insights that aid in understanding many seldom used Hebrew words, since the Ugaritic language, though different, is closely related to Hebrew. The second significant area of help centers in a better understanding of Semitic poetry in terms of structure, rhythm, and turn of phrase. This kind of comparison has been fruitful in studies of poems in the Pentateuch, the historical books, and the Psalter. At the same time, a number of suggestions have been made that have proved to be ill advised.

Some scholars claimed that Psalm 29 was purely a Canaanite hymn in which the only change was the name of the deity from Baal to Yahweh. The psalm is now regarded more as a witnessing hymn that challenges the doctrine of Baal as the lord of nature, boldly proclaiming Yahweh, the creator of nature, as the only true Lord.

Some scholars have claimed that Psalm 104 came from old Egyptian hymns to the sun god. Others have thought it was a reworking of old Babylonian hymns to the sun. Several religious texts from Ugarit include a few expressions almost identical to those in Psalm 104. The tendency now is to see the psalm as thoroughly Hebrew in theological affirmations, though drawing from other cultures certain turns of phrase.

Legal materials from Ugarit throw some light on laws found in the Pentateuch. A particularly strange law is set forth in Exodus 23:19 and Deuteronomy 14:21, "You shall not boil a young goat in its mother's milk." In 1933 the French scholar Virolleaud published one line of Ugaritic which he thought should be translated, "cook a kid in milk." Other scholars took this translation to mean that the biblical law reflects an old Canaanite ritual connected with sex worship and fertility. More recently, scholars have rejected this connection, but they admit the law does prohibit some kind of idolatrous practice.

Several priestly terms and practices are found in both Ugaritic and Hebrew. The words for "priest," "gift," "vow," "altar," "sacrifice," and "offer" are the same in both languages.

The architectural floor plan of temples at Ugarit is basically the same as that of the Israelite tabernacle and temple. Both offered oxen and sheep as sacrifices, neither of which could be crippled or afflicted by blemishes.

Nineveh

Finding the lost capital of the Assyrian empire was not easy; the desert sands had completely covered it and no one remembered exactly where it had been located.

In 1820 C. J. Rich, a British merchant, visited modern Mosul on the west bank of the Tigris River. Suspecting the ruins to be Nineveh, he sketched an outline of mounds on the east bank. He also collected clay tablets on which were strange markings that no one could read.

The two main mounds that caught Rich's attention were known among the natives as Kuyunjik and Nebi-Yunus, the latter in honor of the prophet Jonah. Kuyunjik is approximately ninety feet high, one mile long, and a half mile wide. Both mounds were enclosed by a great wall with a perimeter of eight miles.

In 1842, motivated by the reports of C. J. Rich, a French consular agent to Mosul named Paul E. Botta began to excavate the larger mound of Kuyunjik. Finding little, he moved to another mound, Khorsabad, ten miles north and discovered the ruins of the palace of Sargon II, emperor of Assyria (722–705).

Three years later an Englishman, A. H. Layard, began digging at Calah, also known as Nimrud, located twenty miles south of Kuyunjik, and he had instant success. But the mound could not be identified as Nineveh, so in 1849 he moved to Kuyunjik. His work brought to light the ruins of the palace of Sennacherib (704–681) and the Taylor Prism. The library of Emperor Ashurbanipal (669–633) was discovered in the spring of 1850. In this library and in a collection found in the temple of Nabu there were about 16,000 tablets and fragments. Layard's work continued until 1854.

Excavations led by various archaeologists took place during the following time periods: 1872–75, 1882–91, 1903–05, 1927–32, and 1966 to the present. Soundings to undisturbed soil showed the beginning of the city in the middle of the fifth millennium B.C. There is evidence of Sumerian influence on the city in the third millennium, and through the second millennium it was an important trade and religious center. At various times leaders of the Assyrian Empire made Nineveh a royal city and built palaces there. Tiglath-pileser I (1115–1077); Ashurbanipal II (884–859); Sargon II (722–05); and Sennacherib (705–681), whose successors made it the permanent capital of the empire. The city was utterly destroyed in 612 B.C. by the combined armies of the Babylonians, Medes, and Persians. The site was never occupied again.

The clay tablets of Nineveh are comprised of about 10,000 different documents, some of which are original autographs and others, copies. Many were collected by Sargon and others at Babylon, but most were the fruit of the interest of Ashurbanipal (668–627) in literature. A team of scribes processed the collected tablets and copied many of them. They were carefully cataloged and stored in a library in such a way that any tablet could be retrieved easily.

The tablets cover a range of literary forms: 1) trade records; 2) governmental records of many kinds; 3) training exercises for students and helps such as dictionaries in several languages; 4) laws and court decisions; and 5) religious hymns, epics, myths, rituals, prayers, and lists of gods.

In the religious materials are three sets of tablets which have had significant impact upon Old Testament studies: 1) the "Babylonian Creation Myth," featuring the god Marduk and the goddess Tiamat, recorded on seven tablets and often compared with the first two chapters of Genesis (see pages 91–92); 2) the "Epic of Adapa" (see page 143), which has been compared with the story of Adam and Eve; and 3) the "Epic of Gilgamesh," comprised of twelve tablets, with a flood story on the eleventh tablet (see pages 89–90), which has been compared with the biblical record of Noah and the flood.

The Taylor Prism, made of clay and inscribed with cuneiform symbols, tells the story of Sennacherib's invasion of Palestine in 701 B.C. and his seige of Jerusalem (II Kings 18, 19; Isa. 36, 37). The emperor boasted, "Hezekiah, the Judaean, I shut up in Jerusalem, his royal city, like a bird in a cage." He did not claim he captured the city.

The archives of Nineveh provide the most extensive information about the Assyrian empire available and include a number of references to events connected with Assyria's success in taking control of the coastal lands east of the Mediterranean Sea. Many of the kings of Syria, Northern Israel, and Judah, and most of the cities of Palestine are mentioned, all of which are also referred to in the Old Testament. The result is a more precise correlation between Old Testament history and Assyrian history during the eighth and seventh centuries B.C. than with any other nation in the ancient Near East.

The Dead Sea Scrolls

The discovery in 1948 of leather scrolls in caves in the cliffs west of the Dead Sea was one of the great surprises of archaeological research. The irony is that they were first brought to light, not by archaeologists but by Arab shepherds. Their significance is without rival, because many of the scrolls preserve the oldest manuscripts of the Hebrew Old Testament. They are discussed on pages 209–18.

Tell el-Amarna

Since most of the inscriptions found in Egypt are carved on stone or painted on plaster, few archives are preserved in that land or elsewhere. Some documents written on papyrus prior to New Testament times have come to light.

The only significant collection of clay tablets found in Egypt came from the ancient ruins of the short-lived capital called Tell el-Amarna. The story of how these tablets came to the attention of Western scholars is most interesting.

The setting of the story lies close to the east bank of the Nile River, about 190 miles south of Cairo. The ancient name of the place was Akhetaton and was built in 1365 B.C. by Pharaoh Amenhotep IV as a new capital city to replace Thebes. Akhetaton flourished as a capital for fifty years but was then abandoned; hence there are no layers of debris from previous cities nor of any later city.

In the early 1800s an Arab tribe, the Beni Amran, settled in small villages nearby and used soil from the ruins to fertilize their gardens. In the cliffs just to the east of the villages were old tombs which attracted the attention of European scholars as early as 1821. Visits in 1831 and 1845 resulted in the publication of the art and inscriptions found on the walls of the caves. Included in the twelve-volume set were the ground plans of the streets and portions of a temple wall which could be discerned from the irregular surface of the tell.

Late in 1887 a woman from a nearby village was filling her basket with the rich soil of the site when she found some clay tablets bearing strange looking marks. She sold the objects to a neighbor for ten piasters, the equivalent of fifty cents in U.S. money. Some tablets were sent to J. Oppert in Paris, who immediately recognized the script as cuneiform. He thought they were fraudulent, for whoever heard of genuine cuneiform tablets coming from Egypt? Other scholars agreed with him.

More and more tablets came to light, so an enterprising member of the village put them, with no protective wrapping, in sacks and transported them on the backs of donkeys almost two hundred miles south to Luxor. A number of the tablets, how many no one knows, were completely shattered and reduced to dust, but about 350 survived in fair shape. Later additional tablets were found in the ruins of the tell. All are dated 1365–15 B.C.

A missionary, Chauncy Murch, recognized the value of the tablets and alerted an official of the British Museum, E. A. Wallis Budge, who was touring Egypt at the time. Because several dealers had control of the tablets, Budge could not buy all the tablets for his museum; he had to settle for eighty-two of them. About two hundred of the tablets found their way to the Berlin Museum, sixty to the Cairo Museum, twenty-two to the Ashmolean Museum of Oxford University, six to the Louvre in Paris, two to the Metropolitan Museum in New York City, and one to the Oriental Institute in Chicago. Later, archaeologists found a matching tablet in Palestine at Tell el-Hesi, and four at Taanach.

In 1891 Flinders Petrie, the Englishman who earned his fame as an archaeologist in Egypt, began excavating the ruins of Tell el-Amarna and soon uncovered the main buildings of the ancient capital. In one building he found twenty-two more fragments of tablets. A German team continued the excavation from 1907 to World War I. After that war the digging was under the direction of the Egypt Exploration Society, coming to an end in 1937.

The Amarna tablets were written with cuneiform symbols and were mostly in the Akkadian language. Some tablets were in Hurrian, and others, especially those from Palestine, had some Canaanite words mixed with the Akkadian. The tablets provide evidence that during the Amarna age this script and language were the international media of communication.

About forty of the tablets came from Babylon, Cyprus, Assyria, and from the Hurrians. The remainder came from city-states in Syria, from Phoenicia (Byblos, Beirut, Sidon, and Tyre), and from city-states in Palestine (Acco, Ashkelon, Arvad, Aroer, Ashteroth, Gezer, Gath, Gaza, Jerusalem, Joppa, Keilah, Lachish, Megiddo, Sharon, Shechem, Taanach and Zorah). Most tablets were from local rulers, but a few were reports of Egyptian officials to Pharaoh at Tell el-Amarna.

The tablets are a remarkable witness to the highly developed writing skills in Palestine during the Late Bronze Age. Whether they were written before the Conquest or afterward has been a matter of considerable debate. Some letters from Palestine warn that a people called Apiru (Hapiru) were invading the land from the east. At issue is whether or not these people are the Hebrews or another invading force. None of the names of the city-states mentioned on the tablets are the same as those named in the Book of Joshua. Also, one must recognize that these people are referred to in almost all the archives described above, and thus seem to be a general name for homeless peoples in various places and at different periods of time.

Elephantine

The recovery of ancient papyri is a rare event; apart from a few scraps found in caves near the Dead Sea, most have been found in Egypt. Papyri from Elephantine were first purchased in 1893 by Charles E. Wilbour; more were acquired in later years by other scholars. All the letters were written in the Aramaic language.

Elephantine is an island in the Nile River just below the recently built Aswan Dam in southern Egypt. In ancient times it was a port for boat traffic carrying cargo to the south. The boats could not go farther because the First Cataract was just south of the island. The site was settled about 3000 B.C. and continued as a strong fortress until about 400 B.C.

Israelite refugees from the Babylonian destruction of the Kingdom of Judah (586 B.C.) settled on the island of Elephantine and existed as a strong community during the fifth century B.C. This was the period during which the letters were written.

Excavations by the French started in 1902 and continued for several years. A German team took over the task from 1906–1908, Italian archaeologists worked during the 1920s, and the Egyptian government took charge from 1932–48. Besides the papyri letters, the remains of a temple to Yahu were unearthed.

Apart from Jeremiah 43:7–44:30, the Old Testament has no description of how Jewish refugees fared in Egypt after the Fall of Jerusalem. The Elephantine papyri at least give us a glimpse of life in a Jewish community in Egypt during post-exilic times. They were accepted until they began to collaborate with the Persian oppressors; the result was the destruction of the temple of Yahu.

The content of the papyri indicate that the Jews at Elephantine mixed some of the local polytheism with their worship of Yahweh, but seemed to have observed the Sabbath, celebrated the Feast of Unleavened Bread, and possibly the Passover. One papyrus document names Sanballat as the governor of Samaria (cf. Neh. 2:10; 13:28) and Johanan, son of Joiada, the high priest (Neh. 13:28).

The archives that have been discussed were selected as the most significant collections of inscriptions in specific places which have materials that throw light on Old Testament backgrounds. Some of these documents, such as those at Nineveh and Elephantine, name people and/or events that are recorded in the Old Testament. Numerous inscriptions have been preserved all over the Middle East; many are significant for ancient Near Eastern studies, but not as helpful in terms of Old Testament studies. These sources of information have not been discussed here.

Suggested Books for Further Study

Campbell, Edward F., Jr. "The Amarna Letters and the Amarna Period." *Biblical Archaeologist* 23 (1960): 2–22.

Cowley, A. *Aramaic Papyri of the Fifth Century B.C.* Oxford: The Clarendon Press, 1923.

Craigie, Peter C. *Ugarit and the Old Testament.* Grand Rapids: William B. Eerdmans Publishing Co., 1983.

"The Tablets from Ugarit and Their Importance for Biblical Studies." *Biblical Archaeology Review* 9 (1983): 56–73.

Frymer-Fensky, T. "Patriarchal Family Relationships and Near Eastern Law." *Biblical Archaeologist* 44 (1981): 209–213.

Gelb, I. J. "The Early History of West Semitic Peoples." *The Journal of Cuneiform Studies* 15 (1961): 27–47.

Kapelrud, Arvid S. *The Ras Shamra Discoveries and the Old Testament.* Norman: University of Oklahoma Press, 1963.

Kenyon, Kathleen M. *Royal Cities of the Old Testament.* London: Barrie and Jenkins, 1971.

Kraeling, Emil G. "New Light on the Elephantine Colony." *The Bible Archaeologist* 15 (1952): 50–67.

Lemaire, Andre. "Mari, the Bible, and the Northwest Semitic World." *Biblical Archaeologist* 47 (1984): 101–108.

Matthiae, Paolo. *Ebla: An Empire Rediscovered.* London: Hodder and Stoughton, 1977.

Morrison, M. A. "The Jacob and Laban Narrative in Light of Near Eastern Sources." *Biblical Archaeologist* 46 (1982): 155–164.

Pardee, Dennis. "The Mari Archives." *Biblical Archaeologist* 47 (1984): 88–99.

Parrot, Andre. "Mari." *Archaeology and Old Testament Study* (1967): 136–144.

Pettinato, Giovanni. *The Archives of Ebla: An Empire Inscribed in Clay.* Garden City, NY: Doubleday & Co., 1981.

Pfeiffer, Charles F. *Tell el Amarna and the Bible.* Grand Rapids: Baker Book House, 1963.

_____. *Ras Shamra and the Bible.* Grand Rapids: Baker Book House, 1962.

Vigano, Lorenzo and Pardee, Dennis. "Literary Sources for the History of Palestine and Syria. The Ebla Tablets." *Biblical Archaeologist* 47 (1984): 6–16.

Wise, Michael. "The Dead Sea Scrolls: Part I, Archaeology and Biblical Manuscripts." *Biblical Archaeologist* 49 (1986): 140–154.

Young, Gordon D. *Ugarit in Retrospect.* Winona Lake, IN: Eisenbrauns, 1981.

Index of Authors and Subjects

Index of Scripture References

318